A GUIDE TO ORIENTAL CLASSICS

COMPANIONS TO ASIAN STUDIES

Wm. THEODORE de BARY, editor

A GUIDE TO ORIENTAL CLASSICS

THIRD EDITION

PREPARED BY THE STAFF OF THE
COMMITTEE ON ORIENTAL STUDIES,
COLUMBIA UNIVERSITY

EDITED BY
WM. THEODORE DE BARY
AND AINSLIE EMBREE

THIRD EDITION EDITED BY
AMY VLADECK HEINRICH

COLUMBIA UNIVERSITY PRESS
NEW YORK

Columbia University Press
New York   Oxford
Copyright © 1989 Columbia University Press
All rights reserved

Library of Congress Cataloging-in-Publication Data

A Guide to Oriental Classics.

(Companions to Asian studies)
1. Oriental literature—Bibliography.
2. Oriental literature—Outlines, syllabi, etc.
I. De Bary, William Theodore, 1918–
II. Embree, Ainslie Thomas.
III. Heinrich, Amy Vladeck.
IV. Columbia University. Committee on Oriental Studies.
V. Series.
Z7046.G8   1989   [PJ307]   016.89   88-28538
ISBN 0-231-06674-0

Printed in the United States of America

Casebound editions of Columbia University Press books are Smyth-sewn
and printed on permanent and durable acid-free paper

This edition of the *Guide* is dedicated to
JOHN MESKILL
Professor of Oriental Studies
Barnard College, Columbia University
1960–1988

CONTENTS

Preface to the Third Edition, *by Amy Vladeck Heinrich*   xiii

Introduction, *by Wm. Theodore de Bary*   xv

I. Classics of the Islamic Tradition   1

General Works   3

The Seven Odes (Al-Mu'allaqāt)   13

The Qur'ān (Al-Qur'ān)   17

The Ring of the Dove (Ṭawq al-Ḥamāma), by Ibn
Ḥazm (994–1064)   24

The Maqāmāt of al-Hamadhānī (Maqāmāt al-
Hamadhānī) (968–1008)   27

The Assemblies of al-Ḥarīrī (Maqāmāt al-Ḥarīrī)
(1054–1122)   29

The Thousand and One Nights (Alf Layla wa-Layla)   32

Deliverance from Error (Al-Munqidh min al-Ḍalāl),
by al-Ghazālī (1058–1111)   37

On the Harmony of Religion and Philosophy (Kitāb
faṣl al-maqāl), by Averroes (Ibn Rushd) (1126–
1198)   41

The Conference of the Birds, by Farīd al-Dīn ʿAṭṭār
(*ca.* 1142–*ca.* 1220)   45

The Mystical Poetry of Jalāl al-Dīn Rūmī (1207–1273)   48

The Prolegomena (Al-Muqaddima) of Ibn Khaldūn
(1332–1406)   51

The Shāhnāma   55

The Rubā'iyyāt of ʿUmar Khayyām (eleventh century)   58

The Book of Dede Korkut (Kitab-i Dede Korkut)   60

The Mystical Poetry of Yunus Emre (d. *ca.* 1320)   62

Leylā and Mejnūn, by Fuzūlī (*ca.* 1495–1556)   64

II. Classics of the Indian Tradition   67

General Works   69
The Vedas   75
Upanishads (*ca.* 900–500 B.C.)   79
Mahābhārata (*ca.* fifth century B.C.–fourth century
    C.E.)   82
Bhagavadgītā (*ca.* 100 B.C.–A.D. 100)   86
Rāmāyana of Vālmīki (*ca.* 200 B.C.)   90
Yoga Sūtras of Patañjali (*ca.* A.D. 300)   93
The Vedānta Sūtra with the Commentary of
    Shankārāchārya (*ca.* 780–820)   97
Theravāda Buddhism: The Tipiṭaka   101
Theravāda Buddhism: The Dhammapada (*ca.* 300
    B.C.)   106
Theravāda Buddhism: The Milindapañhā (*ca.* first
    century C.E.)   108
Theravāda Buddhism: The Mahāsatipaṭṭhana Sutta   110
Mahāyāna Buddhism: Prajñāpāramitā (*ca.* 100 B.C.–
    A.D. 400)   112
Mahāyāna Buddhism: The Śrīmālādevisimhanāda
    Sūtra   116
Mahāyāna Buddhism: The Laṅkāvatāra Sūtra   118
Mahāyāna Buddhism: The Sukhavativyūha Sūtras   120
Mahāyāna Buddhism: The Bodhicaryāvatāra of
    Shāntideva (*ca.* 650)   122
Supplementary Readings on Indian Buddhism   124
Shakuntalā (Abhijñānaśakuntalā) of Kālidāsa (*ca.* 400)   126
The Little Clay Cart (Mṙrcchakaṭikā) of Shūdraka (*ca.*
    400)   130
Pañcatantra (*ca.* 200 B.C.) According to Pūrṇabhadra
    (*ca.* 1199)   133
Sanskrit Lyric Poetry   136
Gītagovinda of Jayadeva (*ca.* twelfth century)   140
Indian Devotional Poetry   143

Indo-Islamic Poetry 148
Poems and Plays of Rabindranath Tagore (1861–1941) 152
Autobiography of Mohandas Karamchand Gandhi
  (1869–1948) 155

III. Classics of the Chinese Tradition 159

General Works 161
The Analects (Lun-yü) of Confucius (551–479 B.C.) 168
Mo Tzu, or Mo Ti 173
Lao Tzu, or Tao-te Ching 176
Chuang Tzu 180
Mencius (Meng Tzu, 372–289 B.C.) 184
The Great Learning (Ta-hsüeh) 187
The Mean (Chung-yung) 189
Hsün Tzu, or Hsün Ch'ing 191
Han Fei Tzu 194
Records of the Historian: The *Shih chi* of Ssu-ma
  Ch'ien (*ca.* 145–*ca.* 90 B.C. 197
Texts of Chinese Buddhism 200
The Lotus Sūtra (Saddharma Pundarīka Sūtra, or
  Miao-fa Lien-hua ching) 201
The Vimalakīrtinirdeśa Sūtra (Wei-mo-chieh so-shuo
  ching) 204
The Awakening of Faith in Mahāyāna (Ta-ch'eng ch'i-
  hsin lun) 206
Platform Sutra of the Sixth Patriarch (Liu-tsu t'an
  ching) 208
The Record of Lin-chi (*d.* 866) 210
Supplementary Readings on Chinese Buddhism 212
Works of Chu Hsi (1130–1200) 215
Works of Wang Yang-ming (1472–1529) 218
General Readings in Chinese Fiction 221
The Water Margin, or All Men Are Brothers (Shui-hu
  chuan) 223

Journey to the West, or Monkey (Hsi-yu Chi), by Wu
    Ch'eng-en (*ca.* 1506–1581)   226
The Golden Lotus (Chin P'ing Mei)   230
Dream of the Red Chamber (Hung-lou meng), by
    Ts'ao Hsüeh-ch'in (Ts'ao Chan, *d.* 1763)   233
Chinese Drama   237
Chinese Poetry   240
The Book of Songs (Shih ching)   241
The Songs of the South (Ch'u Tz'u) by Ch'ü Yüan
    and Other Poets   244
Chinese Poets and Poetry   246

IV. Classics of the Japanese Tradition   255

General Works   257
Man'yōshū   262
Court Poetry: The *Kokinshū* and other Imperial
    Anthologies   265
The Pillow Book (Makura no sōshi) of Sei Shōnagon   268
The Tale of Genji (Genji monogatari) by Murasaki
    Shikibu   270
Poetic Diaries and Poem Tales   275
Texts of Japanese Buddhism   279
Writings of Kūkai (Kōbō Daishi, 774–835)   280
Writings of Buddhist Masters of the Kamakura Period   282
Writings of the Zen Master Hakuin (1686–1769)   285
Supplementary Readings in Japanese Buddhism   287
An Account of My Hut (Hōjōki) by Kamo no
    Chōmei (1153–1236)   290
Essays in Idleness (Tsurezuregusa) by Yoshida Kenkō
    (1283–1350)   292
The Tale of the Heike (Heike monogatari)   294
The Nō Plays   297
The Fiction of Ihara Saikaku (1642–1693)   301
The Poetry and Prose of Matsuo Bashō (1644–1694)   304

The Plays of Chikamatsu Monzaemon (1653–1725) 307
The Treasury of Loyal Retainers (Chūshingura, *ca.* 1748), by Takeda Izumo, Miyoshi Shōraku, and Namiki Senryū 310
Kokoro, by Natsume Sōseki (1867–1914) 313

PREFACE

TO THE THIRD EDITION

The third edition of *The Guide to Oriental Classics* has been prepared with the same essential purpose as the earlier editions: to provide an aid to both teachers and students in reading and discussing the major texts of the four traditions represented. In recent years the number of new translations and studies has dramatically increased. This has led us to add sections on major works that were previously unavailable in English, such as the tenth-century Japanese poetry classic, the *Kokinshū*, as well as to expand and refine the lists of translations and secondary readings. The additional sections in the *Guide* mean that to an even greater extent than with earlier editions, there is more material than can be taught in a year's course. However, the greater selection also means that courses can be shaped more specifically to reflect the purposes and interests of particular teachers and students.

Complementing the increase in available translations and studies is an increased interest in teaching these texts more widely, in courses on the traditions they represent, and in a variety of courses on different aspects of world civilizations as well. We have consequently been especially concerned with making the *Guide* as useful as possible to a wider audience of nonspecialists. Many of the brief introductions to the texts have been expanded to clarify the place of each work within its tradition, and the topics for discussion revised to focus even more closely on the texts alone.

As represented here, the Indian, Chinese, and Japanese traditions are broadly defined in geographic and linguistic terms. The Islamic tradition, with its implicit religious basis, cuts across cultural boundaries, and makes defining its canon especially difficult. Here we have defined as "classic" the period of the development of the Islamic tradition from the origins of Islam through about 1500. Most of the texts are in Arabic, but we have included works from Islamic cultures that developed vernacular literature relatively early, such as the Turkish and Persian traditions. The later tradition of Urdu-Islamic poetry has seemed more appropriately placed within the Indian tradition.

This revision has been prepared in conjunction with the Summer Institute on The Great Books of the Major Asian Traditions, conducted at Columbia University under the auspices of the National Endowment for the Humanities, for college faculty from diverse areas of specialization. We are most grateful for the suggestions and responses of the participants, who have provided us with a broader perspective. In addition to those who cooperated in the production of the earlier editions, many people have contributed to the preparation of this version of the *Guide*. I am grateful to Scott Alexander, Peter Awn, Kathleen Burrill, Irene Bloom, Pierre Cachia, Dennis Dalton, Aaron Gerow, Leonard Gordon, John Hawley, Wadad Kadi, Donald Keene, John Meskill, Barbara Stoler Miller, Frances Pritchett, Barbara Ruch, James Russell, Jeanette Wakin, Paul Watt, Philip Yampolsky, Ehsan Yarshater, and Pauline Yu for their contributions to the text, and to Marie Guarino for her invaluable editorial assistance.

Amy Vladeck Heinrich
Acting Librarian
C. V. Starr East Asian Library
Columbia University

INTRODUCTION

TO THE THIRD EDITION

This *Guide* has been compiled as an aid to students and teachers taking up for the first time the major works of Oriental literature and thought. It is designed especially for general education, which emphasizes a careful reading of single whole works and discussion of them in a group. Experience during the past forty years in the Columbia College course in the Oriental Humanities has been drawn upon in making the selections and suggesting the discussion topics offered here.

The assumptions of this course, inherited from the parent Humanities course in the Western tradition, have been basically two: that there were certain great works of intellectual and artistic achievement in the Oriental world which any educated person, whatever his own field of specialization, ought to have read; and that these books could be understood and appreciated without prior initiation into the complexities of scholarly research in each field. The first reading, obviously, was not meant to be a final one. The works were classics or "great books" not only in that they deserved to be read by everyone at least once, but also in that, for most persons, they would repay many readings and, for some, endless study. No one thought of this brief introduction as a substitute for more intensive study. The point in Oriental Humanities was to help the nonspecialist appreciate those qualities in a work that made it worth the scholar's lifetime of study and, moreover, to understand why the scholar's own perplexities with certain texts could be resolved only through such exacting research.

Time and experience in teaching the Oriental Humanities have not caused us to abandon these basic assumptions. We learned very early, however, that they would need special qualification in regard to some Oriental texts. Professor Trilling, recalling the debate in Columbia College over special competence versus general intelligence as qualifications for the Humanities teacher, says that it

> was settled in favor of the party which believed that the purposes of the course . . . would be adequately served by the general intelligence and enlightenment of the teacher. . . . The books that would make the substance of the course were to be chosen because they were no less pertinent now than when they had first been written, and also because their authors were men speaking to men, not to certain men who were specially trained to understand them but to all men. . . . It seemed to us a denial of their nature to suppose that any sort of "secondary material" was needed to make them comprehensible.[1]

Accepting this point of view, we nevertheless came to see that "general intelligence and enlightenment of the teacher" took for granted, perhaps more than one at first realized, acquaintance with a common cultural tradition in the West. In the East this common culture did not exist. We were dealing with many traditions, not one, and few scholars in Chinese literature could be presumed also to have read and thought about important works in the Islamic tradition. Nor had Muhammad, on the other hand, ever read Confucius. In this respect, then, Oriental Humanities was not carrying on a "great conversation" among the great minds of the past, but rather trying to get a new conversation started.

As regards the teacher, this implied no less need for "general intelligence and enlightenment," and we have always been glad when seasoned teachers of the Western Humanities joined our colloquium (especially since among Western students it would

[1] Lionel Trilling, preface to *The Proper Study: Essays on Western Classics,* edited by Quentin Anderson and Joseph Mazzeo (New York: St. Martin's Press, 1962), p. vi.

be unnatural and stultifying to exclude from the conversation their own tradition). But this general intelligence was most often helpful insofar as it brought specific disciplines to bear on these diverse works, and it functioned most effectively when recourse could be had to the more specialized knowledge of others concerning the subject at hand. The nonspecialist himself, no matter how adventurous and wide-ranging, found it reassuring to have on hand a guide thoroughly familiar with the cultural terrain.

A mixed staff, representing different disciplines and competence in different traditions, provided part of the answer to this situation. Each class section has been conducted by a pair of instructors, one of them acquainted with the language and history of the tradition concerned and the other a knowledgeable outsider. Obviously, however, there are more languages and cultures tributary to the main traditions of Asia than could be represented by a team of teachers, unless either the teachers were to outnumber the students or the students were to be subjected to a kind of Chautauqua series. The classroom instructors or the Colloquium team, therefore, could work best if their individual talents were pooled in a larger staff that met regularly for consultation and that even had the benefit of special lectures by authorities on particularly difficult subjects. (One such subject, perennially, was the *Gathas* of the Avesta, which successive authorities finally convinced us were so obscure and unmanageable as to be poorly suited to this type of course.)

The matter was further complicated by the number of exceptions that our texts provided to the definition of a classic or great book as "addressed to all men." Professor Trilling himself allows that Spinoza was an exception, since he specified that his writing was for a limited group with "strong minds" rather than for the general public. Among Oriental writers, there are a few, like Averroes, who would share Spinoza's feeling and make it explicit. There are many more for whom it is implicit.

This does not mean that their works, any more than Spinoza's, are lacking in universal appeal or significance. But it does mean that the reader was presumed to have had some prior initiation or preparation for the reading. Especially is this true of certain religious scriptures, and particularly of the traditions arising in India, where the esoteric character of religious truth is strongly emphasized and the written text is often considered only an adjunct to personal training and experience under the guidance of a master. In the Far East, Zen texts exemplify the extreme of this type. But this is true not only in religion. The Nō drama of Japan, in its own way, is quite esoteric, and the effect intended is only to a small degree conveyed by the written text.

In such cases, where the text is an enigma without its context, unless the latter is somehow provided in secondary material, the reader will be forced to make his own conjectures, with results that can rarely be happy. If important works like the *Yoga Sutra* of Patanjali or the *Analects* of Confucius are too often overlaid with commentary, so that their essential meaning is lost in a philological maze, the alternative is not to dispense with commentary altogether. Interpretation and exegesis arise naturally and inevitably from the nature of the text itself.

A careful translation with adequate introduction will normally incorporate as much of this traditional scholarship as is needed to make the text understandable. Readers of the more cryptic Oriental classics, however, soon become aware that there may be several such translations available for certain texts, no one of which can necessarily be canonized as the sole definitive version, while for other texts there may be none that can be considered authoritative. At this point the judgment of experts will be of help to them. Thus something more than a bare reading list has been found desirable for teachers and students in the Oriental Humanities. We could not hold to the principle, as Professor Trilling puts it, "that there were to be no background lectures or readings, no 'guides,' either in textbook or outline form, no 'secondary material' of any kind—all was to be primary."[2] The teachers, no less than the students, felt a need for precisely such background material or scholarly guidance in areas outside their own immediate competence.

It is out of this realization that the present *Guide* has been conceived, but conceived in such a way as to reinforce the basic purposes of general education, not to compromise them. Above all, it is a guide which should help to focus the reader's attention on the central issues or essential qualities of a work, relieving the honest mind, insofar as possible, of doubts that these books have something to say to him personally, rather than only to readers in some other time or place. Or it may help to avoid misconceptions, perhaps historical, economic, or sociological, which obscure the issues and sometimes blunt the thrust of a writer's point. There are more than enough clichés about the Orient that can be invoked to explain away an uncomfortable idea. How often, for instance, is Buddhism disposed of as simply another manifestation of Indian pessimism, and Indian pessimism as merely an abnormal state of mind reflecting the age-old, extreme poverty of the land.

If some such questions of context are diversionary, though nonetheless sincere, the answers to them—or the direction in which to look for answers—may be suggested by a "guide" designed to provide the essential background, without permitting this to preempt the forefront of group discussion. But such a guide can do more than dispose of questions that would otherwise distract the reader or obstruct the discussion. For not all questions of context are ultimately irrelevant, to be refined out of the discussion until we are left alone with some supposedly pure essence of a work in universal terms. If each of these books is a "classic" because there is something eternal and unchanging in it, to which the constant nature of man responds, each is also unique, the product of a singular intelligence reflecting particular historical circumstances. And it is precisely in

[2] *Ibid.*, p. v.

their peculiarity that the appeal of many works lies. Reading them becomes an adventure for us when we identify ourselves with the human spirit as it moves through strange surroundings. Similarity and difference illuminate one another, as we come to appreciate the manifold forms and situations in which human sensibility has found expression.

Unfortunately there is no certain criterion, in East or West, by which to judge once and for all which works possess these enduring qualities of greatness. Durability is one obvious test, but the continuing popularity of Shankara with the type of limited audience to which Spinoza appeals may, depending upon the taste of the reader, count for more than the popularity of a Chinese play with generations of common folk. There will always be room for debate over the books that have been put on or kept off our list. This much may be said: over the years it has been a fairly stable list, with the original selections, based largely on the standing of the works in their own tradition, confirmed in at least eight or nine cases out of ten by their perennial success with readers in Oriental Humanities. In the remaining cases there is almost perennial dispute among our staff, and since the addition of a new title can be effected only by the removal of another, the dispute is sure to be intense. Yet even here there is a recurring pattern and a kind of consensus in the end—books stricken from the list in this year's reform are likely to be put forward and reinstated by other reformers a few years hence.

In this *Guide* we have included somewhat more titles than could be assigned in a given year, providing a range of selection that covers the likely candidates over the years. We have also tried to represent the major genres of literature, thus giving a balanced selection of scriptures, philosophical texts, poetry, drama, and fiction. It should be remembered, however, that these genres were not developed to an equal degree by each of the various Oriental traditions, and we have felt no obligation to include a sample of Indian or Islamic fiction simply because the Chinese and Japanese novel held a prominent place on the list, nor have we hunted for a specimen of epic poetry in China and Japan to place beside the *Mahābhārata* or *Rāmāyana* of India. Our selection aims at representing what has been most valued in these traditions, whatever the form, not at presenting a survey that covers every type of literature, whatever its quality.

One gap, however, is not wholly a matter of choice. Iranian literature is inadequately represented. This revision of the *Guide* makes an improvement on earlier ones by including the poet Rumi, the *Shāhnāma*, and a few other works of Iranian literature, but no doubt some readers will feel strongly about other glaring omissions.

We realize that not all teachers and students will make the same use of the *Guide*. Those whose concerns are more religious than literary will perhaps draw more heavily on the Indian readings than upon the Chinese, while those with more literary tastes may bypass Shankara to get at Chinese drama and Japanese haiku. There should be enough of both types here for each, given the richness and variety we have to draw upon. What really matters, however, is not whether we have fully satisfied individual tastes, but whether we have included all the basic works which anyone should read.

Clearly, then, this *Guide* is selective rather than exhaustive. It deals with the most immediate problems of the teacher and student rather than those of the researcher. Our judgment has been exercised upon the translations and secondary works most readily available for use in general education and upon the kind of topic that would best lend itself to group discussion. The topics themselves we have tried to formulate as simply and concisely as possible, for the reason that they are meant to open discussion and not settle it. Their chief value, as we conceive it, is to suggest the essential ideas, issues, or qualities of a work that a reader ought to look for or a satisfactory discussion to touch upon. Granted that interpretations vary, and that some will find much more of significance in a work than others do, still the central questions or features can usually be identified, if only because they are the ones most often in dispute. No speculation or interpretation, however intriguing, should be allowed to take precedence over such basic questions as: what the author is trying to say, what means he chooses to express it, how he defines his problem or his purpose, to what audience he addresses himself, and so forth. Only when these points are clearly understood is it safe to proceed to more general consideration.

For similar reasons the suggested topics do not lean heavily in the direction of comparisons with the Western tradition. It is only natural that such comparisons should be made, since so much of our knowledge is gained or assimilated that way, and one would not seek to avoid in class what arises so spontaneously and irrepressibly in any discussion. Obviously, however, the problem is not to stimulate or suggest comparisons, when so many abound, but rather to keep them within limits. Comparative analysis of several works can be fruitful only if it deals with specific features or concepts in each work for which the grounds of comparability are well established and explicitly defined. Comparisons of whole traditions or religions are almost always risky, and can only be treated in a most tentative way in general education. Indeed, exposure to the complexities of different cultural traditions and religious systems should make the student increasingly conscious that such questions, while not insignificant, require a depth of scholarly study and fullness of treatment quite beyond an introductory course. It is not upon their solution that the value of such a course depends, but upon the opening up of the mind and stretching of the imagination that the reading of these books demands of one.

Wm. Theodore de Bary

A GUIDE TO ORIENTAL CLASSICS

I. Classics of the Islamic Tradition

GENERAL WORKS

Basic Bibliographies and Reference Works

Brice, William, ed. *An Historical Atlas of Islam*. Leiden: Brill, 1981.

A companion volume to *The Encyclopaedia of Islam*, below.

Ede, David et al. *Guide to Islam*. Boston: Hall, 1983.

A well-annotated guide divided into five sections (historical development; religious thought; Islamic institutions; art and architecture; research aids) with subject and author index.

Encyclopaedia of Islam, The. New Edition. 5 vols. and continuing. Leiden: Brill, 1954– .

Contains the most recent authoritative articles in all fields of Islamic studies. Gradually replacing the *First Edition*, 4 vols. and *Supplement*, Leiden: Brill, 1913–38.

Encyclopedia Iranica. 2 vols. and continuing. London, New York, and Henley: Routledge and Kegan Paul, 1985– .

Jean Sauvaget's Introduction to the History of the Muslim East: A Bibliographic Guide. Recast by Claude Cahen. Berkeley: University of California Press, 1965.

A valuable annotated guide.

Pearson, James Douglas, ed. *Index Islamicus, 1906–1955*. Cambridge: Heffert, 1958; London: Mansell, 1972, 1974. *Index Islamicus Supplement 1956–60*. Cambridge: Heffert, 1962. *Second Supplement, 1961–65*, 1967, and *Third Supplement, 1966–70*, with Anne Walsh. London: Mansell, 1972. *Fourth Supplement, 1971–75*, 1977, and *Index Islamicus, 1976–1980*. Part I: *Articles;* Part II: *Monographs*, with Wolfgang Behn, London: Mansell, 1983.

A classified and exhaustive list of articles dealing with Islamic subjects.

The Quarterly Index Islamicus. Compiled by G. J. Roper. London: Mansell, 1976– .

Ajami, Mansour. *The Neckveins of Winter: The Controversy Over Natural and Artificial Poetry in Medieval Arabic Literary Criticism.* Leiden: Brill, 1984.

Discusses an important topic in Arabic literary theory.

Andrews, Walter G. *Poetry's Voice, Society's Song: Ottoman Lyric Poetry.* Seattle and London: University of Washington Press, 1985.

A study that challenges some earlier views of the poetry of the "high" Ottoman Islamic tradition and attempts to link it more generally to the Turkish cultural environment.

Arberry, A. J., trans. *Arabic Poetry: A Primer for Students.* Cambridge University Press, 1965.

A short bilingual anthology.

—— *Aspects of Islamic Civilization as Depicted in the Original Texts.* London: Allen and Unwin, 1964. Pbk ed., Ann Arbor: University of Michigan Press, 1967.

An anthology with commentary.

Bombaci, Alessio. *Histoire de la littérature turque.* Translated by I. Mélikoff from *Storia della letteratura turca,* Milan, 1956. Paris: C. Klincksieck, 1968.

A survey of the literature of the Turks from Central Asia to modern Turkey.

Browne, E. G. *A Literary History of Persia.* 4 vols. Cambridge University Press, 1928–30; reprint, 1956–59.

A detailed account that includes many translations and material on Persian history in general.

Cambridge History of Arabic Literature, The. Vol. 1: *Arabic Literature to the End of the Umayyad Period.* Edited by A. F. L. Beeston, T. M. Johnstone, R. B. Sargeant, and G. R. Smith. New York and London: Cambridge University Press, 1984.

The first volume in a projected series of definitive essays.

de Bary, Wm. Theodore, ed. *Approaches to the Oriental Classics:*

Asian Literature and Thought in General Education. New York: Columbia University Press, 1959; 2d rev. ed., 1989.

Includes essays on representative works.

Gibb, E. J. W. *A History of Ottoman Poetry.* 6 vols. London: Luzac, 1900–1909; reprint, London: Luzac, 1958–67.

The standard reference work; translations are sometimes labored, but indexes on technical terms and on subjects are useful.

Gibb, H. A. R. *Arabic Literature: An Introduction.* London: Oxford University Press, 1926; 2d rev. ed., Oxford: Clarendon Press, 1963.

Excellent survey of all varieties of Arabic writings up to the eighteenth century. Includes a selected bibliography of literature in translation.

Ibn Qutayba. *Introduction au livre de la poésie et des poètes.* Translated and edited by M. Gaudefroy-Demombynes. Paris: Société d'editions "Les Belles lettres," 1947.

The introduction to a voluminous anthology, this is a useful early statement of Arabic poetic theory.

Khaial-Jāḥiẓ, ʿAmr ibn Bahr. *The Life and Works of Jāḥiz; Translations of Selected Texts by Charles Pellat.* Translated from the French by D. M. Hawke. Berkeley: University of California Press, 1969.

Khairallah, As'ad E. *Love, Madness, and Poetry: An Interpretation of the Magnun Legend.* Beirut: Orient-Institut der Deutschen Morgenländischen Gesellschaft; Weisbaden: Franz Steiner, 1980.

Kramer, Joel. *Humanism in the Renaissance of Islam.* Leiden: Brill, 1986.

A thoughtful history of the flowering of Islamic philosophical and literary humanism, stressing individualism in literary creativity, in Bagdad during the Buyid age (945–1055).

Kritzeck, J. *Anthology of Islamic Literature.* New York: Holt, Rinehart, and Winston, 1964. Pbk ed., New York: New American Library, Mentor, 1966.

Short selections from Islamic literature to 1800.

Levy, Reuben. *An Introduction to Persian Literature*. New York: Columbia University Press, 1969.

A useful short survey.

Lichtenstadter, Ilse. *Introduction to Classical Arabic Literature*. New York: Twayne, 1974. Reprint ed., New York: Schocken, 1976.

Menemencioglu, Nermin, ed., in collaboration with Fahir Iz. *The Penguin Book of Turkish Verse*. Harmondsworth: Penguin, 1978.

An excellent selection from classical *divan,* folk, and mystic poetry as well as the works of twentieth-century poets.

Monroe, James Y., comp. *Hispano-Arabic Poetry*. Berkeley: University of California Press, 1974.

A useful bilingual anthology.

Nicholson, R. A. *A Literary History of the Arabs*. 2d ed. Cambridge University Press, 1930; pbk ed., 1969.

A standard work, well informed and richly documented.

Rosenthal, Franz, ed. and trans. *The Classical Heritage in Islam*. Translated from the German by Emile Marmorstein and Jenny Marmorstein. Berkeley: University of California Press, 1975.

Rypka, Jan. *History of Iranian Literature*. Dordrecht: D. Reidel, 1968.

A comprehensive work.

Schimmel, Annemarie. *As Through a Veil: Mystical Poetry in Islam*. New York: Columbia University Press, 1982.

Schroeder, Eric. *Muhammad's People*. Portland, ME: Wheelwright, 1955.

A selection of Islamic writings on a variety of subjects, artfully translated.

Trabulsi, Amjad. *La Critique poétique des Arabes jusqu'au V° siècle de l'Hégire*. Damascus: Institut français de Damas, 1955.

An excellent account of Arabic literary theory and literary criticism.

Usāma ibn Munqidh. *Memoirs of an Arab-Syrian Gentleman, or An Arab Knight in the Crusades*. Translated by Phillip K. Hitti.

New York: Columbia University Press, 1929. Beirut: Khayat, 1964.

One of a very few Arabic autobiographies, with interesting sidelights on the society of the period.

Islamic Religion and Philosophy

Anawati, G. C. "Philosophy, Theology and Mysticism," in Joseph Schacht, with C. E. Bosworth, eds., *The Legacy of Islam*. 2d ed. Oxford: Clarendon Press, 1974; New York: Oxford University Press, 1974; pbk ed., 1979.

Arberry, A. J. *Revelation and Reason in Islam*. London: Allen and Unwin, 1957; New York: Macmillan, 1957.

A readable discussion of the conflict between reason and revelation and its resolution in Islam.

—— *Sufism: An Account of the Mystics of Islam*. New York: Harper and Row, 1970. Pbk ed., London and Boston: Unwin, Mandala Books, 1979.

A general introduction to the history of Sufi thought and writing.

Bravmann, M. M. *The Spiritual Background of Early Islam*. Leiden: Brill, 1972.

Penetrating analyses of a number of key themes, many drawn from poetry, stressing the conceptual continuity between early Islamic thought and the pre-Islamic Arab background.

Chittick, William, ed. and trans. *A Shiʿite Anthology*. London: Routledge and Kegan Paul, 1986; New York: Methuen, 1986.

Translations of selections from an important branch of Islam.

Cragg, Kenneth and R. Marston Speight. *Islam from Within: Anthology of a Religion*. Belmont, CA: Wadsworth, 1980.

A brief but fine collection of representative samples of Islamic literature in areas such as scripture, tradition, law, theology, art and architecture, mysticism, and selected contemporary issues.

De Boer, T. J. *The History of Philosophy in Islam*. Translated by

Edward R. Jones. London: Luzac, 1903. Pbk ed., New York: Dover, 1967.

While much new research has been done, this older account still provides a useful framework.

Fakhry, Majid. *A History of Islamic Philosophy*. New York: Columbia University Press, 1970; 2d ed., Columbia University Press and Longman, 1983.

A good general study with well-written expository sections on the thought of the major medieval Islamic philosophers.

Gardet, Louis. "ʿIlm al-kalām," in *The Encyclopaedia of Islam, New Edition*, 3:1141–50. Leiden: Brill, 1954– .

Gardet, Louis and M.-M. Anawati. *Introduction à la théologie musulmane*. Paris: J. Vrin, 1948.

Gibb, H. A. R. *Mohammedanism: An Historical Survey*. 2d ed., London: Oxford University Press, 1953. Pbk eds., New York: New American Library, Mentor, 1955; New York: Harper, Galaxy, 1962.

A brief, graceful survey by a distinguished authority.

Goldziher, Ignáz. *Introduction to Islamic Theology and Law*. Translated by Andras and Ruth Hamori. Modern Classics in Near Eastern Studies. Princeton University Press, 1981.

An excellent study by a premier scholar.

Guillaume, Alfred. *Islam*. Harmondsworth: Penguin, 1954.

A background study that expertly examines the great religious doctrines and practices in historical context.

—— "Philosophy and Theology," in T. W. Arnold and A. Guillaume, eds., *The Legacy of Islam*, pp. 239–83. Oxford: Clarendon Press, 1931; reprint, 1952.

An excellent brief account of the influence of Islamic thought on Europe and its transmission through Spain.

Hourani, George F. *Reason and Tradition in Islamic Ethics*. Cambridge University Press, 1985.

A readable collection of the author's articles in this area of Islamic philosophy.

Hyman, Arthur and James J. Walsh, eds. *Philosophy in the Middle Ages: The Christian, Islamic, and Jewish Traditions,* 2d ed. Indianapolis: Hackett, 1983.

Part 2 contains excellent selections from major Islamic philosophical writings as well as equally excellent relevant bibliographic material.

Jeffery, Arthur. *A Reader on Islam.* The Hague: Mouton, 1962.

Valuable collection of translations from Arabic writings, with notes, illustrating Islamic beliefs and practices.

Kelly, Marjorie, ed. *Islam: The Religious and Political Life of a World Community.* New York: Praeger, 1984.

Essays on a broad range of topics on classical and modern Islam, by a number of American scholars.

Lerner, Ralph and Muhsin Mahdi, eds. *Medieval Political Philosophy: A Sourcebook.* Glencoe, IL: Free Press, 1963.

Part 1 gives selections from Islamic philosophy.

McNeill, William H. and Marilyn R. Waldman, eds. *The Islamic World.* New York: Oxford University Press, 1973. Pbk ed., University of Chicago Press, 1984.

This anthology includes selections from the seventh through the twentieth centuries, from original Arabic, Persian, Indian, and Turkish sources.

Momen, Moojan. *An Introduction to Shi'i Islam.* New Haven: Yale University Press, 1985.

Ormsby, Eric L. *Theodicy in Islamic Thought: The Dispute Over al-Ghazālī's "Best of All Possible Worlds."* Princeton University Press, 1984.

Surveys a range of opinions illustrating the diversity of thought on this interesting problem.

Rahman, Fazlur. *Islam.* 2d ed. University of Chicago Press, 1979. Pbk ed.

An excellent introduction to Islam.

Savory, R. M., ed. *Introduction to Islamic Civilization.* New York: Cambridge University Press, 1976.

A collection of articles by Canadian scholars on faith, law, literature, art, science, relations with the West, etc.

Schacht, Joseph. *An Introduction to Islamic Law*. Oxford: Clarendon Press, 1964; reprint, 1982. Pbk ed.

The basic and most authoritative work on the subject.

Schimmel, Annemarie. *And Muhammad Is His Messenger: The Veneration of the Prophet in Islamic Piety*. Chapel Hill: University of North Carolina Press, 1985. Pbk ed.

The important role of the Prophet in popular piety, religious devotions, and cultural expression, by an eminent specialist.

—— *Mystical Dimensions of Islam*. Chapel Hill: University of North Carolina Press, 1975. Pbk ed.

The best and most authoritative account of Islamic spirituality; special emphasis is placed on Sufism in Islamic poetry.

Sharif, M. M., ed. *A History of Muslim Philosophy: With Short Accounts of Other Disciplines and the Modern Renaissance in Muslim Lands*. 2 vols. Wiesbaden: Harrassowitz, 1963–66.

Swartz, Merlin L., ed. and trans. *Studies on Islam*. New York: Oxford University Press, 1981.

A collection of important articles, translated from German, which reveal the major theses and trends of twentieth-century Islamic studies; a very useful book.

Von Grunebaum, G. E. *Islam: Essays in the Nature and Growth of a Cultural Tradition*. Menasha, WI: American Anthropological Association, 1955. 2d ed., London: Routledge and Kegan Paul, 1961.

Walzer, Richard. *Greek into Arabic: Essays on Islamic Philosophy*. Oxford: Cassirer, 1962. Los Angeles: University of Southern California Press, 1969.

Contains some important articles, but see especially an excellent summary on pp. 1–28.

Watt, W. Montgomery. *Islamic Philosophy and Theology*. Edinburgh University Press, 1962.

A clear, concise outline with excellent bibliographies.

—— *The Formative Period of Islamic Thought.* Edinburgh University Press, 1973.

A comprehensive treatment of the development of early Islamic thought from 632–945.

Williams, John Alden, ed. *Themes of Islamic Civilization.* Berkeley: University of California Press, 1971. Pbk ed.

An anthology of short translations that attempts to expound the essence of the Muslim religious and political world view.

Wolfson, H. A. *The Philosophy of the Kalam.* Cambridge: Harvard University Press, 1976.

A masterful study of the key debated issues of classical Islamic theology.

Islamic History

Arnold, T. W. and Alfred Guillaume, eds. *The Legacy of Islam.* Legacy Series. Oxford: Clarendon Press, 1931.

Contains many authoritative articles on Islamic religious thought, science, and art, and their influence upon Europe. See Schacht, ed., below.

Dunlop, D. M. *Arab Civilization to A.D. 1500.* New York: Praeger, 1971.

A readable and useful work, thematically arranged.

Gibb, H. A. R. *Studies on the Civilization of Islam.* S. J. Shaw and J. R. Polk, eds. Boston: Beacon Press, 1962. Pbk ed., 1968. Pbk reprint, Princeton University Press, 1982.

Hitti, Philip K. *History of the Arabs, from the Earliest Times to the Present.* 8th ed. London: Macmillan, 1963. Pbk ed., New York: St. Martin's Press, 1963.

A standard work based on the Arabic sources, best up to the period of the Mamlūks.

Hodgson, Marshall G. S. *The Venture of Islam: Conscience and History in a World Civilization.* Vol. 1, *The Classical Age of*

Islam. Vol. 2, *The Expansion of Islam in the Middle Periods*. Vol. 3, *The Gunpowder Empires and Modern Times*. University of Chicago Press, 1974.

The best and most detailed discussion of Islamic history and institutions.

Holt, P. M. *The Age of the Crusades: The Near East from the Eleventh Century to 1517*. London and New York: Longman, 1986.

An important interpretation.

Inalcik, Halil. *The Ottoman Empire: The Classical Age, 1300–1600*. Translated by Normal Itzkowitz and Colin Imber. London: Weidenfeld and Nicolson, 1973.

A survey of the period when the Ottoman Empire dominated the Islamic world.

Makdisi, George. *The Rise of Colleges: Institutions of Learning in Islam and the West*. University of Edinburgh Press, 1981.

A fundamental work on Muslim scholarship, scholastic method, and the milieu in which these took place.

Saunders, J. J. *A History of Medieval Islam*. London: Routledge and Kegan Paul, 1965; New York: Barnes and Noble, 1965. Reprint, 1982. Pbk ed.

A brief and well written history up to the period of the Mongols.

Schacht, Joseph, with C. E. Bosworth, eds. *The Legacy of Islam*. 2d ed. New York: Oxford University Press, 1974; pbk ed., 1979.

A new collection of articles on the influence and the transmission of Islamic culture to the West. See Arnold and Guillaume, eds., above.

Von Grunebaum, G. E., ed. *Unity and Variety in Muslim Civilization*. University of Chicago Press, 1955.

A collection of essays on Islamic literature, history, and institutions.

THE SEVEN ODES (AL-MU'ALLAQĀT)

This collection, the most celebrated among several, has exerted a lasting influence on Islamic poetry. The poems are traditionally assigned to the sixth and early seventh centuries.

TRANSLATIONS

Complete

Arberry, A. J., trans. *The Seven Odes.* London: Allen and Unwin, 1957; New York: Macmillan, 1957.

> A vigorous yet sensitive prose rendering which tends to follow in simple, clear English the rhythm of the original. Introductions are mainly concerned with the history of translation.

Blunt, Anne and Wilfred S. Blunt, trans. *The Seven Golden Odes of Pagan Arabia, Known Also as the Moallakat.* London: the Translators, 1903. (Translated from the original Arabic by Lady Anne Blunt; done into English verse by Wilfred S. Blunt.)

> A verse translation in archaistic English that takes as a model FitzGerald's very freehanded method of rendering the *Rubā'iyyāt.*

Jones, William, trans. *The Moallakát or Seven Arabian Poems, Which Were Suspended on the Temple at Mecca.* London, 1783. Also available in Sir William Jones, *Works* (London, 1799), 4:245–335.

> The pioneer translation in formal eighteenth-century prose.

Selections

Lyall, C. J., trans. *Translations of Ancient Arabian Poetry, Chiefly Pre-Islamic.* London: Williams and Norgate, 1930; New York: Columbia University Press, 1930.

13

Verse translations of an excellent collection chiefly from early Arab poetry, which attempt to imitate the original meters, with a useful introduction and notes.

Nicholson, R. A., trans. *Translations of Eastern Poetry and Prose,* pp. 1–27. Cambridge University Press, 1922.

The first twenty-five selections are translations of short passages from ancient Arabian poetry ranging from a free to a more literal rendering.

SECONDARY READINGS

Bateson, Mary Catherine. *Structural Continuity in Poetry: A Linguistic Study of Five Pre-Islamic Arabic Codes.* The Hague: Mouton, 1970.

Blachère, Régis. *Histoire de la littérature arabe.* 3 vols. Paris: Maisonneuve, 1952–66.

The first two volumes constitute the best account of pre-Islamic and early Islamic literature.

Cantarino, Vicente. *Arabic Poetics in the Golden Age: Selection of Texts Accompanied by a Preliminary Study.* Leiden: Brill, 1975.

Encyclopaedia of Islam, The. New Edition. Leiden: Brill, 1954– .

Articles "ᶜArabiyya" (Arabic Language and Literature, 1:561–603, especially pp. 583–86); "(Djazīrat) al-ᶜArab" (Arabian Peninsula, 1:533–56); "Badw" (Nomad, 1:872–92); "ᶜArūḍ" (Metrics, by G. Weil, 1:667–77); and "Kaṣīda" (Ode, by F. Krenkow, G. Lecomte et al., 4:713–16).

Also see articles under names of individual poets.

Gabrieli, Francesco. "Ancient Arabic Poetry," in *Diogenes* 40 (Winter 1962):82–95.

Gibb, H. A. R. *Arabic Literature,* pp. 1–31. 2d rev. ed., Oxford: Clarendon Press, 1963.

Hitti, Philip K. *History of the Arabs, from the Earliest Times to the Present.* 8th ed., London: Macmillan, 1963. Pbk ed., New York: St. Martin's Press, 1963.

Chapters 1, 2, and especially 3.

Nicholson, R. A. *A Literary History of the Arabs.* 2d ed., Cambridge University Press, 1930. Pbk ed., 1969.
  Chapters 1, 2, and especially 3.
Stetkevych, Suzanne Pinckney. "The Ṣuʿlūk and His Poem: A Paradigm of Passage Manqué," in *Journal of the American Oriental Society* 104 (1984)4:661–78.
Von Grunebaum, G. E. "Arabic Poetics," in H. Franz and G. L. Anderson, eds., *Indiana University Conference on Oriental-Western Literary Relations,* pp. 27–46. Chapel Hill: University of North Carolina Press, 1955.
Zwettler, Michael. *The Oral Tradition of Classical Arabic Poetry: Its Character and Implications.* Columbus: Ohio State University Press, 1978.

TOPICS FOR DISCUSSION

1. The special place of Arabian poetry: the Arab love of poetry; the poet and his role in pre-Islamic society; poetry as a model of literary excellence, as a record of the past, and as a mirror of Bedouin life.

2. The natural setting: desert background and pastoral life; the Arab's feeling for nature as shown through concrete, sensuous imagery and use of local color.

3. The Bedouin spirit: nomadic love of freedom and independence; chivalry, generosity, and tribal loyalty as dominant ideals.

4. Arab paganism and hedonism; underlying pessimism and signs of a religious awakening.

5. Intense subjectivity of the poet; his personal experience always central.

6. Structure and style: metrical complexity and elaborateness; the highly conventionalized nature of the odes (stereotyped beginning, common themes, epithets, figures of speech); casual mood and spontaneity of expression; lack of unified theme.

15

7. Special qualities of individual poets:
   a. Imr al-Qais: his love adventures, daring, feeling for nature.
   b. Ṭarafa: his passionate tone, hedonism.
   c. Zuhair: moral earnestness and depth of religious feeling.
   d. Labīd: his feeling for the desert, pessimism.
   e. ʿAntara: heroism and chivalry.
   f. ʿAmr: glorification of self, family, and tribe.
   g. Ḥārith ibn Ḥilliza: panegyric; conception of justice.

THE QUR'ĀN (AL-QUR'ĀN)

The revelations to the Prophet Muhammad, compiled soon after his death, are accepted by Muslims as God's final Word; the Qur'ān is indispensable to all reading in the later tradition.

TRANSLATIONS

Complete

Ali, Abdullah Yusuf, trans. *The Holy Qurān: Text, Translation, and Commentary*. Brentwood, MD: Amana, 1983.

An annotated translation giving background and interpreting passages in the light of modern Muslim thought.

Arberry, A. J., trans. *The Koran Interpreted*. 2 vols. London: Allen and Unwin, 1955; New York: Macmillan, 1955.

An attempt to popularize the Qur'ān and to do justice to the rhetoric and artistry of the original text; of all the translations into English it is recommended for general extended reading.

Bell, Richard, trans. *The Qur'ān. Translated, with a Critical Rearrangement of the Surahs*. 2 vols. Edinburgh: Clark, 1937–39.

The best scholarly translation available in English; attempts a chronological rearrangement of the *sūras* (chapters) as well as the verses within each *sūra*. Especially recommended for brief, exact quotations and for more specialized uses.

Blachère, Régis, trans. *Le Coran*. 3 vols. Paris: Maisonneuve, 1949–51.

A distinguished scholarly translation into French that attempts to reconstruct the probable chronological order of the verses. With notes and a detailed subject index; Vol. 1 is an introduction.

Palmer, Edward H., trans. *The Qur'an*. Sacred Books of the

17

East, vols. 6, 9. Oxford: Clarendon Press, 1880. (Also available under the title *The Koran,* with an introduction by R. A. Nicholson. Oxford University Press, 1928; reissued in World's Classics ed.)

An early translation, rather literal, but deserving of mention.

Pickthall, M. M., trans. *The Meaning of the Glorious Koran: An Explanatory Translation.* London: Knopf, 1930; New York: Knopf, 1931. Pbk ed., New York: New American Library, Mentor, 1953.

A sensitive rendering, although with a tendency to archaize, by an English Muslim convert. Valuable for presenting the modern orthodox interpretation of the teachings of the Qur'ān. The version preferred by English-speaking Muslims.

Rodwell, J. M., trans. *The Koran.* London, 1861; revised ed., London: Dent, Everyman's Library, 1953. Reissue of 1909 ed., New York: Dutton, 1953.

A literal version rendered in a biblical style of English which has the *sūras* arranged in roughly chronological order, with useful short footnotes.

Sale, George, trans. *The Koran with Notes and a Preliminary Discourse.* London, 1734 (new eds., 1825, 1857, 1878); Philadelphia, 1870. Reprinted with introduction by Sir Edward Dennison Ross, London: F. Warne, 1921.

An early and literal rendering valuable for its attempt to adhere to the traditional orthodox interpretation.

Selections

Arberry, A. J. *The Holy Koran: An Introduction with Selections.* Ethical and Religious Classics of East and West, no 9. London: Allen and Unwin, 1953; New York: Macmillan, 1953.

Short Quranic selections freely rendered; designed for the general reader.

Dawood, N. J., trans. *The Koran.* Classics Series. Baltimore: Penguin, 1956. Pbk ed.

Jeffery, Arthur, trans. *The Koran: Selected Suras.* New York: Heritage Press, 1958.

An excellent, scholarly selection with useful introduction and notes. Jeffery's *A Reader on Islam* (see General Works, above) also contains selections from the Qur'ān.

Schroeder, Eric. *Muhammad's People,* pp. 24–144. Portland, ME: Wheelwright, 1955.

Short selections, interspersed with traditions relating the passages to episodes in the life of Muhammad. A sensitive, if somewhat free, translation.

SECONDARY READINGS

Andrae, Tor. *Mohammed, the Man and His Faith.* Translated from the German by T. Menzel. London: Allen and Unwin, 1956; New York: Barnes and Noble, 1957. Pbk ed., New York: Harper, Torchbooks, 1960.

A modern biography from the point of view of religious psychology, and emphasizing possible Christian influences on Muhammad.

Ayoub, Mahmoud. *The Qur'ān and Its Interpreters.* Vol. 1. Albany: State University of New York Press, 1984.

This is the first volume of a multivolume work which proposes to translate and interpret the classical and modern commentary literature on each verse of the Qur'ān. Included in this volume is commentary on the first two *sūras.*

Cragg, Kenneth. *The Event of the Qur'ān: Islām and its Scripture.* London: Allen and Unwin, 1971.

Attention is paid to put the Qur'ān in its historical context in this intelligent effort at recounting the history of the birth of Islam from a Quranic perspective.

—— *The Mind of the Qur'ān: Chapters in Reflection.* London: Allen and Unwin, 1973.

A collection of chapters each of which focuses on one or

another Quranic theme with a particular emphasis on the function of the Qur'ān in the Muslim faith experience.

Encyclopaedia of Islam, The. New Edition. Leiden: Brill, 1954– . Article "al-Kur'ān" by A. T. Welch, 5:400–29.

Gätje, Helmut. *The Qur'ān and Its Exegesis: Selected Texts with Classical and Modern Muslim Interpretation*. Translated and edited by Alford T. Welch. Islamic World Series. Berkeley: University of California Press, 1977.

This work is useful in that it contains representative selections drawn from medieval Muslim exegesis.

Guillaume, Alfred, trans. *The Life of Muhammad: A Translation of Ibn Isḥāq's Sīrat Rasūl Allāh*. Oxford University Press, 1955.

The classical, authoritative Muslim biography, dating from the early ninth century but preserving earlier material, reconstructed in a scholarly translation.

Haykal, Muḥammad Ḥusayn. *The Life of Muḥammad*. Translated from the 8th ed. by Isma'il Rāgī A. al-Fārūqi. [Philadelphia?]: American Trust Publications, 1976.

This biography by a modern Egyptian literary figure has achieved great popularity in the Arab world, and reflects contemporary popular understanding of the Prophet.

Izutsu, Toshihiko. *The Structure of the Ethical Terms in the Koran: A Study in Semantics*. Tokyo: Keio Institute of Philological Studies, 1959. Revised ed., *Ethico-Religious Concepts in the Qur'ān*. Studies in the Humanities and Social Relations, vol. 2. Montreal: McGill University Press, 1966.

—— *God and Man in the Koran: Semantics of the Koranic Weltanschauung*. Tokyo: Keio Institute of Cultural and Linguistic Studies, 1964. Reprint, Salem, NH: Ayer, 1980.

Both works by Izutsu are important and highly illuminating semantic studies of some key concepts and the world view of the Qur'ān.

Jeffery, Arthur. "The Qur'ān," in Wm. Theodore de Bary, ed., *Approaches to the Oriental Classics*, pp. 49–61. New York: Columbia University Press, 1959.

—— *The Qur'ān as Scripture*. New York: Russell Moore, 1952. Reprint, New York: AMS Press, n.d. Islam Series, Salem, NH: Ayer, 1980.

Lings, Martin. *Muhammad: His Life Based on the Earliest Sources*. New York: Inner Traditions International, 1983.

Rahman, Fazlur. *Major Themes of the Qur'an*. Minneapolis: Bibliotheca Islamica, 1980. Pbk ed.

The best discussion of the content and message of the Qur'ān by an outstanding and original scholar. The themes are discussed synthetically rather than verse by verse.

Sherif, Faruq. *A Guide to the Contents of the Qur'an*. London: Ithaca Press, 1985.

A useful and complete index, arranging the themes in sixty-seven sections and citing the relevant verses.

Watt, W. Montgomery. *Companion to the Qur'ān*. London: Allen and Unwin, 1967.

A commentary intended for the general reader, prepared for use with Arberry's translation.

—— *Muhammad at Mecca*. Oxford: Clarendon Press, 1953.

—— *Muhammad at Medina*. Oxford: Clarendon Press, 1956.

—— *Muhammad, Prophet and Statesman*. London: Oxford University Press, 1961; pbk ed., 1964.

Like the author's other two works on Muhammad, of which this is an abridgement, an attempt to understand the Prophet's activity within his own social and economic environment.

—— *Bell's Introduction to the Qur'an*. (Revised and enlarged). Edinburgh University Press, 1970; Chicago: Aldine, 1970. Pbk ed.

The best brief guide to problems concerning the history of the text and features of style. Contains a valuable index to the contents of the Qur'ān.

TOPICS FOR DISCUSSION

1. The Qur'ān as a book: Muhammad as Prophet and the Qur'ān as scripture, the final revelation. The Qur'ān as literature: form and style. In which sense is it original or distinctive? Is it a unified work? Is chronology an unavoidable problem (within the text, in the history of the text, etc.)? What about the development of Muhammed's own thought, his personal involvements, his authorial presence (if any) in the work?

2. The unity and transcendence of Allah as the central conception of the Qur'ān: His majestic aloofness in contrast to his tender compassion. His absolute freedom as against his involvement in a moralistic system which insures retribution or reward for every action.

3. Man's relation to God: Man face to face with God; is there no mediator here? Fear *(wara')* as the essential element of faith and basis of piety *(taqwā)*. Man's unconditional allegiance to Allah: Islam as submission to Allah's will. Equality of all men in their creaturely relation to God. Man's nature: created good but weak and prone to sin. The definition of unbelief and the unbeliever (*kāfir*, literally, "ingrate").

4. Salvation: subjectively through piety; objectively through submission to Allah's will. Predestination and free will. The idea of God "misleading whom he will."

5. The question of the origin of evil in the Qur'ān.

6. The Qur'ān as the basis of the social order: Life in this world as a means to salvation in the next. Emphasis upon "works and obedience." The Qur'ān as the source of all law.

7. The text as a prescription for an Islamic society. The tension between the prophetic view versus the legal/scholarly understanding of Islam. The patriarchal conception of the divine as a basis for human society. The place and role of women.

8. Islamic fundamentalism—literal interpretation and/or prophetic inspiration?
9. Holy war and the resort to violence: how are these to be understood?
10. The view in the Qur'ān of Judaism and Christianity: "The People of the Book."

THE RING OF THE DOVE
(ṬAWQ AL-ḤAMĀMA),
BY IBN ḤAZM (994–1064)

A book on the anatomy of love, by an Andalusian Muslim scholar.
Personal experience and direct observation lend depth and psychological
truth to this outstanding example of an Arabic literary genre.

TRANSLATIONS

Arberry, A. J., trans. *The Ring of the Dove: A Treatise on the Art
and Practice of Arab Love.* London: Luzac, 1953.
   A superior translation that conveys the spirit of the original.
Bercher, Léon, trans. *Le Collier du pigeon ou de l'amour et des
amants.* Algiers: Editions Carbonels, 1949.
Gabrieli, Francesco, trans. *Il collare della colomba, sull'amore e gli
amanti.* Bari: Giuseppe Laterza e Gigli, 1949.
García Gómez, E., trans. *El collar de la Paloma.* Madrid: La
Sociedad de Estudios y Publicaciones, 1952.
   Contains an appendix devoted to works on the *Ṭawq.*
Nykl, A. R. *A Book Containing the Risāla Known as the Dove's
Neck-Ring about Love and Lovers.* Paris: Paul Geuthner, 1931.
   A pioneer effort, although the translation is somewhat awk-
ward. The important introduction discusses the relationship
between the Arabic work and the writings of the Troubadors.
Weisweiler, Max, trans. *Halsband der Taube, über die Liebe und
die Liebenden.* Leiden: Brill, 1944.

SECONDARY READINGS

Abel, Armand. "Spain: Internal Division," in G. E. von
Grunebaum, ed., *Unity and Variety in Muslim Civilization,* pp.
207–30. University of Chicago Press, 1956.

Contains an interesting interpretation of Ibn Ḥazm's *Ṭawq al-Ḥamāma*.

Arberry, A. J. *Moorish Poetry*. Cambridge University Press, 1953.

An English translation of an anthology compiled by Ibn Sa'īd in 1243, called *The Pennants*. Parts of the Arabic work were translated by E. García Gómez, *Poemas arábigoandaluces*, Madrid, 1930 and 1943.

Encyclopaedia of Islam, The. New Edition. Articles "Ibn Ḥazm" by R. Arnaldez (3:790–99); "al-Andalus" by E. Levi-Provencal (1:486–503); and "'Arabiyya" (appendix, Arabic literature in Spain, pp. 599–603).

Gibb, H. A. R. *Arabic Literature: An Introduction*. 2d rev. ed., Oxford: Clarendon Press, 1963.

Chapter 5, pp. 108–16; chapter 6, pp. 136–40; chapter 7, pp. 149–55. See the bibliography for related works in translation.

Hitti, Philip K. *History of the Arabs, from the Earliest Times to the Present*. 8th ed., London: Macmillan, 1963. Pbk ed., New York: St. Martin's Press, 1963.

See Part 4, "The Arabs in Europe: Spain and Sicily," pp. 493–615.

Nykl, A. R. *Hispano-Arabic Poetry and its Relations with the Old Provençal Troubadors*. Baltimore, MD: J. H. Furst, 1946.

A survey of Andalusian poetry with information on poets and translations of selected passages.

Scheidlin, Raymond P. *Form and Structure in the Poetry of Al-Mu'tamid ibn 'Abbād*. Leiden: Brill, 1974.

An excellent introduction to Arabic poetry through the work of one Andalusian figure.

—— *Wine, Women, and Death: Medieval Hebrew Poems on the Good Life*. Philadelphia: Jewish Publication Society of America, 1986.

Sensitive and scholarly translations from the major Hebrew poets of Spain, with commentaries showing the extent to

25

which they shared the literature and culture of the Muslim poets.

Watt, W. Montgomery and Pierre Cachia. *A History of Islamic Spain*. Islamic Surveys, 4. Edinburgh University Press, 1965. Pbk ed., New York: Doubleday, Anchor, 1967.

An excellent short survey, with useful bibliography, covering the period from 711 to 1492. Special sections deal with poetry and prose literature.

TOPICS FOR DISCUSSION

1. Ibn Ḥazm as a psychologist and observer of the human scene. His use of examples drawn from personal experience. The nature of the *Ṭawq* as entertainment, as literature, and as instruction. The author's preoccupation with language and the apparent and hidden meanings of words. Its picture of life and manners in eleventh century Cordova.

2. Ibn Ḥazm's moral and ethical views. The increasing seriousness of the work and the significance of the last chapters. Hints of pessimism and bitterness. The standards of conduct portrayed; do they conform to or oppose those considered proper in the orthodox Muslim world?

3. Techniques and organization of the work. Systematic treatment of the material: the various categories of love; nature and essence of love; causes, symptoms and effects; the tragedies of love.

4. The significance of the work in relation to European troubador poetry and ideas of courtly love. The themes of the martyrs of love and chaste love. Ibn Ḥazm's theory of profane love.

5. Relationship between profane love and the divine love of the Muslim martyrs. Is there an anti-ascetic and anti-mystical trend in the *Ṭawq?*

THE MAQĀMĀT OF AL-HAMADHĀNĪ
(MAQĀMĀT AL-HAMADHĀNĪ)
(968–1008)

A major work of classical Arabic literature, in fifty-two maqāmas, *or rhetorical anecdotes, portraying the adventures of a sophisticated bohemian and a credulous bourgeois. The satire of medieval manners and morals is accomplished with a much-admired linguistic virtuosity. Al-Hamadhānī created the genre that was to be imitated in all languages of the Muslim world until modern times.*

TRANSLATIONS

Complete

Prendergast, W., trans. *The Maqāmāt* by Badī' al-Zamān al-Hamadhānī. Madras, 1915; reissued, with Introduction by C. E. Bosworth. London: Curzon Press, 1973.

Selections

Blachère, R. and P. Masnou, trans. *Choix de maqāmāt, traduites de l'arabe avec une étude sur le genre.* Paris: Klincksieck, 1957.
A translation of fifteen anecdotes by al-Hamadhānī, with a valuable introductory essay on the genre.

SECONDARY READINGS

Abu-Haydar, Jareer. "*Maqāmāt* Literature and the Picaresque Novel," in *Journal of Arabic Literature* 5 (1974):1–10.
Beeston, A. F. L. "The Genesis of the *Maqāmāt* Genre," in *Journal of Arabic Literature* 2 (1971):1–12.
Bosworth, C. E. *The Medieval Underworld: The Banū Sāsān in Arabic Society and Literature.* 2 vols. Leiden: Brill, 1976.

A masterly work, which includes valuable material on the genre of *maqāmāt*.

Encyclopaedia of Islam, The. New Edition. Articles "al-Hamadhānī" (3:106–7); and "Maḵāma," by C. Brockelmann and C. Pellat (6:107–115).

Ettinghausen, Richard. *Arab Painting.* Treasures of Asia. [Geneva?]: Skira, 1962.

Malti-Douglas, Fedwa. *"Maqāmāt* and *Adab*: 'Al-Maqāma al-Maḏīriyya' of Al-Hamadhānī," in *Journal of the American Oriental Society* 105 (1985)2:247–258.

A structural analysis of one of the anecdotes.

—— *Structures of Avarice: The Bukhalā' in Medieval Arabic Literature.* Leiden: Brill, 1985. See especially chapters 4 to 7.

A structuralist approach to literary anecdotes about misers.

Monroe, James T. *The Art of Badīʿ al-Zamān al-Hamadhānī as Picaresque Narrative.* Center for Arab and Middle East Studies, American University of Beirut Press, 1983.

Stresses the unified conception of the stories, and brings out their picaresque and ironic features.

Nicholson, Reynold A. *A Literary History of the Arabs,* chapter 7, especially pp. 328–36. 2d ed. Cambridge University Press, 1930. Pbk ed., 1969.

TOPICS FOR DISCUSSION

See below, *The Assemblies of Al-Ḥarīrī.*

THE ASSEMBLIES OF AL-ḤARĪRĪ (MAQĀMĀT AL-ḤARĪRĪ) (1054–1122)

A major work of classical Arabic literature, in fifty episodes, which illustrates some of the tensions between piety and civilization, the desert and the city in Islamic culture, and reflecting the Arab love of linguistic dexterity.

TRANSLATIONS

Complete

Chenery, Thomas and F. Steingass. *The Assemblies of al-Ḥarīrī.* Vol. 1 translated by Chenery, vol. 2 by Steingass. (Oriental Translation Fund, New Series, 3, 1867; 9 [reissue of vol. 1] and 10 [vol. 2], 1898.) 2 vols. London: Williams, 1867–98; reprint, 1969.

An excellent literal rendering in prose, with a lengthy introduction and notes.

Selections

Nicholson, Reynold A. *Translations of Eastern Poetry and Prose.* Cambridge University Press, 1922; selections 112, 113.

A strict literal translation in rhymed prose of two assemblies (nos. 11 and 12), which keeps to the original form.

Preston, Theodore. *"Makāmāt" or Rhetorical Anecdotes of Al-Ḥarīrī of Basra.* London, 1850.

A free translation of twenty assemblies rendered in a mixture of prose and verse, together with notes and a summary of the untranslated assemblies.

29

SECONDARY READINGS

Blachère, R. and P. Masnou. *Choix de maqāmāt, traduites de l'arabe avec une étude sur le genre.* Paris: Klincksieck, 1957.

A translation of fifteen assemblies by an earlier author, al-Hamadhānī. Contains a valuable introductory essay on the genre.

Encyclopaedia of Islam, The. New Edition. Article "al-Ḥarīrī" (3:221–22).

Monroe, James T. *The Art of Badī' az-Zamān al-Hamadhānī as Picaresque Narrative.* Center for Arab and Middle East Studies, American University of Beirut Press, 1983.

Stresses the unified conception of the stories, and brings out their picaresque and ironic features.

Nicholson, Reynold A. *A Literary History of the Arabs.* 2d ed. Cambridge University Press, 1930. Pbk ed., 1969.

Chapter 7, especially pp. 328–36.

Von Grunebaum, G. E. *Islam: Essays in the Nature and Growth of a Cultural Tradition.* London: Routledge and Kegan Paul, 1955.

Chapter 5, pp. 95–110: "The Spirit of Islam as Shown in Its Literature," especially pp. 104–9.

—— *Medieval Islam: A Study in Cultural Orientation.* 2d ed. University of Chicago Press, 1953; pbk ed., Phoenix, 1961.

Chapter 8, pp. 258–93: "Self-Expression: Literature and History."

TOPICS FOR DISCUSSION

1. Abū Zayd as the central figure of the *Assemblies;* the problematic character of Abū Zayd as hero or anti-hero and of al-Ḥārith as his foil. Abū Zayd's "hypocrisy" and final repentance. How does he justify his actions, his livelihood?
2. The *Assemblies* as a picture of the life of medieval Islam in a more sedentary, urbanized setting and sophisticated culture.

3. The *Assemblies* as an expression of the Arab love of eloquence and scholarship.
4. The *Assemblies* as a literary form: what are the functions of
   a. the alternation of rhymed prose and poetry in each assembly;
   b. the quick transition from one subject to another and from seriousness to jest;
   c. the episodic character of the work; lack of sustained narrative development;
   d. the combination of thematic simplicity with linguistic and literary complexity;
   e. the use of stereotyped characters and situations as vehicles for the display of literary technique and linguistic virtuosity.
5. The *Assemblies* as expressions of the Islamic spirit: the raw spirit of the desert and the sophisticated indulgence of the town.
   a. the use of the *Assemblies* for the exposition of Muslim doctrine: the relation of entertainment to instruction; al-Ḥarīrī's claim to be one "who composes stories for instruction, not for display," and "who assents to doctrine and 'guides to the right path' ";
   b. the repetition of characteristic Islamic themes and images: the mosque, pilgrimage, graveyard, etc.;
   c. Qur'anic verses and imagery, and the relating of Ḥadīth (traditions concerning the Prophet).

THE THOUSAND AND ONE NIGHTS (ALF LAYLA WA-LAYLA)

A collection of imaginative tales for popular audiences, dating from the fourteenth century although probably containing older elements. The genres include fairy tales, romances, legends, didactic stories, humorous tales, and anecdotes. The stories have entertained European audiences since they were introduced to them in the eighteenth and nineteenth centuries.

TRANSLATIONS

Complete

Burton, Richard F., trans. *The Arabian Nights' Entertainments; or, The Book of a Thousand Nights and a Night.* 16 vols. Benares: 1885–88. Besides the Smithers edition in 12 vols. (London: 1894–97) and Lady Burton's edition in 6 vols. (London: 1886), there were several complete reprints of this translation, including those of the Limited Editions Club (6 vols., 1934) and the Heritage Press (6 vols. in 3, 1956).

A literal translation rendered in a mixture of archaic and slang expressions, attempting to reproduce the oriental flavor of the original. The work borrows extensively from Payne's translation (below).

Littmann, E., trans. *Die Erzählungen aus den Tausendundein Nächten, zum ersten Mal nach dem arabischen Urtext der Calcuttaer Ausgabe aus dem Jahre 1839 übertragen.* 6 vols. Leipzig: 1923–28. Reprint, Wiesbaden: Insel-Verlag, 1954.

A distinguished translation by one of the leading scholars of the *Nights*. Conveys the proper tone and character of the original.

Payne, John, trans. *The Book of the Thousand Nights and One Night*. 9 vols. London: 1882–84; 4 supplementary vols., 1884–88. There have been several complete reprints.

The first complete translation in English, noted for its strict literal rendering of the original. It suffers from the lack of explanatory notes and from the use of obscure slang expressions.

Selections

Arberry, A. J., ed. *Scheherezade: Tales from the Thousand and One Nights*. London: Allen and Unwin, 1953. Pbk ed., New York: New American Library, Mentor, 1955.

A lively, up-to-date, free rendering in modern colloquial language of four well-known and representative tales.

Campbell, Joseph, ed. *The Portable Arabian Nights*. New York: Viking, 1952.

Selections from Payne's translation with a summary of all the plots. The edition is marred by a poor introduction.

Dawood, N. J., ed. *The Thousand and One Nights: The Hunchback, Sindbad, and Other Tales*. Harmondsworth: Penguin, 1954.

—— *Alladin and Other Tales from the 1001 Nights*. Harmondsworth: Penguin, 1957.

Selections in modern prose.

Lane, Edward W. *The Thousand and One Nights: The Arabian Nights' Entertainment*. 4 vols. London: C. Knight, 1839–41; 2d ed., 1847. New edition, edited by E. S. Poole, 4 vols., London: Bickers, 1877.

The earliest important translation, rendered into archaic English. Though incomplete and literal, it is valuable for its accuracy and its extensive commentary.

SECONDARY READINGS

Elisséeff, Nikita. *Thèmes et motifs des mille et une nuits: essai de classification*. Beirut: Imprimerie Catholique, 1949.
> Contains an extensive bibliography.

Encyclopaedia of Islam, The. New Edition. Leiden: Brill, 1954–86. "Alf Layla wa-Layla" by E. Littmann (1:358–64).

Gerhardt, Mia I. *The Art of Story-Telling*. Leiden: Brill, 1963.
> The best comprehensive literary study of the *Nights*.

Hamori, Andras. *On the Art of Medieval Arabic Literature*. Princeton University Press, 1974.
> A collection of studies, of which the last two (pp. 145–80) are on aspects of the *Arabian Nights*.

Horovitz, J. "The Origins of the Arabian Nights," translated from the German, in *Islamic Culture* 1 (1927):36–57.

Lane, Edward W. *Arabian Society in the Middle Ages: Studies from The Thousand and One Nights*. Edited by Stanley Lane-Poole. London: Chatto and Windus, 1883.

Mahdi, Muhsin. "Remarks on the 1001 Nights," in *Interpretation* (The Hague), 3 (Winter 1973)3:157–68.

Pellat, Charles. "Alf Layla wa Layla," in *The Encyclopaedia Iranica*, 1:831–35. London and Boston: Routledge and Kegan Paul, 1982–85.
> An authoritative article with bibliography.

Additional Readings in Folk Literature

'Antarah ibn Shaddād. *Anatar, a Bedoueen Romance*. Translated by Terrick Hamilton. 4 vols. in 2; 2d ed., London: J. Murray, 1819. Delmar, NY: Scholars' Fascimiles and Reprints, 1981.

Blunt, Wilfred Scawen and Lady Anne. *The Celebrated Romance of the Stealing of the Mare*. London: Reeves and Turner, 1892. Also W. S. Blunt. *Poetical Works*. 2:129–217. London: Macmillan, 1914. Grosse Pointe, MI: Scholarly Press, 1968.
> An episode from the Antar cycle in Victorian verse.

Connelly, Bridget. *Arabic Folk Epic and Identity*. Berkeley and Los Angeles: University of California Press, 1986.

The best informed discussion of the Arabic folk epic, especially as a means to cultural self-definition.

Encyclopaedia of Islam, The. New Edition. "[Sīrat] ʿAntar" by B. Heller (1:518–21); "Dhū'l-Himma" (the heroine of a romance of Arab chivalry) by M. Canard (2:233–39).

Galley, Micheline and Abderrahman Ayoub. *Histoire des Beni Hilal et de ce qui leur advint dans leur march vers l'Ouest*. Versions Tunisiennes de la Geste Hilalienne. Paris: Armand Colin, Classiques Africains 22, 1983.

Three texts, accompanied by a general history of the Banū Hilāl, maps, genealogies, etc.

Norris, H. T. *The Adventures of Antar: An Early Arabic Epic*. Warminster: Aris and Phillips, 1980.

Translation of a selection, with a critical introduction.

Paret, Rudi. *Sīrat Saif ibn Dhī Jazan, ein arabischer Volksroman*. Hannover: Lafaire, 1924; Orient-Buchhandlung, 1924.

Mainly a summary of the text.

TOPICS FOR DISCUSSION

1. Origin and authorship; the *Nights* as a product of the popular imagination.
2. The *Nights* as an example of the storytelling art; the frame story and the question of structural unity.
3. The *Nights* as a vivid expression of the mood and temper of medieval Islam and a portrayal of its way of life.
4. The supernatural element; the role of magic and *jinn* in the *Nights* as compared to the Qur'ān.
5. Religion as expressed in the form and spirit of the *Nights*.
6. The morality of the *Nights*. Is there any consistent ethical viewpoint?
7. The role of women in the *Nights,* as reflections of popular views.

8. The concept of the hero: whether the *Nights* are stories of character, accident, or fate; character analysis of Judar, Aladdin, etc.
9. Love and the pursuit of pleasure.
10. The impact of the *Nights* on the West and the reasons for its popularity.

DELIVERANCE FROM ERROR
(AL-MUNQIDH MIN AL-DALĀL),
BY AL-GHAZĀLĪ (1058–1111)

A very personal spiritual autobiography, by one of the greatest Islamic theologians, concerning the relation of mystical experience to theology and the rational sciences.

TRANSLATIONS

Jabre, Farid, trans. *Al-munquidh min Adalāl (Erreur et déliverance).* Collection UNESCO d'Oeuvres représentatives. Beirut: Commission internationale pour la Traduction des Chefs-d'oeuvres, 1959.

An excellent translation with an extensive introduction and useful notes.

McCarthy, Richard Joseph, trans. *Freedom and Fulfillment: An Annotated Translation of al-Ghazālī's al-Munqidh min al-dalāl and Other Relevant Works of Ghazālī.* International Studies and Translations Program Series. Boston: G. K. Hall, Twayne, 1980.

The most scholarly and sensitive of all the translations of this famous work. Includes a fine introduction, notes, an extensive bibliography, and short translations of relevant works by al-Ghazālī.

Watt, W. M., trans. *The Faith and Practice of Al-Ghazālī.* London: Allen and Unwin, 1953.

A somewhat literal rendering of al-Ghazālī's *Al-Munqidh* and the *Bidāya;* but a reliable translation.

SECONDARY READINGS

Arberry, A. J. *Sufism: An Account of the Mystics of Islam.* London: Allen and Unwin, 1950.

Bousquet, G. H. *Ih'yā 'Ouloum ed-Dîn ou Vivification des Sciences de la foi: Analyse et Index*. Paris: M. Besson, 1955.

A summary translation of al-Ghazālī's great work.

Encyclopaedia of Islam, The. New Edition. Leiden: Brill, 1954–1986. "al-Ghazālī" by W. Montgomery Watt (2:1038–41).

Faris, Nabih Amin. *The Book of Knowledge, Being the Translation of the Kitāb al-ᶜIlm.* Lahore: Ashraf, 1962.

The first sections of al-Ghazālī's *Revivification of the Religious Sciences.*

Gairdner, W. H. T., trans. *Al-Ghazzālī's Mishkāt al-Anwār (The Niche for Lights).* London: Royal Asiatic Society, 1924. Reprint, Lahore: Ashraf, 1952.

al-Ghazālī. *The Book of Fear and Hope.* Translated by W. McKane. Leiden: Brill, 1962.

This is a translation of vol. 4, book 3, of al-Ghazālī's *Revivification of the Religious Sciences,* one of many translations of parts of his great opus.

—— *Ninety-Nine Names of God in Islam.* Translated by R. C. Stade. Ibadan: Daystar, 1970.

A translation of the major portion of al-Ghazālī's *Al-Maqṣad al-Asnā.*

—— *Tahāfut al-Falāsifah or Incoherence of the Philosophers.* Translated by S. A. Kamali. Lahore: Pakistan Sabih Ahmad Philosophical Congress, 1958, 1963.

Hourani, George F. "A Revised Chronology of Ghazālī's Writings," in *Journal of the American Oriental Society* 104 (1984)2:289–302.

Surveys al-Ghazālī's works and helps explain the development of his thought.

Jabre, Farid. *La notion de certitude selon Ghazālī dans ses origins psychologiques et historiques.* Paris: Éditions Les Lettres Orientales, 1958.

An authoritative and interesting discussion of one of al-Ghazālī's major themes.

Makdisi, George. "Ashᶜarī and the Ash'arites in Islamic Religious History," in *Studia Islamica* 17 (1962), pp. 37–80; and 18 (1963), pp. 19–39.

A fundamental article on the doctrinal school to which al-Ghazālī belonged.

—— *The Rise of Colleges: Institutions of Learning in Islam and the West.* University of Edinburgh Press, 1981.

A fundamental work on Muslim scholarship, scholastic method, and the milieu in which these took place.

Nicholson, R. A. *The Mystics of Islam.* The Quest Series. London: G. Bell, 1914. Reprint, London: Routledge and Kegan Paul, 1966.

Rahman, Fazlur. *Prophecy in Islam: Philosophy and Orthodoxy.* London: Allen and Unwin, 1958.

A readable and lucid exposition of a central theme in al-Ghazālī's work.

Sabbagh, Toufic, ed. and trans. *Lettre au Disciple (Ayyuhā 'l-Walad).* Collection UNESCO d'Oeuvres représentatives. Beirut: Commission internationale pour la Traduction des Chefs-d'oeuvres, 1959.

An epistolary guide by al-Ghazālī to the mystic's life.

Schimmel, Annemarie. *Mystical Dimensions of Islam.* Chapel Hill: University of North Carolina Press, 1975. Pbk ed.

Sherif, Mohamed Ahmed. *Ghazālī's Theory of Virtue.* Albany: State University of New York Press, 1975.

Watt, W. Montgomery. *Muslim Intellectual: A Study of al-Ghazali.* Edinburgh University Press, 1963.

A biography placing al-Ghazālī in his intellectual and social milieu.

Wensinck, A. J. *La pensée de Ghazali.* Paris: Adrien-Maisonneuve, 1940.

An important and lucid introduction to al-Ghazālī's thought.

TOPICS FOR DISCUSSION

1. The question of *Al-Munqidh* as an autobiographical or apologetic work; prescriptive rather than descriptive? His awareness that religious belief is conditioned by cultural differences. Does he claim to rise above them? In any case, does he succeed?

2. Al-Ghazālī's informal and engaging style; his clarity of presentation; his wide resources and knowledge; his power of illustration and extensive use of imagery.

3. Al-Ghazālī's dilemma: rational versus lively faith (certitude) concerning ultimate religious truths *(awwalīyāt)*.

   a. His evaluation of sense perception, intellect, and faith based on "blind acceptance" *(taqlīd)* as sources of "certain" knowledge *(yaqīn)*.

   b. The various approaches to knowledge, namely, philosophy, theology, "authoritative instruction" *(ta'līm)*, and mysticism. The place of the philosophic and mathematical sciences in relation to the religious sciences. The usefulness and limitations of these approaches in arriving at certain knowledge of ultimate religious truths. Is mystic intuitive knowledge *(kashf)* the only means of achieving such certitude?

4. The reconciliation of mysticism and revealed tradition (prophetic revelation).

5. The relation of the mystical experience to prophetic inspiration and ordinary religious experience. The relation of these in turn to the practical conduct of life.

ON THE HARMONY
OF RELIGION AND PHILOSOPHY
(KITĀB FAṢL AL-MAQĀL),
BY AVERROES (IBN RUSHD, 1126–1198)

A classic attempt to reconcile religion and philosophy.

TRANSLATIONS

Gauthier, Leon, ed. and trans. *Traité décisif (Façl al-maqāl) sur l'accord de la religion et de la philosophie, suivi de l'appendic (Dhamīma)*. 3d ed. Algiers: Editions Carbonel, 1942.

A concise, dependable translation in French by a recognized authority, with the Arabic text, a helpful introduction, and notes.

Hourani, George F., trans. *On the Harmony of Religion and Philosophy: A Translation, with Introduction and Notes, of Ibn Rushd's Kitāb faṣl al-maqāl, with its Appendix (Damīma) and an Extract from Kitāb al-kashf ʻan manāhij al-adilla*. E. J. W. Gibb Memorial Series. London: Luzac, 1961.

An accurate translation, faithful to the author's meaning, and especially valuable for its precise, systematic rendering of technical terms. Useful introduction, summaries, and notes.

SECONDARY READINGS

Allard, M. "Le rationalisme d'Averroès d'après une étude sur la création," in *Bulletin d'Etudes Orientales* 14 (1952–54):7–59.

Arberry, A. J. *Avicenna on Theology*. Wisdom of the East series. London: John Murray, 1951.

—— *Revelation and Reason in Islam*. London: Allen and Unwin, 1957; New York: Macmillan, 1957.

Arnaldez, Roger. "La Pensée religieuse d'Averroès," in *Studia Islamica* 7, 8 (1957), 10 (1959).

Averroes. *Averroes' Middle Commentaries on Aristotle's Categories and De Interpretatione*. Translated, with Introduction and Notes, by Charles E. Butterworth. Princeton University Press, 1983.

—— *Averroes' Middle Commentary on Aristotle's Poetics*. Translated, with Introduction and Notes, by Charles E. Butterworth. Princeton University Press, 1986.

—— *Tahāfut al-tahāfut (The Incoherence of the Incoherence)*. Translated by Simon van den Bergh. 2 vols. London: Luzac, 1954.

An authoritative translation. The second volume consists of valuable notes.

Daniel, Norman. *The Arabs and Medieval Europe*. 2d ed., London and New York: Longman, 1979; Beirut: Librarie du Liban, 1979.

See especially chapters 10 and 11 on Arabic science and philosophy in Europe.

Encyclopaedia of Islam, The. New Edition. "Ibn Rushd" (3:909–20), and "Falsafa" (2:769–75) by R. Arnaldez; "Ibn Sīnā" by A.-M. Goichon (Avicenna, 3:941–47).

Fakhry, Majid. "Philosophy and Scripture in the Theology of Averroes," in *Medieval Studies* 30 (1968):78–89.

—— *A History of Islamic Philosophy*, chapter 9, especially pp. 270–92. 2d ed., London: Longmans, 1983; New York: Columbia University Press, 1983.

A clear and concise exposition of Averroes' thought.

Gauthier, L. "Scolastique musulmane et scolastique chrétienne," in *Revue d'Histoire de la Philosophie* 2 (1928):221–53, 333–65.

Goodman, Lenn E., trans. *Ibn Ṭufayl's Ḥayy Ibn Yaqzān*. New York: Twayne, 1972.

An excellent English translation with extensive notes.

Guillaume, Alfred. "Philosophy and Theology," in T. W. Arnold and A. Guillaume, eds., *The Legacy of Islam*, pp. 238–83. Oxford: Clarendon Press, 1931; reprint, 1952.

Contains remarks on the influence of Averroes on European thought and his role in the transmission of Aristotle to Europe.

Hourani, George F. "Averroes on Good and Evil," in *Studia Islamica* 16 (1962), pp. 13–40; reprinted in his *Reason and Tradition in Islamic Ethics,* pp. 249–68. New York and Cambridge: Cambridge University Press, 1985.

Leaman, Oliver. "Ibn Rushd on Happiness and Philosophy," in *Studia Islamica* 52 (1981):167–81.

Maimonides (Moses ben Maimon). *The Guide of the Perplexed.* Translated by Shlomo Pines. University of Chicago Press, 1963. (Also, *The Guide for the Perplexed,* translated by M. Friedländer. 2d ed., 1904; 4th ed., 1927; pbk ed., New York: Dover, 1956.)

Makdisi, George. *The Rise of Colleges: Institutions of Learning in Islam and the West.* University of Edinburgh Press, 1981.

A fundamental work on Muslim scholarship, scholastic method, and the milieu in which these took place.

TOPICS FOR DISCUSSION

1. Averroes' concept of philosophy as a "science" and its relation to revelation.
2. The defense of philosophy and the philosophers against the attacks of the theologians.
3. The legal approach of the treatise.
4. Averroes' theory of allegorical interpretation.
5. The view that agreement with philosophy is the ultimate criterion for correct interpretation. Its intellectual and religious implications; the accuracy of philosophy and revelation; the necessity of scripture; the predetermination of the meaning of scripture by philosophical requirements extrinsic to it.

6. The intellectual and moral significance of the doctrine that philosophical interpretations of scripture should not be taught to the majority.
7. Averroes' attitude towards Islam; towards Greek philosophy.
8. The question of the eternity of God's knowledge.

THE CONFERENCE OF THE BIRDS
OF FARĪD AL-DĪN ʿAṬṬĀR
(*ca.* 1142–*ca.* 1220)

A sophisticated literary treatment, in fable form, of the stages of religious experience in man's contemplative journey toward union with God, by a Persian Sufi.

TRANSLATION

Darbandi, A. and D. Davis, trans. *The Conference of the Birds.* London: Penguin Classics, 1984.

The best translation, recommended for general education.

SECONDARY READINGS

ʿAṭṭār, Farīd al-Dīn. *The Ilāhi-Nāma; or, Book of God of Farīd al-Dīn ʿAṭṭār.* Translated by John A. Boyle. Manchester University Press, 1976.

—— *Le livre de l'épreuve (Musībatnāma).* Translated by Isabelle de Gastines. Paris: Fayard, 1981.

—— *Le livre des secrets (Asrār-Nāma).* Translated by Christiane Tortel. Paris: Les Deux Océans, 1985.

—— *Muslim Saints and Mystics: Episodes from the Tadhkirat Al-Auliyā ("Memorial of the Saints").* Translated by A. J. Arberry. London: Routledge and Kegan Paul, 1966; reprint, 1976.

Excerpts from ʿAṭṭār's *Tadhkirat al-Awliyā.*

—— *Pend-Nāmeh (Le livre des conseils).* Translated and edited by Silvestre de Sacy. Paris: L'imprimerie Royale, 1819.

Awn, Peter J. *Satan's Tragedy and Redemption: Iblīs in Sufi Psychology.* Leiden: Brill, 1983.

Contains an analysis of ʿAṭṭār's sophisticated treatment of the Islamic devil figure.

Encyclopaedia of Islam, The. New Edition. "ʿAṭṭār, Farīd al-Dīn," by H. Ritter (3:752–55).

al-Hujwīrī, ʿAlī ibn ʿUthmān. *Kashf Al-Maḥjūb.* Translated by Reynold A. Nicholson. London: Luzac, 1911; reprint ed., New Delhi: Taj, 1982.

Levy, Reuben. *An Introduction to Persian Literature.* New York: Columbia University Press, 1969.

A useful short survey.

Meier, Fritz. "The Spiritual Man in the Persian Poet ʿAṭṭār," in *Spiritual Disciplines: Papers from the Eranos Yearbooks.* Translated by R. Manheim. New York: Pantheon, 1960.

Nasr, Seyyed Hossein. "The Spiritual States in Sufism," in *Essays in Sufism,* pp. 68–83. London: Allen and Unwin, 1972. Albany: State University of New York Press, 1973.

Rice, Cyprian. *The Persian Sufis.* London: Allen and Unwin, 1964.

Ritter, Helmut. *Das Meer der Seele.* Leiden: Brill, 1955.

The best overall treatment of ʿAṭṭār's work.

—— "Muslim Mystics' Strife with God," in *Oriens* 5 (1952): 1–15.

Schimmel, Annemarie. *As Through a Veil: Mystical Poetry in Islam.* New York: Columbia University Press, 1982.

TOPICS FOR DISCUSSION

1. ʿAṭṭār's technique: the function of the anecdotes; the story as an allegory of the Sufi path. The role of the Hoopoe; the meaning of the birds, of the valleys; the excuses of the birds.
2. To what extent does the structure of the work reflect the content? The text as an epic poem that evokes the Sufi way. How does it compare with al-Ghazālī's more rational presentation of the matter?

3. The relationship between love and suffering, reason and the irrational; the function of the madman.
4. ʿAṭṭār's conception of the world; of existence; of the soul.
5. The problem of man's access to God; of man's ability to attain communion with God; the role reason plays in this quest.
6. The significance of the anecdote of the moth and the flame; of the final scene of recognition and union.

THE MYSTICAL POETRY OF JALĀL AL-DĪN RŪMĪ (1207–1273)

The greatest mystical poet of Persia.

TRANSLATIONS

Complete: Mathnawī

Nicholson, R. A., trans. *The Mathnawí of Jalálu'ddín Rúmí*. 8 vols. Gibb Memorial Series, n.s. 4. London: Luzac, 1925–40. Vols. 1, 3, 5 Persian text; vols. 2, 4, 6, translation; vols 7, 8 commentary.

    A literal prose translation, with an extensive commentary.

Selections: Mathnawī

Arberry, A. J., trans. *Tales from the Masnavi*. London: Allen and Unwin, 1961

—— *More Tales from the Masnavi*. London: Allen and Unwin, 1963.

Nicholson, R. A., trans. *Rumi, Poet and Mystic*. Ethical and Religious Classics of the East and West Series. London: Allen and Unwin, 1950.

    A brief collection of selections from the Mathnawī.

Whinfield, E. H., trans. *Masnavi i Ma'navi*. 2d ed., London: Trubner, 1898. Reprint, London: Octagon Press, 1973.

    A prose translation of selected passages from all six books.

Wilson, C. E., trans. *The Masnavi*. 2 vols. London: Probsthain, 1910.

    An accurate prose translation of Book 2 only with extensive commentary.

Selections: Divān of Shams-e Tabrizi

Arberry, A. J., trans. *Mystical Poems of Rūmī.* University of Chicago Press, 1968. Pbk ed.

Davis, F. H. *The Persian Mystics: Jalalu'd-Din Rumi.* Wisdom of the East series. London: J. Murray, 1907.

Nicholson, R. A., trans. *Selected Poems from the Dīvāni Shamsi Tabrīz.* Cambridge University Press, 1898; reprint, 1952.

Selections: Quatrains

Arberry, A. J., trans. *Mystical Poems of Rumi. Second Selection: Poems 201–400.* Persian Heritage Series, no. 23. Boulder: Westview Press, 1983.

—— *The Rubā'iyāt of Jalāl al-Dīn Rūmī.* London: Walker, 1949.

—— *Rumi: Mystical Poems.* Persian Heritage Series, nos. 3, 23. Vol. 1, poems 1–200, University of Chicago Press, 1974

SECONDARY READINGS

Arberry, A. J. *The Discourses of Rumi.* London: J. Murray, 1961. Reprint, New York: Weiser, 1972.

Arberry, A. J., trans. *The Mystical Poems of Ibn al-Farid.* London: Walker, 1952; Dublin: Walker, 1956.

Bausani, Alessandro. "The Religious Thought of Maulānā Jalāludīn Rūmī," in *Iqbal* 13 (1965):61–86.

—— "Theism and Pantheism in Rumi," in *Iranian Studies* 1 (Winter 1967)1:8–24.

Chelkowski, Peter J., ed. *The Scholar and Saint: Studies in Commemoration of Abu'l-Rayhan al-Biruni and Jalal al-din al-Rumi,* pp. 169–306. New York University Press, 1975.

    Six of the essays in this volume are devoted to Rumi.

Chittick, William C., trans. *The Sufi Path of Love: The Spiritual Teachings of Rumi.* Albany: State University of New York Press, 1983.

An excellent introduction to Rumi's thought, with selected translations.

Friedlander, Ira. *The Whirling Dervishes: Being an Account of the Sufi Order Known as the Mevlevis and Its Founder the Poet and Mystic Mevlana Ja'alu'ddin Rumi*. New York: Macmillan, 1975.

Halman, Talat. "Jalāl al-Din Rumi: Passions of the Mystic Mind," in E. Yarshater, ed., *Persian Literature*, chapter 11. Albany, NY: Bibliotheca Persica, 1987.

Schimmel, Annemarie. *As Through a Veil: Mystical Poetry in Islam*. New York: Columbia University Press, 1982.

—— *The Triumphal Sun: A Study of the Works of Jalāloddin Rumi*. London: Fine Books, 1978. Rev. ed., London: East-West Publications, 1980.

An excellent study of Rūmī's poetry.

TOPICS FOR DISCUSSION

1. How does Rūmī present his message? What are his strongest images? From what are they derived?
2. What does Rūmī mean when he speaks of wine and drunkenness? Of silence?
3. Rūmī's attitude toward reason; the self; this world. How do his attitudes on these matters compare with ʿAṭṭār's on the same subjects?
4. In Rūmī's mysticism, what roles do the following play: love, sacred and profane; the beloved; beauty?
5. What might Rūmī's reaction have been to al-Ghazālī's *Deliverance from Error*?
6. The form and content of the *ghazals*: the general independence of each line. The expression of a self-contained idea in each line, and its relation to the content.

THE PROLEGOMENA
(AL-MUQADDIMA) OF IBN KHALDŪN
(1332–1406)

One of the most remarkable philosophies of history ever written, Ibn Khaldūn's encyclopedic discourses on the historical factors in the rise and fall of civilizations is a classic among modern world historians.

TRANSLATIONS

Complete

Rosenthal, Franz, trans. *The Muqaddimah: An Introduction to History*. 3 vols. Bollingen Series 43. New York: Pantheon, 1958; London: Routledge and Kegan Paul, 1958.

Includes a selected bibliography compiled by Walter J. Fischel. The first complete English translation. Aims at presenting a text comprehensible to the general reader, combining literal translation with a judicious use of modernized terminology.

Slane, W. M. C. de, trans. *Les Prolégomènes historiques d'Ibn Khaldoun,* in *Notices et extraits des manuscrits de la Bibliothèque Nationale* (Académie des Inscriptions et Belles-Lettres), vols. 19–21. Paris: L'Institut de France, 1862–68. Reissued under the title *Les Prolégomènes d'Ibn Khaldoun*. 3 vols. Paris: Geuthner, 1934–38.

The pioneer translation in French. Highly readable version, freely rendered, but generally faithful to the original.

Selections

Dawood, N. J., ed. *Ibn Khaldūn: The Muqaddimah, an Introduction to History*. Translated from the Arabic by Franz Rosenthal. Princeton University Press, 1969; pbk ed., 1981.

Excerpts from the Rosenthal translation, abridged and edited by N. J. Dawood.

Issawi, Charles, trans. *An Arab Philosophy of History: Selections from the "Prolegomena" of Ibn Khaldun of Tunis.* Wisdom of the East series. London: John Murray, 1950.

A selection of brief excerpts rearranged under topical headings and freely rendered in modernized style and terminology, which emphasizes the modern scientific character of the thought of Ibn Khaldūn and presents his ideas on many subjects.

SECONDARY READINGS

al-Azmeh, Aziz. *Ibn Khaldūn: An Essay in Reinterpretation.* London and Totowa: Frank Cass, 1982.

A systematic presentation of the structure of Ibn Khaldūn's thought, locating this within his own coherent cultural and intellectual tradition.

Bouthoul, Gaston. *Ibn Khaldoun: sa philosophie sociale.* Paris: Geuthner, 1930.

—— "L'Esprit de corps selon Ibn-Khaldoun," in *Revue internationale de sociologie* (Paris) 40 (1932):217–21.

Enan, Muhammad Abdullah. *Ibn Khaldun: His Life and Work.* Translated from the Arabic. Lahore: Ashraf, 1962.

Encyclopaedia of Islam, The. New Edition. "Ibn Khaldūn" by M. Talbi (3:825–31).

Gibb, H. A. R. "The Islamic Background of Ibn Khaldūn's Political Theory," in *Bulletin of the School of Oriental Studies* (London), 7(1933–35):23–31. Reprinted in S. J. Shaw and W. R. Polk, eds., *Studies on the Civilization of Islam,* pp. 166–76. Boston: Beacon, 1962; pbk ed., 1968.

Lacoste, Y. *Ibn Khaldoun; naissance de l'histoire, passé du tiers-monde.* Paris: F. Maspero, 1966.

An interesting Marxist interpretation.

Mahdi, Muhsin. *Ibn Khaldūn's Philosophy of History: A Study in the Philosophic Foundation of the Science of Culture.* London:

Allen and Unwin, 1957; New York: Macmillan, 1957. Pbk ed., University of Chicago Press, Phoenix, 1964.

An original and detailed study of the historian.

Makdisi, George. *The Rise of Colleges: Institutions of Learning in Islam and the West*. University of Edinburgh Press, 1981.

A fundamental work on Muslim scholarship, scholastic method, and the milieu in which these took place.

Nassar, Nassif. *La Pensée realiste d'Ibn Khaldūn*. Paris: Press universitaire de France, 1967.

Rosenthal, E. I. J. *Political Thought in Medieval Islam: An Introductory Outline*. Cambridge University Press, 1958. Pbk ed., 1962.

See especially pp. 84–109: "The Theory of the Power-State: Ibn Khaldun's Study of Civilization."

Talbi, Mohammed. "Ibn Ḥaldūn et le sens de l'histoire," in *Studia Islamica* 26 (1967):73–148.

TOPICS FOR DISCUSSION

1. The question of Ibn Khaldūn's modernity: consider his systematic method and critical approach, as compared to uncritical and uncoordinated accounts of earlier historians; his contribution of a new technical vocabulary for the description of social phenomena; his identification of problems which preoccupy modern social sciences today; his concern with the objective criteria governing social institutions rather than with passing moral judgment on them.

2. Ibn Khaldūn's originality, not so much in specific ideas, as in the achievement of a monumental synthesis of Islamic learning with man and his social institutions as its focus.

3. Man in his "ordinary" environment the center of Ibn Khaldūn's thought; Ibn Khaldūn's preoccupation with the end, the good, and the happiness of man; comparison between Ibn Khaldūn's classical concept of the nature of man and society and that of modern science.

4. The supernatural (its divine and magical aspects) in Ibn Khaldūn's thought; the limitation of its influence to the "extraordinary" in human affairs; the relationship between the supernatural and the ordinary forms and functioning of human social institutions. Does this remove God from history, religion from government?
5. The conflict between reason and revelation as guides to human action; the central problem of Islamic thought. Ibn Khaldūn's reconciliation of the conflict.
6. Ibn Khaldūn's concept of *aṣabīya* (social solidarity or group feeling) as the basis of human society; religion as a powerful component of *aṣabīya*.
7. The juxtaposition of nomadic and urban ways of life as a basic polarity of Ibn Khaldūn's thought.
8. The centrality of the state in Ibn Khaldūn's formulation of social, historical, and economic laws; the four phases in the life of a state and the question of their applicability to nondynastic states.
9. Does Ibn Khaldūn's view of history allow for the cumulative progress of world civilization, or is it purely cyclical in character? What are the possibilities of fundamental reform? Of Islam playing a part in it?
10. "The individual plays a negligible part in Ibn Khaldūn's philosophy; since the individual's tastes and beliefs are conditioned by his environment and education, and since the great men of history have a very minor influence on the course of events" (Issawi, *Ibn Khaldun,* p. 7, note citing Bouthoul).
11. Ibn Khaldūn's disqualification of philosophers as kings.

THE SHĀHNĀMA, BY FIRDAWSĪ
(940–1020)

*A major epic and the greatest monument of Persian language and
literature composed by the poet Firdawsī in the tenth century on the
basis of pre-Islamic prototypes. It comprises the mythical, legendary,
and factual history of Iran from earliest times to the Arab conquest.*

TRANSLATIONS

Complete

Warner, A. G. and E. Warner. *The Shahnama of Firdausi*. 9 vols.
Trubner Oriental Series. London: Kegan Paul, Trench, Trubner, 1905–25.

> A translation in verse.

Selections

Arnold, Matthew. *Sohrab and Rustum*. New York: Longmans,
Green, 1910; reprinted in many editions of the *Collected Works
of Matthew Arnold*.

> Although an abridged and free adaptation of an episode of
the *Shāhnāma*, it catches the tone and the spirit of the original
better than the other translations.

Atkinson, James A. *The Shah Nameh of the Persian Poet Firdausi*.
London: 1892; reprinted many times, among others in *Persian
and Japanese Literature,* vol. 2, London and New York: Colo-
nial Press, 1900; and in *The Sacred Books and Early Literature of
the East,* 7:155–401. New York and London: Parke, Osten
and Lipscomb, 1917.

> Translated and abridged in prose and verse with notes and
illustrations.

—— "Soorab, A Poem; Freely Translated from the Original

Persian of Firdousee," in N. H. Dole and B. M. Walker, eds., *Flowers from Persian Poets.* Vol. 1. New York: T. Y. Crowell, 1901.

Levy, Reuben. *The Epic of the Kings, Shah-nama; The National Epic of Persia by Ferdowsi.* University of Chicago Press, 1967. 4th ed., pbk ed., London: Routledge and Kegan Paul, 1985.

An abridged translation in prose with summaries of omitted sections.

Pavry, B. *The Heroines of Ancient Persia: Stories Retold from the Shahnamah of Firdusi.* Cambridge University Press, 1930, 1954.

Pickard, Barbara Leonie. *Tales of Ancient Persia Retold of the Shah-Nama of Firdausi.* London: Oxford University Press, 1972.

Abridged translation in prose of selected episodes.

SECONDARY READINGS

Banani, Amin. "Firdawsi and the Art of Tragic Epic," in E. Yarshater, ed., *Persian Literature,* chapter 6. Albany, NY: Bibliotheca Persica, 1987.

Bogdanov, L., trans. *The Iranian National Epic; or, The Shahnamah.* Translated from the German of Theodor Nöldeke. Philadelphia: Porcupine Press, 1979.

Encyclopaedia of Islam, The. New Edition. "Firdawsī" by V. L. Ménage (2:918–21).

Grey, Basil. *Persian Painting.* New York: Rizzoli, 1977; Geneva: Skira, 1977.

Hanaway, William Jr. "Epic Poetry," in E. Yarshater, ed., *Persian Literature.* Persian Heritage Series. Albany: State University of New York Press, 1986. Pbk ed.

Rypka, Jan. *History of Iranian Literature.* Dordrecht: D. Reidel, 1968.

Swietochowski, Marie Lukens, and Suzanne Boorsch, comps. *A King's Book of Kings, The Houghton Shah-nameh: Synopses of the Stories Illustrated in the Exhibition A King's Book of Kings,*

May 4–October 31, 1972. New York: Metropolitan Museum of Art, 1972.

Welch, Stuart Cary. *A King's Book of Kings: The Shah-nameh of Shah Tahmasp.* New York: Metropolitan Museum of Art, 1972.

Yarshater, Ehsan. "Iranian National Tradition," in *The Cambridge History of Iran,* vol. 3, part 1, pp. 359–477. Cambridge University Press, 1985.

    Contains the background material and an analysis of the content of the *Shāhnāma.*

TOPICS FOR DISCUSSION

1. The major themes of the *Shāhnāma:* the feud between Iran and Turan; Iranian heroic ages; the institution of kingship and the defense of the Iranian land.
2. The characters of the *Shāhnāma;* the culture-heroes and the transformation of mythical figures into world-kings; the Keyanian epic-cycle and the legends of the Keyanian kings.
3. Aspects of Iranian nationalism in the *Shāhnāma.*
4. The character of the noble warrior in the *Shāhnāma;* the exploits of kings and warriors; primitive forms of combat; heroic conceits; the Rostam cycle.
5. The great tragedies in the *Shāhnāma* and their character.
6. Moral values of the *Shāhnāma.* The role of the national epic in maintaining the ideals of the society.
7. The *Shāhnāma* as the mainstay of Iranian identity.

THE RUBĀ'IYYĀT OF
'UMAR KHAYYĀM (eleventh century)

The Rubā'iyyāt *represents a persistent trend of skepticism and reflections on the transience of the world in Persian lyric poetry, and forms an important aspect of its poetic sensibilities.*

TRANSLATIONS

Avery, Peter and John Heath-Stubbs, trans. *The Ruba'iyat of Omar Khayyam*. London: Penguin Classics, 1984.

> The latest translation and the result of a collaboration between an Iranist and a poet.

FitzGerald, E. G., trans. *The Ruba'iyat of Omar Khayyam*. Classics Series. 1st ed., London: Bernard Quaritate, 1859. New York: Airmont, 1969.

> A free translation of exceptional merit which captures the spirit of Khayyām, conveys his message, and reflects much of his imagery.

Graves, Robert and Omar Ali-Shah, trans. *The Rubaiyyat of Omar Khayyam*. London: Cassell, 1967.

> Based on a dubious manuscript, and attributing mystical thought to Khayyām, which runs counter to the consensus on this skeptic poet.

SECONDARY READINGS

Arberry, A. J. *The Romance of Ruba'iyat*. London: Allen and Unwin, 1959.

> Includes a reprint of FitzGerald's first edition.

Browne, E. G. *A Literary History of Persia*. 4 vols. Cambridge University Press, 1928–30; reprint, 1956–59; vol. 2.

Dashti, Ali. *In Search of Omar Khayyam*. Translated by L. P. Elwell-Sutton. New York: Columbia University Press, 1971. An authoritative work by a Persian critic dealing with both the questions of textual criticism and Khayyamian thought.

Elwell-Sutton, L. P. "'Omar Khayyām," in E. Yarshater, ed., *Persian Literature,* chapter 8. Albany, NY: Bibliotheca Persica, 1987.

TOPICS FOR DISCUSSION

1. The form of *rubā'ī* (quatrain) and its terse and epigrammatic characters.
2. The Khayyamian thought; Khayyām's skepticism in the face of religious dogmatic certainty; his agnosticism and his perception of human helplessness and ignorance.
3. The nature of Khayyamian hedonism; comparison with epicurean thought. The underlying melancholy of Khayyām's mode of thinking.
4. Lyrical aspects of the *Rubā'iyyāt;* their affinity with contents of *ghazal* poetry.

THE BOOK OF DEDE KORKUT
(KITAB-I DEDE KORKUT)

Twelve epic tales in prose and verse as presented in sixteenth-century manuscripts. An Islamic coloring is superimposed on a setting that reflects the pre-Islamic heroic age of the Oghuz Turks.

TRANSLATIONS

Lewis, Geoffrey. *The Book of Dede Korkut.* Baltimore: Penguin, 1974. Pbk ed.

 A sensitive translation with map, introduction, and notes.

Sumer, Faruk, with Ahmet E. Uysal and Warren S. Walker. *The Book of Dede Korkut: A Turkic Epic.* Austin and London: University of Texas Press, 1972.

 Translation with map, introduction, notes and bibliography.

SECONDARY READINGS

Başgöz, Ilhan. "The Turkist Folk Stories about the Lives of Minstrels," in *Journal of American Folklore* 65 (1952):331–39.

Bombaci, Alessio. *Histoire de la littérature Turque,* pp. 185–99. Translated by I. Mélikoff. Paris: C. Klincksieck, 1968.

Boratav, Pertev N. "Notes sur 'Azrail' dans le folklore turc," in *Oriens* 4 (1951):58–79.

Burrill, Kathleen R. F. "Karajuk, Mini-Hero of a Dede Korkut Story," in *Proceedings of the Thirty-First International Congress of Human Sciences in Asia and North Africa,* 1:541–42. Edited by Yamamoto Tatsuro. Tokyo: Tōhō Gakkai, 1984.

Encyclopaedia of Islam, The. New Edition. Articles on "Dede Korkut" by Fahir Iz (2:200); "Ḥikāya," by P. N. Boratav ("The narrative genres of Turkish literature and folklore") (section iii.-, 3:173–75); and "Khiḍr-Ilyās" by P. N. Boratav (5:5).

Mundy, C. S. "Polyphemus and Tepegöz," in *Bulletin of the School of Oriental and African Studies* 18 (1956)2:279–302.

—— "The Cyclops in Turkish Tradition: A Study in Folktale Transmission," in Kurt Ranke, ed., *Internationaler Kongress der Volkserzählungsforscher in Kiel und Kpenhagen: Fortrage und Referale*. Berlin: Walter de Bruyter, 1961.

TOPICS FOR DISCUSSION

1. The *Dede Korkut* stories as literature: prose and verse format; conventions of the narrative technique; description and metaphor.
2. What do the stories reveal about the role of the musician-storyteller among the Oghuz Turks?
3. The *Dede Korkut* stories as an expression of the Oghuz ethos and way of life: how do the stories exemplify Orhuz attitudes toward heroism, rulership, loyalty, women, family relationships, childlessness, nature, fortune, and death?
4. The *Dede Korkut* stories as a reflection of the spread of Islam among the Turks.
5. Common themes in the epic material of the classical Greek and Oghuz Turkish traditions.

THE MYSTICAL POETRY OF YUNUS
EMRE (*d. ca.* 1320)

*One of the most important of Anatolian Turkish mystic poets, Yunus
Emre was also one of the first to use Turkish as a serious literary
language.*

TRANSLATIONS

Halman, Talât Sait, ed. *Yunus Emre and His Mystical Poetry.*
Bloomington: Indiana University Turkish Studies, 1981.
 Verse translations of forty-six poems, preceded by six arti-
cles contributed by scholars in Great Britain, Turkey, and the
United States.
Menemencioğlu, Nermin, ed., in collaboration with Fahir Iz.
The Penguin Book of Turkish Verse, pp. 13, 123–28. Baltimore:
Penguin, 1978.

SECONDARY READINGS

Birge, John Kingsley. "Yunus Emre: Turkey's Great Poet of
the People," in *The MacDonald Presentation Volume,* pp. 43–
60. Princeton University Press, 1933.
—— *The Bektashi Order of Dervishes,* pp. 53–55 and 107–109.
London: Luzac, 1937.
Bombaci, Alessio. *Histoire de la Littérature Turque,* pp. 228–41.
Translated by I. Melikoff. Paris: Librairie C. Klincksieck,
1968.
Cahen, Claude. *Pre-Ottoman Turkey.* London: Sidgwick and
Jackson, 1968. See especially Part 4, 11, pp. 347–360, "Intel-
lectual and Artistic Life in Asia Minor in the Time of the
Mongols."

Gibb, E. J. W. *A History of Ottoman Poetry*. 1:164–75. London: Luzac, 1900.

Halman, Talât Sait. "Imitations and Mutations: The Impact of Islam on Turkish Poetry," in *Yearbook of Comparative Literature*. Bloomington: Indiana University Press, 1971.

Schimmel, Annemarie. *Mystical Dimensions of Islam*, pp. 328–43. Chapel Hill: University of North Carolina Press, 1975. Pbk ed.

Sofi Huri. "Yunus Emre: In Memoriam," in *Muslim World* 46 (1959):111–23.

TOPICS FOR DISCUSSION

1. The relation between the poetry of Rūmī and Yunus Emre, both products of thirteenth/fourteenth century Anatolia.
2. The place of Yunus Emre in the literature of the Turks and Turkish Islam.
3. Yunus Emre's language and literary technique.
4. Yunus Emre's mystic imagery.
5. Yunus Emre's philosophy of humanism and universalism.

LEYLĀ AND MEJNŪN, BY FUZŪLĪ
(ca. 1495–1556)

The story of Leylā and Mejnūn stems from an old Arabic legend of unrequited love among the Bedouins. Its first appearance as a verse romance (mathnawī) *was in 1133 in a Persian work by Nezami, who developed the story according to the ascetic theory of love. Fuzūlī's beautiful treatment of it as a mystic allegory is the best-known Turkish version of the romance.*

TRANSLATIONS

Nizāmī, Ḥarīm. *Layla and Majnūn.* Translated from the Persian and edited by R. Gelpke. English Version, E. Matthew and G. Hill, trans. Boulder, CO: Shambala, 1978.

Sofi Huri, trans. (from the Turkish). *Leylā and Mejnūn by Fuzūlī.* With an Introduction, notes and a bibliography by Alessio Bombaci (translated from the Italian by Elizabeth Davies). London: George Allen and Unwin, 1970.

A verse translation with detailed history of the poem.

SECONDARY READINGS

Andrews, Walter G. *Poetry's Voice, Society's Song: Ottoman Lyric Poetry,* pp. 36–88. Seattle and London: University of Washington Press, 1985.

Bombaci, Alessio. *Histoire de la Littérature Turque,* pp. 31–62, 203–15. Translated by I. Melikoff. Paris: Librairie C. Klincksieck, 1968.

Encyclopaedia of Islam, The. New Edition. Articles on "Fuḍūlī" by Abdülkadir Karahan (2:937–39); and "Madjnūn Laylā" by Ch. Pellat, J. T. P. de Bruijn, B. Flemming, and J. A. Haywood (5:1102–07).

Gibb, E. J. W. *A History of Ottoman Poetry*. 1:11–26, 33–83, 104–24; 3:70–107. London: Luzac, 1958.

Schimmel, Annemarie. *Mystical Dimensions of Islam*, pp. 287–343. Chapel Hill: University of North Carolina Press, 1975. Pbk ed.

TOPICS FOR DISCUSSION

1. The origin of the Leylā and Mejnūn story, its development and treatment in Islamic literature.
2. Fuzūlī's *Leylā and Mejnūn* as a literary work. Its place in the development of the *mathnawī* genre. Fuzūlī's use of convention and innovation in format and style.
3. Fuzūlī's *Leylā and Mejnūn* as a mystic allegory of the passage from "metaphoric" to "true" love. In what way does its presentation of the paradigm of love, lover, and beloved differ from that of Nizami's romance? What are the roles of Nevfel, Ibni Salam, and Zayd? How does Fuzūlī regard the world? Fortune? What significance is given to beauty, human desire and abstinence, sorrow and joy, madness and reason, union and separation?
4. To what extent does Fuzūlī present environment and characters of *Leylā and Mejnūn* realistically?

II. Classics of the Indian Tradition

GENERAL WORKS

Basic Bibliographies

Dell, David J. et al., eds. *Guide to Hindu Religion.* Boston: Hall, 1981.

A useful annotated bibliography.

Emeneau, M. B. *A Union List of Printed Indic Texts and Translations in American Libraries.* American Oriental Series, vol. 7. New Haven: American Oriental Society, 1935.

A standard reference work listing available translations at that time from Indic languages.

Patterson, Maureen L. P. *South Asian Civilizations: A Bibliographic Synthesis.* University of Chicago Press, 1982.

The best bibliography of English works.

Potter, Karl H., ed. *The Encyclopedia of Indian Philosophies.* 2d rev. ed., Delhi: Motilal Banarsidass, and Princeton University Press, 1983– .

Przyluski, Jean M. Lalou et al. *Bibliographie bouddhique, fasç. 1–31.* Fasç. 1–3 (January 1928–May 1931), Paris: Geuthner, 1930–33; fasç. 4–31 (May 1931–May 1958), Paris: Maissonneuve, 1934–61.

An annotated survey of publications on Buddhism throughout the world from January 1928 through May 1958.

Reynolds, Frank E. et al., eds. *Guide to Buddhist Religion.* Boston: Hall, 1982.

Indian Literature

Chaitanya, Krishna. *A New History of Sanskrit Literature.* New York: Asia Publishing Co., 1962.

A general survey of major works.

De, S. K. *History of Sanskrit Literature.* University of Calcutta, 1947.

Comprehensive survey of the literary works of the classical Indic tradition.

—— *Sanskrit Poetics as a Study of Aesthetics.* The Tagore Memorial Lectures. Berkeley: University of California Press, 1963.

A good introduction to the major issues of Indian aesthetic theory.

de Bary, Wm. Theodore, ed. *Approaches to the Oriental Classics: Asian Literature and Thought in General Education.* New York: Columbia University Press, 1959; 2d rev. ed., 1989.

A collection of essays on various Oriental classics and their significance for general education.

Dimock, Edward C. et al. *The Literatures of India: An Introduction.* University of Chicago Press, 1974.

A collection of excellent critical essays on aspects of Indian literature, with reference to major Indian critical theories.

Gargi, Balwant. *Theatre in India.* New York: Theatre Arts Books, 1962.

An introductory survey of Sanskrit drama as well as the popular and modern theater.

Gonda, J., ed. *History of Indian Literature.* 10 vols. Wiesbaden: Harrassowitz, 1975–81.

See especially vol. 1, fasç. 2, R. S. MacGregor, ed., *Hindi Literature of the 19th and Early 20th Centuries,* 1984; vol. 10, fasç. 1, Kamil Zvelebil, ed., *Tamil Literature,* 1974; vol. 9, fasç. 3, Dusan Zbavitel, ed., *Bengali Literature,* 1976.

Keith, Arthur Berriedale. *A History of Sanskrit Literature.* Oxford: Clarendon Press, 1928.

—— *The Sanskrit Drama: Its Origin, Development, Theory, and Practice.* Oxford: Clarendon Press, 1924.

The two titles by Keith were standard works in English on classical Indian literature and dramaturgy, but are now somewhat outdated.

Macdonell, Arthur A. *A History of Sanskrit Literature.* New York: Appleton, 1900; London: Heinemann, 1900.

Useful survey of Sanskrit literary works.

Warder, Arthur K. *Indian Kavya Literature*. 3 vols. Delhi: Motilal Banarsidass, 1972–77.

Analysis of Sanskrit literature in terms of classical Indian criticism.

Winternitz, Moriz. *A History of Indian Literature*. Translated from the German by S. Ketkar and H. Kohn. Vols. 1–2, University of Calcutta, 1927–33; vol. 1, part 1, 2d ed., 1959. Vol. 3, part 1, Delhi: Motilal Banarsidass, 1963.

The most complete treatment in English of Indian literature.

Indian Thought and Religion

Brown, William Norman. *Man in the Universe: Some Continuities in Indian Thought*. The Tagore Memorial Lectures. Berkeley: University of California Press, 1966.

A suggestive discussion of major themes in Indian culture.

de Bary, Wm. Theodore et al. *Sources of Indian Tradition*. New York: Columbia University Press, 1958; pbk ed., 2 vols., 1964; rev. ed., 1988.

Dhavamony, Mariasusai. *Love of God according to Śaiva Siddhānta: A Study in the Mysticism and Theology of Śaivism*. Oxford: Clarendon Press, 1971.

A detailed study of Hindu theology according to an important sect of Shaivism.

Dimmett, Cornelia and J. A. B. van Buitenan, eds. *Classical Hindu Mythology: A Reader in the Sanskrit Purānas*. Philadelphia: Temple University Press, 1978.

Eck, Diana L. *Darśan: Seeing the Divine in India*. Focus on Hinduism and Buddhism Series. Chambersburg, PA: Anima Books, 1981.

A fine first view of Hinduism.

Edgerton, Franklin. *The Beginnings of Indian Philosophy: Summing Up After a Lifetime of Philological Study and Reflection*. Cambridge: Harvard University Press, 1965.

An introduction to Indian thought, with translations from

71

the Vedas, the Upanishads, the *Bhagavadgītā,* and the Mokshadharma section of the *Mahābhārata.*

Eliade, Mircea, ed. *A History of Religious Ideas.* 2 vols. Translated from the French by William R. Trask. University of Chicago Press, 1978–82.

Embree, Ainslie, ed. *The Hindu Tradition.* New York: Modern Library, 1966.

> An introduction to major aspects of Indian civilization through selected readings.

Farquhar, J. N. *An Outline of the Religious Literature of India.* London: Oxford University Press, 1920.

> A useful survey with good bibliography.

Hastings, James, ed. *Encyclopaedia of Religion and Ethics.* 13 vols. Edinburgh: Clark, 1908–26. New York: Scribner's, 1913–27; 13 vols. in 7; New York: Scribner's, 1951.

> The articles on Indic subjects are still useful even though some are outdated. The Index (vol. 13) is quite complete and locating pertinent Indic themes is easy.

Hawley, John Stratton and Donna Marie Wulff, eds. *The Divine Consort: Rādhāa and the Goddesses of India.* Berkeley: Berkeley Religious Studies Series, 1982. Pbk ed., Boston: Beacon, 1986.

Hopkins, E. Washburn. *Ethics of India.* New Haven: Yale University Press, 1924.

> Somewhat outdated but still interesting.

Kinsley, David. *Hindu Goddesses: Visions of the Divine Feminine in the Hindu Religious Tradition.* Berkeley and Los Angeles: University of California Press, 1986.

O'Flaherty, Wendy. *The Origins of Evil in Hindu Mythology.* Berkeley: University of California Press, 1976.

O'Flaherty, Wendy, ed. and trans. *Hindu Myths: A Sourcebook.* Baltimore: Penguin, 1975.

Potter, Karl H. *Presuppositions of India's Philosophies.* Englewood Cliffs, NJ: Prentice-Hall, 1963.

> An introduction to the systematic philosophies of India,

considered in terms of key topics rather than the traditional "six systems."

Radhakrishnan, Sarvepalli and Charles A. Moore, eds. *A Source Book in Indian Philosophy*. London: Oxford University Press, 1957; Princeton University Press, 1957.

Useful anthology of Indian philosophical texts. The quality of the translations varies greatly, and Buddhism is weakly represented.

Raghavan, V. *The Indian Heritage: An Anthology of Sanskrit Literature*. Bangalore: Indian Institute of Culture, 1956.

Free translations of Hindu religious works with lengthy introductory survey of basic texts.

Shulman, David Dean. *Tamil Temple Myths: Sacrifice and Divine Marriage in South India*. Princeton University Press, 1980.

Zimmer, Heinrich. *Philosophies of India*. Edited by Joseph Campbell. Bollingen Series 26. New York: Pantheon Books, 1951; London: Routledge and Kegan Paul, 1951. Pbk eds., New York: Noonday Press, Meridian, 1956; Princeton University Press, 1969.

A readable but not always reliable generalization of main themes in Indian thought.

Indian Cultural History and Geography

Basham, Arthur Llewellyn. *The Wonder That Was India: A Survey of the Culture of the Indian Sub-continent Before the Coming of the Muslims*. London: Sidgwick and Jackson, 1954. Pbk ed., New York: Grove, Evergreen, 1959.

Excellent coverage of the early period of India's cultural history.

Brown, William Norman, ed. *India, Pakistan, Ceylon*. Ithaca, NY: Cornell University Press, 1950. Rev. ed., Philadelphia: University of Pennsylvania Press, 1960, 1964.

Series of articles on India, reprinted from the *Encyclopedia Americana*.

Davies, Cutherbert Collin. *An Historical Atlas of the Indian Peninsula*. Bombay: Oxford University Press, 1949; 2d ed., Madras and Calcutta: Oxford University Press, 1959; rev. ed., 1965.

A useful collection of sketch maps and historical summaries.

Garratt, G. T., ed. *The Legacy of India*. Oxford: Clarendon Press, 1937; rev. ed., 1951.

Gordon, Leonard A. and Barbara Stoler Miller. *A Syllabus of Indian Civilization*. Companions to Asian Studies. New York: Columbia University Press, 1971. Pbk ed.

Majumdar, R. C., ed. *The History and Culture of the Indian People*. Vols. 1–10. Bombay: Bharatiya Vidya Bhavan, 1951–1965.

Covers the period from the Vedic Age to the twentieth century.

Renou, Louis et al. *L'inde classique: Manuel des études indiennes*. 2 vols. Vol. 1, Paris: Payot, 1949. Vol. 2, Paris: Imprimerie Nationale, 1953. English translation by Philip Spratt under titles *Classical India* and *Vedic India*, Calcutta: Gupta, 1957.

Comprehensive survey.

Schwartzberg, Joseph, ed. *A Historical Atlas of South Asia*. University of Chicago Press, 1978.

Authoritative texts and maps.

Thapar, Romila. *A History of India*. Vol. 1. Baltimore: Penguin, 1965–66; reprint, 1972.

Reliable overview from earliest times to about 1500.

THE VEDAS

Ritual hymns that are the earliest source for the fundamental concepts of the Hindu tradition.

TRANSLATIONS

Complete

Geldner, Karl F. *Der Rigveda.* Harvard Oriental Series. Vols. 33–36. Vol. 36: Index. Cambridge: Harvard University Press, 1951–57.

The best complete German translation; includes copious notes, many of which are based on Sayana's Commentary.

Griffith, Ralph T. H. *The Hymns of the Rigveda.* 2 vols. 3d ed., Benares: E. J. Lazarus, 1920–26.

The most complete English translation, but the language is archaic and there are numerous errors in the translation itself.

Selections

Bose, Abinash Chandra. *Hymns from the Vedas.* New York: Asia Publishing House, 1966.

A good selection of hymns from the *Atharva Veda,* the *White Yajur Veda,* and the *Sama Veda,* as well as the *Rig Veda.* The verse translations read well but are colored by the editor's personal interpretations of the hymns.

Edgerton, Franklin. *The Beginnings of Indian Philosophy: A Summing up After a Lifetime of Philological Study and Reflection.* Cambridge: Harvard University Press, 1965.

Rig Veda translations, pp. 51–75; *Atharva Veda* translations, pp. 79–132.

Macdonell, Arthur A. *Hymns from the Rigveda, Selected and Metrically Translated.* Heritage of India Series. London: Oxford

University Press, 1922; Calcutta: Association Press, 1922.
Good selection and translations.

Max Müller, Friedrich. *Vedic Hymns.* Sacred Books of the East, vol. 32. Oxford: Clarendon Press, 1891.
Translations of hymns to the Maruts, Ruda, Vayu, and Vata.

O'Flaherty, Wendy. *The Rig Veda.* Baltimore: Penguin, 1981. Pbk ed.
Readable, modern translations.

Oldenberg, Hermann. *Vedic Hymns.* Sacred Books of the East, vol. 46. Oxford: Clarendon Press, 1897.
Translations of hymns to Agni from books 1–4 of the *Rig Veda.*

Panniker, Raimundo. *The Vedic Experience.* Pomona: Auromere, 1983.

Smith, H. Daniel, ed. *Selections from Vedic Hymns.* Berkeley: McCutchan, 1968. Pbk ed.
Selections from the translations of Griffith and from Maurice Bloomfield's translation of the *Atharva Veda.* (*Hymns of the Atharva Veda,* Sacred Books of the East, vol. 42, Oxford: Clarendon Press, 1897.)

SECONDARY READINGS

Bloomfield, Maurice. *The Religion of the Veda: The Ancient Religion of India.* London and New York: Putnam, 1908.
Still useful introduction.

Brown, W. Norman. "Agni, Sun, Sacrifice, and Vāc: A Sacerdotal Ode by Dīrghatamas (Rig Veda 1.164)," in *Journal of the American Oriental Society* 88 (1968):199–218.
Four creative scholarly articles on major themes of the *Rig Veda.*

—— "The Creation Myth of the Ṛigveda," in *Journal of the American Oriental Society* 62 (1942):85–98.

—— "The Rigvedic Equivalent for Hell," in *Journal of the American Oriental Society* 61 (1941):76–80.

—— "The Sources and Nature of *Puruṣa* in the *Puruṣasūkta*," in *Journal of the American Oriental Society* 41 (1931):108–18.

Keith, Arthur Berriedale. *The Religion and Philosophy of the Veda and Upanishads*. Harvard Oriental Series, vols. 31, 32. Cambridge: Harvard University Press, 1925; London: Oxford University Press, 1925.

 The standard survey in English, but somewhat outdated.

Macdonell, Arthur A. *Vedic Mythology*. Strassburg: Trübner, 1897. Reprint, Varanasi: Indological Book House, 1963.

 Good introduction to the Vedic gods.

Renou, Louis. *Religions of Ancient India*. London: Athlone, 1953, pp. 1–45. Pbk ed., New York: Schocken, 1968.

 Brief introductory summary.

Staal, Fritz et al. *Agni: The Vedic Ritual of the Fire Altar*. 2 vols. + tapes (2 cassette recordings). Berkeley: Asian Humanities Press, 1983.

 Monumental case study of a Vedic ritual.

TOPICS FOR DISCUSSION

1. The nature of prayer in the *Rig Veda* and the power of language. The metrical hymns of the *Rig Veda* as literature and scripture. What kind of revelation is this, especially as compared to prophetic revelation in the Semitic religions?

2. The religion of the Vedas has been called a "naturalistic polytheism, with an elaborate mythology treated henotheistically." What does this mean? What does it (or the hymns themselves) reveal about how people relate to the gods through ritual, or tell us about the Vedas as expressive or formative of an Indian world view?

3. The crucial role of sacrifice as creative process. Agni and

Soma, as links between earthly priests and the gods. In what way are people, the community, involved?

4. Cosmogonic speculations treated in mythological (e.g., Indra-Vritra myth), naturalistic (e.g., Heaven-Earth), and abstract (e.g., *puruṣa*, being-nonbeing) terms, as early evidence of the speculative drive emerging in the Upanishads.

5. The place of gods and man in a universe governed by ordinances (*dharma*) and truth (*ṛta*).

UPANISHADS (*ca.* 900–500 B.C.)

The concluding portion of the Vedic texts dealing with, and setting the foundation for, classical Hindu philosophical and religious speculation.

TRANSLATIONS

Complete

(Although traditionally there are 108 Upanishads, ten to thirteen are early and fundamental.)

Hume, Robert E. *The Thirteen Principal Upanishads.* 2d ed. London: Oxford University Press, 1931.

   The best translation into English of the major Upanishads.

Max Müller, Friedrich. *The Upanishads.* Sacred Books of the East, vols. 1, 15. Oxford: Clarendon Press, 1879; 1884. Reprint, New York: Dover Publications, 1961.

   A good but somewhat outdated rendition.

Nikhilananda, Swami. *The Upanishads.* 4 vols. New York: Harper, 1949–59; London: Phoenix House, 1951–59. (Abridged ed., 1 vol., London: Allen and Unwin, 1963; New York: Harper, Torchbook, 1964.)

   A translation of the principal Upanishads, with a modern Vedantin interpretation, based on the commentaries of Shankarāchārya.

Radhakrishnan, Sarvepalli. *The Principal Upanishads.* London: Allen and Unwin, 1953; New York: Harper, 1953.

   A very useful edition, containing the transliterated Sanskrit text.

Selections

de Bary, Wm. Theodore et al. *Sources of Indian Tradition*, chapter 3. New York: Columbia University Press, 1958; pbk ed., 2 vols., 1964; 2d ed., 2 vols., 1988.

79

A very short but useful translation of several excerpts from the Upanishads with introductory notes.

Zaehner, R. C. *Hindu Scriptures,* pp. 33–245. New York: Dutton, Everyman's Library, 1966.

Readable translations of major portions of the larger Upanishads and complete translations of the smaller Upanishads.

SECONDARY READINGS

Burch, George Bosworth. "The Upanishads," in Wm. Theodore de Bary, ed., *Approaches to the Oriental Classics,* pp. 84–94. New York: Columbia University Press, 1959.

An enthusiastic account by a contemporary philosopher.

Deussen, Paul. *The Philosophy of the Upanishads.* Translated from the German by A. S. Geden. Edinburgh: Clark, 1906. Pbk ed., New York: Dover, 1966.

The principal philosophical concepts of the Upanishads interpreted from the point of view of Shankara's nondualism (*advaita*).

Edgerton, Franklin. *The Beginnings of Indian Philosophy: A Summing Up After a Lifetime of Philological Study and Reflection,* pp. 135–93. Cambridge: Harvard University Press, 1965.

—— *The Bhagavad Gītā,* 39:3–33. Harvard Oriental Series. Cambridge: Harvard University Press, 1944; London: Oxford University Press, 1944.

One of the best summaries of Upanishadic thought as background to the *Bhagavad Gītā.*

—— "Sources of the Filosofy of the Upaniṣads," in *Journal of the American Oriental Society* 36 (1916):197–204.

An authoritative statement of Upanishadic thought.

Keith, Arthur Berriedale. *Religion and Philosophy of the Veda and Upanishads,* 2:489–600. Harvard Oriental Series, vol. 32. Cambridge: Harvard University Press, 1925; London: Oxford University Press, 1925.

Radhakrishnan, Sarvepalli. *The Philosophy of the Upanishads.* 2d ed. London: Allen and Unwin, 1935.

TOPICS FOR DISCUSSION

1. Do the Upanishads represent a systematic philosophical statement or a consistent philosophical viewpoint? Or do they demonstrate a method, perhaps even a form, of religious praxis?
2. Concern for death and the avoidance of transmigration through knowledge and discipline (*yoga*) with increasing emphasis on monism and monotheism.
3. The equation of two apparently dissimilar elements as a basic characteristic of the Upanishads: e.g., Dawn and the head of the sacrificial horse. What is the point of such speculations?
4. The symbolic interpretation of sacrifices and the stress on understanding their meaning rather than on the performance of them; knowledge as power.
5. The view of language and the power of the word. The significance of Om.
6. The methods of dialectical graded teaching and reduction of plurality to unity. Concepts of the nature of the world: the problem of plurality.
7. Investigation of the individual soul or self (*ātman*), its origin, states of consciousness, constituent elements (e.g., breath, intelligence, desire, food, etc.) leading to the identification of universal power (*brahman*) with *ātman*.

MAHĀBHĀRATA
(*ca.* fifth century B.C.–fourth century C.E.)

The longer of the two major Indian epics, it is primarily a folk epic that includes many religious poems, didactic passages, myths, and legends, and as such is the major encyclopedic source for the significant themes of Indian civilization.

TRANSLATIONS

Complete

Dutt, Manmatha Nath, ed. *A Prose English Translation of the Mahabharata.* 8 vols. Calcutta: H. C. Dass, 1895–1905. Reprint, New Delhi: 1960.

    A fair translation of this monumental work.

Ganguli, Kisari Mohan and Protap Chandra Roy. *The Mahabharata of Krishna-Dwaipayana Vyasa.* 11 vols. Calcutta: Bharata Press, 1883–96. Calcutta: Datta Bose, 1919–30. Calcutta: Oriental Publishing Co., 1956.

    An ambitious translation only slightly inferior to that of Dutt. Both are flawed by unidiomatic expressions, but manage to convey something of the grandeur and structure of the original.

Van Buitenen, J. A. B. *The Mahābhārata.* Books I-V, 3 vols. University of Chicago Press, 1973–78.

    Van Buitenen's complete translation of the first five of the eighteen major books of the *Mahābhārata*, based on the Poona critical edition. Work on books unfinished at the time of his death is being carried on by other scholars. (See also Van Buitenen's translation of *Bhagavadgītā.*)

Selections

Arnold, Edwin. *Indian Idylls*. Boston: Roberts Brothers, 1883; London: Trübner, 1883.

A blank verse translation of eight stories from the *Mahābhārata*, including the well-known Sāvitrī episode, Nala and Damayantī, the Birth of Death, etc.

Brough, John. *Selections from Classical Sanskrit Literature*, pp. 22–69. London: Luzac, 1951.

The best prose translation of the popular Sāvitrī episode, which treats of the ideal faithful Hindu wife and her conquest of Death.

Dutt, Romesh C. *The Ramayana and the Mahabharata*. London: Dent, 1910; New York: Dutton, Everyman's Library, 1910.

A rhymed translation of the main episodes of the story.

Lal, P. *The Mahābhārata*. Calcutta: Writers Workshop, 1968.

A free translation in modern English.

Monier-Williams, M., ed. *Nalopākhyānam: Story of Nala*. Chowkhamba Sanskrit Studies, vol. 53. 2d ed. Oxford: Clarendon Press, 1879.

Sanskrit text, accompanied by a metrical English translation of the famous love story of Nala and Damayantī, translated by H. H. Milman.

Narasimhan, C. V. *The Mahābhārata*. New York: Columbia University Press, 1964.

A literal prose translation of the main story that preserves the flavor of the original.

Narayan, R. K. *Gods, Demons, and Others*. New York: Viking Press, 1964. Reprint, New York: Bantam Books, 1986.

Stories from the epics retold by India's leading novelist.

—— *The Mahabharata: A Shortened Prose Version of the Great Indian Epic*. New York: Viking, 1978. Pbk ed.

Retelling of major stories.

Nott, S. C., ed. *The Mahābhārata of Vyasa Krishna Dwaipayana*.

New York: Philosophical Library, 1956; London: James Press, 1956.

Selected incidents from the Ganguli and Roy translation.

Subramaniam, Kamala. *Mahābhārata*. Bombay: Bharatiya Vidya Bhavan, 1965.

A prose translation of literary merit.

Yohannan, John D., ed. *A Treasury of Asian Literature*, pp. 91–111. New York: John Day, 1956; London: Phoenix House, 1958. Pbk ed., New York: New American Library, Mentor, 1960.

A reprint of the Edwin Arnold translation of the Sāvitrī story.

SECONDARY READINGS

See below under Secondary Readings for *Rāmāyana* of Vālmīki: Antoine, Hopkins, Macdonell, Monier-Williams, Nivedita, and Vora.

Fausbøll, M. V. *Indian Mythology, According to the Mahābhārata, in Outline*. London: Luzac, 1903.

'Ghoshal, U. N. *A History of Indian Political Ideas: The Ancient Period and the Period of Transition to the Middle Ages*. London: Oxford University Press, 1959.

Hiltebeitel, Alf. *The Ritual of Battle: Krishna in the Mahabharata*. Symbol, Myth, and Ritual series, Victor Turner, general ed. Ithaca, NY: Cornell University Press, 1976.

Places *Mahābhārata* in the tradition of Indo-European epics and mythology. A good synthesis of modern scholarship.

Hopkins, E. Washburn. *The Great Epic of India*. New York: Scribner's, 1901.

—— *Legends of India*. New Haven: Yale University Press, 1928.

A poetical "reinterpretation" of several popular legends.

Jacobi, Hermann. *Mahābhārata Inhaltsangabe, Index und Concordanz der Calcuttaer und Bombayer Ausgaben*. Bonn: Friedrich Cohen, 1903.

A survey of the contents, plus a comprehensive index to the epic.

Macdonell, Arthur A. *A History of Sanskrit Literature,* pp. 277–98. New York: Appleton, 1900, 1929.

A short but scholarly statement of the origin of the epic, its date, and the main narrative and episodes.

Sharma, Ram Karan. *Elements of Poetry in the Mahābhārata.* Berkeley: University of California Press, 1964.

Sukthanker, V. S. *On the Meaning of the Mahābhārata.* Asiatic Society of Bombay, 1957.

Four papers on aspects of the epic.

TOPICS FOR DISCUSSION

1. The *Mahābhārata* as an epic in its Indian context: localization of place, but not of time; the secret of its great national appeal through easily identifiable motifs and symbols; allegorical qualities, especially in the Krishna legends.
2. A living mythology: men and gods as part of an ordered scheme of life; the character of its chief figures: men or gods?
3. Concept of the hero. Comparison to Homeric figures, Hector, Achilles, Odysseus, et al.
4. The ethics of the *Mahābhārata*; chivalry and the warrior's code; group loyalty.
5. The expression of human emotions; married love and devotion.
6. Attitudes toward fate and death.
7. The importance of asceticism and the power of vows, curses, and truth.
8. The function of kingship and the social order.

BHAGAVADGĪTĀ (*ca.* 100 B.C.–A.D. 100)

The Bhagavadgītā *is a religious and philosophic synthesis of many aspects of Indian thought. It is the central text of Hindu devotion as well as the classic statement of Hindu social ethics.*

TRANSLATIONS

Arnold, Edwin. "The Song Celestial" (text of 2d ed., 1886), in Franklin Edgerton, *The Bhagavad Gītā.* Harvard Oriental Series, vol. 39. Cambridge: Harvard University Press, 1944; London: Oxford University Press, 1944.

A literary translation in blank verse at the expense of literal accuracy. This version is available in numerous other editions, including the following: Allahabad: Kitabistan, 1944; Bombay: Jaico, 1957.

Deutsch, Eliot. *The Bhagavad Gītā.* New York: Harcourt, Brace, 1968. Pbk ed.

Readable translation intended for academic use.

Edgerton, Franklin. *The Bhagavad Gītā.* Harvard Oriental Series, vol. 38. Cambridge: Harvard University Press, 1944; London: Oxford University Press, 1944. Pbk ed., New York: Harper, Torchbook, 1964.

An accurate English translation.

Hill, W. Douglas P. *The Bhagavadgītā.* London: Oxford University Press, 1928. 2d, abridged ed. (lacking Sanskrit text). Madras: Oxford University Press, 1953.

Accurate translation, with particular emphasis on the religious context of the work. Extensive critical notes and an excellent introduction.

Miller, Barbara Stoler. *The Bhagavad Gita: Krishna's Counsel in Time of War.* New York: Bantam Books/Columbia University Press, 1986. Pbk. ed., New York: Bantam, 1986.

An excellent verse translation with introduction, lexicon of key words, and essay on the influence of the *Gita* on American transcendentalists: "Why did Henry David Thoreau Take the Bhagavad Gita to Walden Pond?"

Nikhilananda, Swami. *The Bhagavad Gita.* New York: Ramakrishna-Vivekananda Center, 1944.

A devotional translation with copious notes by the translator and references on each stanza to Shankara's commentary.

Radhakrishnan, Sarvepalli. *The Bhagavadgītā.* London: Allen and Unwin, 1948; New York: Harper, 1948. 2d ed., London: Allen and Unwin, 1956.

Influenced by other existing versions, but valuable for its verse by verse commentary giving references to world philosophical and religious thought.

Telang, Kashināth Trimbak. *The Bhagavadgītā, with the Sanatsujātīya and the Anugītā.* Sacred Books of the East, vol. 8. Oxford: Clarendon Press, 1882.

A good translation by a devout Hindu. It includes two similar philosophical or religious texts of the *Mahābhārata.*

Van Buitenen, J. A. B. *The Bhagavadgītā in the Mahābhārata: A Bilingual Edition.* University of Chicago Press, 1981. Pbk ed.

Prose versions by translator of longer epic.

Zaehner, R. C., ed. *The Bhagavad-gītā, with Commentary based on Original Sources.* London: Oxford University Press, 1969. Pbk ed.

Coherent English translation with good critical notes.

SECONDARY READINGS

Most of the translations cited above contain useful introductions or commentary.

Aurobindo, Ghose (Sri Aurobindo). *Essays on the Gītā.* New York: Dutton, 1950.

A detailed analysis of the concepts of the *Bhagavadgītā*, from the philosophical rather than historical or philological point of view, by one of modern India's most provocative thinkers.

Bhave, Vinoba. *Talks on the Gita.* New York: Macmillan, 1960; London: Allen and Unwin, 1960.

A series of eighteen short essays on the message of the *Bhagavadgītā* for modern life. These essays were originally talks given to Bhave's fellow prisoners in 1932 during the Indian independence movement.

Dasgupta, Surendra Nath. *A History of Indian Philosophy.* 2:437–552. Cambridge University Press, 1932.

A provocative study of the basic philosophical ideas of the *Bhagavadgītā.*

Desai, Mahadev, trans. *The Gospel of Selfless Action; or, The Gita According to Gandhi.* Ahmedabad: Navjivan, 1956.

Introductory essays by both author and translator give insights into Gandhi's own unorthodox interpretations of Hinduism as well as indicate the meaning the *Gītā* has for the more orthodox.

Edgerton, Franklin. *The Bhagavad Gītā.* Harvard Oriental Series, vol. 39. Cambridge: Harvard University Press, 1944; London: Oxford University Press, 1944.

Short critical essays on the background, philosophy, religion, and significant concepts of the text, based on internal and historical evidence.

Gandhi, Mohandas Karamchand. See above, under Desai, Mahadev.

Jñānadeva (Jñāneśvara, also known as Shri Dnyāndev). *Bhāvārtha-Dīpikā, Otherwise Known as Dnyānesgwarī.* Translated by R. K. Bhagwat, revised by S. V. Pandit and V. V. Dixit. 2 vols. Poona: Dnyaneshwari English Rendering Publishing Association, 1953–54.

Roy, Satis Chandra. *The Bhagavad-Gītā and Modern Scholarship.* London: Luzac, 1941.

An illuminating historical study of critical interpretations and background aspects of the *Bhagavadgītā*.

Tilak, B. G. *Śrimad Bhagavadītā Rahasya*. 2 vols. Poona: R. B. Tilak, 1935–36.

Interesting for relation to Tilak's political philosophy.

Van Buitenen, J. A. B. *Rāmānuja on the Bhagavadgītā: A Condensed Rendering of His Gītā bhāsya*. The Hague: H. L. Smits, 1953.

A fine scholarly translation of one of the most important classical Hindu commentators on the *Bhagavadgītā*.

TOPICS FOR DISCUSSION

1. What is the significance of the *Gita* as a drama; as a philosophical poem? In what sense could it be considered revelation? What is the source of the text's authority?
2. Arjuna's question: the dilemma of fighting and killing to save human civilization. How can one control, or be responsible for, the consequences of one's actions?
3. Krishna's answer in terms of the relation of action to the real self and the Supreme Lord.
4. Implications concerning the value of individual human life and action. Concepts of individual duty or social obligation (*dharma*), social class (*varna*), individual action (*karma*), and inaction as a form of action.
5. Nature and spirit: concept of nature or matter with its qualities; the relation of man to the world.
6. Ways to release: concept of yoga; the three disciplines of action/sacrifice, knowledge/meditation, and devotion.
7. Philosophical and religious synthesis: Sāṁkhya philosophical analysis, yoga practice, Vedānta metaphysics. How does it reconcile the Upanishadic view to the world of action?
8. Nature of the Godhead: Krishna as charioteer, teacher, and Supreme Lord. The concept of the Avatar; preeminent manifestations and universal form of the Godhead.
9. The conception of the Three Strands or *Gunas*.

RĀMĀYANA OF VĀLMĪKI (*ca.* 200 B.C.)

The earlier of the two major Indian epics and the best known in Indian art and legends, this work is primarily a court epic that exemplifies fundamental values and tensions in the classical tradition and forms the basis for many later religious texts.

TRANSLATIONS

Complete

Goldman, Robert P., ed. and trans. *The Rāmāyana of Vālmīki: An Epic of Ancient India.* Vol. 1, Balakānda. Princeton University Press, 1984.

 The first of seven volumes that will present a complete and fully annotated prose translation of the epic.

Griffith, Ralph T. H. *The Rámáyan of Valmiki.* 5 vols. London: Trübner, 1870–74; Benares: E. J. Lazarus, 1870–1874. Reprint, London: Luzac, 1895; Benares: Lazarus, 1895.

 A good verse translation which, in spite of somewhat archaic language, preserves some of the flavor of the original.

Shastri, Hari Prasad. *The Ramayana of Valmiki.* 3 vols. London: Shanti Sadan, 1952–59.

 A prose translation that is fairly reliable as well as readable. Detailed glossaries of Sanskrit proper names and epithets are included in each volume.

Selections

Buck, William. *Ramayana.* Berkeley and Los Angeles: University of California Press, 1976. Pbk ed. New York: New American Library, Mentor, 1978.

 An imaginative retelling of the epic that captures much of its flavor.

Dutt, Romesh C. *The Ramayana and the Mahabharata*. London: Dent, 1910; New York: Dutton, Everyman's Library, 1910; reprint 1929.

A fairly good, but somewhat monotonous, metrical translation of the main narrative elements of the epic. In many respects, this is a useful abridgment.

SECONDARY READINGS

Antoine, Robert. "Indian and Greek Epics," in Wm. Theodore de Bary, ed., *Approaches to the Oriental Classics*, pp. 95–112. New York: Columbia University Press, 1959. "Comments on the Rāmāyana and Mahābhārata" by George T. Artola, pp. 113–18.

Hopkins, Edward Washburn. *Epic Mythology*. Strassburg: Trübner, 1915.

A scholarly reference work on the Indian epics, with detailed index of deities, sages, etc.

Jacobi, Hermann. *The Rāmāyana*. Translated from the German by S. N. Ghosal. Baroda: Oriental Institute, 1960.

Analytical study of the epic, with special concern for the origin and composition of the text.

Macdonell, Arthur A. *A History of Sanskrit Literature*, pp. 302–17 passim. New York: Appleton, 1900, 1929.

Monier-Williams, M. *Indian Epic Poetry*. London: Williams and Norgate, 1863.

An older account of the epics with comparative references to Western literature.

Narayan, R. K. *The Rāmāyana: A Shortened Modern Prose Version of the Indian Epic Suggested by the Tamil Version of Kamban*. New York: Viking, 1972.

An Indian novelist's recreation of the Tamil epic, which was based on Vālmīki's.

Vora, Dhairyabala P. *Evolution of Morals in the Epics*. Bombay: Popular Book Depot, 1959.

A good survey of marriage customs, *karma*, and socioethical concepts in the *Rāmāyana* and *Mahābhārata*.

TOPICS FOR DISCUSSION

1. The *Rāmāyana* as a court epic: scope of the work in terms of geography and time; alternation between urban and forest environments; intrigues, tournaments, and wars.
2. The *Rāmāyana* as a dramatic tragedy, history, and allegory.
3. Levels of interpretation: the role of fate or destiny; personal responsibility for action. Mythological and supernatural elements and their relationship to human life.
4. The plot and narrative as contributing factors to dramatic tension.
5. Typical Hindu motifs: the conflict between duty (*ahamsa*) and desire (*kāma*). A Brahman's curse; asceticism and hermitages; the socially ordered life; concept of truth as the ultimate criterion for action; didactic elements.
6. Descriptions of battles and nature as contributing to the literary interest of the work.
7. Characters of Rāma and Sītā: real people or idealized concepts? the role of human feelings and emotions; Rāma as king or god; Sītā as an ideal wife; Sītā's ordeals.
8. The roles and characters of secondary figures such as Rāvana, Lakshmana, Hanumāan.
9. Factors contributing to the popular appeal of the *Rāmāyana*.

YOGA SŪTRAS OF PATAÑJALI
(*ca.* A.D. 300)

The classical Hindu philosophical treatise on the discipline of yoga, which, though one of the oldest concepts of Indian civilization, continues to attract the serious attention of the Western world.

TRANSLATIONS

Hauer, J. W. *Der Yoga, ein indischer Weg zum Selbst.* Stuttgart: Kohlhammer, 1958.

A careful German translation of the *Yoga Sūtras.*

Prabhavananda, Swami and Christopher Isherwood. *How To Know God: The "Yoga Aphorisms" of Patanjali.* New York: Harper, 1953; London: Allen and Unwin, 1953.

A readable, but not always accurate, translation, with the authors' comments on each sūtra and a lengthy introduction.

Vivekananda, Swami. *Rāja Yoga, or, Conquering the Internal Nature.* Calcutta: Swami Trigunatita, 1901; London: Luzac, 1937; 2d ed. rev., New York: Ramakrishna-Vivekananda Center, 1956. Also in Lin Yutang, *The Wisdom of China and India,* pp. 115–32 (New York: Random House, 1942), and Swami Nikhilananda, ed., *Vivekananda: The Yogas and Other Works,* pp. 577–694, rev. ed. (New York: Ramakrishna-Vivekananda Center, 1953).

This translation (first published in 1899) is quite readable and fairly accurate. Each sūtra is commented upon by the Swami in the light of his neo-Vedantic orientation.

Weiler, Royal W. *Patañjali's Yogasūtras.* Dittographed; Committee on Oriental Studies, Columbia University.

Exact, scholarly translation with good introduction.

Woods, James Haughton. "The Yoga-Sūtras of Patañjali as Illustrated by the Comment Entitled the Jewel's Lustre or

93

Maniprabhā," in *Journal of the American Oriental Society* 34 (1914):1–114.

In several respects this edition, with its commentary, is superior to the following. It is somewhat more readable.

—— *The Yoga-System of Patañjali; or, the Ancient Hindu Doctrine of Concentration of Mind, Embracing the Mneomonic Rules, Called Yoga-Sūtras, of Patañjali.* Harvard Oriental Series, vol. 17. 2d ed., Cambridge: Harvard University Press, 1927.

This edition includes a fairly accurate translation of Veda-Vyāsa's commentary and Vācaspati's *Tattva-vaiśāradī* (gloss). The translation of the sūtras themselves is accurate, but not readily comprehensible.

SECONDARY READINGS

Behanan, Kovoor T. *Yoga: A Scientific Evaluation.* New York: Macmillan, 1937; London: Secker and Warburg, 1937. New York: Dover, 1960.

A provocative analysis of yoga practice in the light of modern Western scientific standards, especially those of psychology and psychoanalysis.

Coster, Geraldine. *Yoga and Western Psychology: A Comparison.* London: Oxford University Press, 1934; reprinted, 1945.

A comparative study of the *Yoga Sūtras* of Patañjali in terms of Western psychology, especially the theories of Freud and Jung.

Dasgupta, Surendranath. *History of Indian Philosophy,* 1:208–73. 4 vols. Cambridge University Press, 1932–49.

A scholarly analysis of the fundamental principles of the Sāṃkhya and yoga philosophies.

—— *Yoga as Philosophy and Religion.* London: Kegan Paul, Trench, Trübner, 1924; New York: Dutton, 1924.

A commentary on Patañjali's *Yoga Sūtras* on the basis of traditional commentaries. The emphasis is on metaphysics, ethics, and practice.

Eliade, Mircea. *Yoga: Immortality and Freedom.* Translated from the French by Willard R. Trask. New York: Pantheon, 1958; London: Routledge and Kegan Paul, 1958.

A comprehensive survey of yoga, its origin and development. There are several minor philological inaccuracies in this detailed work.

Gervis, Pearce. *Naked They Pray*. London: Cassell, 1956; New York: Duell, Sloan and Pearce, 1957.

An unpretentious personal account of the author's contact with yogis in northwest India. These experiences are described with admirable simplicity and open-mindedness.

Hopkins, E. Washburn. "Yoga-Technique in the Great Epic," in *Journal of the American Oriental Society* 22(1901):333–79.

An account of the concept of yoga as it appears in the *Mahābhārata* prior to its formulation into a philosophical system by Patañjali.

Sivananda, Swami. *Practice of Bhakti-Yoga*. Amritsar, 1937.

This is perhaps the best of the countless books on the practical application of the ancient Indian concept of yoga to the life of modern Western man.

—— *Practical Lessons in Yoga*. Lahore: Motilal Banarsi Dass, 1938.

Woodroffe, Sir John G. (Arthur Avalon, pseud.) *The Serpent Power*. London: Luzac, 1919; 2d rev. ed., Madras: Ganesh, 1924; fifth ed. enl., Madras: Ganesh, 1953.

A translation and commentary on two short post-Patañjali yoga texts dealing with *laya-yoga,* which is concerned primarily with psychic energy and psychic centers in the body. There is a lengthy introduction discussing the theoretical details of the practice.

TOPICS FOR DISCUSSION

1. Psychological aspects: the nature of the mind or thought, its activities or fluctuations; the senses; residual impressions (the subconscious).

2. The control of the mind through yoga discipline: the eight-limbs; the importance of dispassion or asceticism and regular practice.
3. Meditation: the practice of controlled contemplation, including stages of concentration, meditation, and trance.
4. The nature of trance (*samādhi*).
5. Philosophical elements: the spirit or "seer" entangled in matter or nature based on dualistic Sāṁkhya philosophy (see *Bhagavadgītā*, above); the concept of God.
6. The goal of yoga as "isolation."
7. The significance of supernatural powers in the course of yoga practice.
8. The place of ethics and morality in the *Yoga Sūtras*.

THE VEDĀNTA SŪTRA WITH THE COMMENTARY OF SHANKĀRĀCHĀRYA (ca. 780–820)

Shankārāchārya, or Shankara, is the most influential of Indian philosophers, representing nondualistic philosophy based on the Upanishads *(Vedānta), the form of Indian thought best known in the West.*

TRANSLATIONS

Apte, Vasudeo Mahadeo. *Brahma-sūtra Shankara-bhāshya.* Bombay: Popular Book Depot, 1960.

An accurate translation of Shankara's commentary on the *Brahma Sūtras.*

Deussen, Paul. *Die Sūtra's des Vedānta, oder die Çāriraka-Mīmāṅsā des Bādarāyana, nebst dem vollständigen Commentare des Çaṅkāra.* Leipzig: Brockhaus, 1887.

A German translation of Shankara's commentary by an early Western authority on the Vedānta philosophy.

Radhakrishnan, Sarvepalli. *The Brahma Sūtra: The Philosophy of Spiritual Life.* New York: Harper, 1960; London: Allen and Unwin, 1960.

A translation that includes references to the various commentaries, as well as translator's remarks and a lengthy introduction.

Thibaut, George. *The Vedānta-Sūtras of Bādarāyana, with the Commentary by Śaṅkara.* Sacred Books of the East, vols. 34, 38. Oxford: Clarendon Press, 1890. 2 vols., New York: Dover, 1962.

This is still probably the best complete translation in English.

SECONDARY READINGS

Dasgupta, Surendranath. *History of Indian Philosophy,* 1:406–94; 2:1–82. Cambridge University Press, 1932.

A detailed survey of the main philosophical problems of the Vedānta system according to Shankara.

—— *Indian Idealism,* pp. 149–98. Cambridge University Press, 1933.

A short, somewhat generalized discussion of the Vedānta and related systems as idealism.

Deussen, Paul. *Outline of the Vedanta System of Philosophy, According to Shankara.* Translated from the German by J. H. Woods and C. B. Runkle. London: Oxford University Press, 1927; Cambridge: Harvard University Press, 1927.

A short but very useful essay on the concepts of Vedānta in terms of theology, cosmology, psychology, migration of the soul, and emancipation.

—— *The System of the Vedānta.* Translated from the German by Charles Johnston. Chicago: Open Court, 1912.

A systematic and detailed study of the Vedānta as expressed in the *Brahma Sūtras* and Shankara's commentary. This is probably the best book available on the subject.

Deutsch, Eliot. *Advaita Vedānta: A Philosophical Reconstruction.* Honolulu: East-West Center Press, 1969.

The insights of modern Western philosophy are used to elucidate the meaning of the Indian system.

Ghate, V. S. *The Vedānta.* Poona: Bhandarkar Oriental Research Institute, 1926; 2d ed., 1960.

A critical analysis of the classical commentaries of Shankara, Rāmanūja, Nimbārka, Madhva, and Vallabha on the *Brahma Sūtras.* This scholarly study differentiates the five classical schools of Vedānta based on their respective interpretations.

Mahadevan, T. M. P. *Gaudapāda: A Study in Early Advaita.* University of Madras Press, 1952.

A study of the major pre-Shankara Vedantin that illuminates Shankara's dialectics.

Max Müller, Friedrich. *The Vedanta Philosophy*. Calcutta: Susil Gupta, 1955. Originally published as *Three Lectures on the Vedanta Philosophy* (London: Longmans, 1894).

A series of three essays (originally lectures) on the origin of Vedānta, its treatment of the soul and god, and similarities and differences between Indian and European philosophy.

Menon, Y. Keshava and R. F. Allen. *The Pure Principle: An Introduction to the Philosophy of Shankara*. East Lansing: Michigan State University Press, 1960.

Shankarāchāraya. *Upadésāsahasrī: A Thousand Teachings*. Translated by Swami Jagadananda. 1st ed., Hollywood: Vedanta Society of Southern California, 1949. 3d ed., Mylapore and Madras: Sri Ramakrishna Math, 1961.

A considerably shorter work than the commentary on the *Brahma Sūtras,* this text sets forth Shankara's philosophy somewhat more concisely. The work is written in both prose and verse.

Thibaut, George. *The Vedānta-Sūtras, with the Commentary of Rāmānuga*. Sacred Books of the East, vol. 48. Oxford: Clarendon Press, 1904.

A standard translation of Rāmānuja's commentary, which is second only to Shankara's in importance to the Vedānta.

Vivekananda, Swami. *Jñāna Yoga*. 2d rev. ed., New York: Ramakrishna-Vivekananda Center, 1955. Also in Swami Nikhilananda, ed., *Vivekananda: The Yogas and Other Works*, pp. 201–399. New York: Ramakrishna-Vivekananda Center, 1953.

The essays on *māya* and "practical Vedānta" are particularly illuminating.

TOPICS FOR DISCUSSION

1. Shankara's interpretation of the Upanishads in terms of non-duality (*advaita*) or a monistic system of philosophy.

2. The use of scriptural authority and exegesis to counter ignorance, refute contrary philosophies (e.g., Buddhism, Sāṁkhya, etc.), and reconcile textual inconsistencies. How can Shankara reconcile his stress on mystical, nonconceptual knowledge with the authority of scripture?
3. The nature of the Self (*ātman*) and its involvement with the senses; "superimposition"; the function of intelligence or reason as a means to release (*mokṣa*); the Self in dream and deep sleep.
4. The nature of ignorance or nescience; its origin in the concept of illusion (*māya*) and its removal through the knowledge of Brahman. The impossibility that those who know reality can be aware of ignorance.
5. The individual soul and god in terms of bondage (*saṁsāra*) and release (*mokṣa*); the meaning of "That thou art" (*tat tvam asi*); the place of devotion in this context.
6. The problem of cause and effect: how can they be identical? If the prime cause is the only reality, what is the status, if any, of secondary causes?
7. The ethical implication of Shankara's philosophy: moral prerequisites to undertaking the study of Vedānta; the relation of action to knowledge; the concept of a single, unitary Self as a basis for moral action; the social behavior of a liberated man. If one has achieved ultimate liberation, is he not free from the obligations of dharma? If one is unified in the Brahman, what need is there to act?

THERAVĀDA BUDDHISM: THE TIPIṬAKA

*The canon of Buddhist texts in Pāli is the oldest complete and extant collection of Buddhist scriptures. It belongs to one of the earliest traditions within Buddhism, the "Way of the Elders" (*Theravāda*). This tradition is still dominant in Sri Lanka, Burma, Thailand, and Kampuchea. The canon itself—the "Three Baskets" (*Tipiṭaka*)—is a lengthy anthology of the Buddha's teachings in three parts: the* Vinaya-piṭaka, *which consists of the rules of discipline for monks and nuns and narrations of the incidents which prompted the Buddha to declare those rules; the* Sutta-piṭaka, *containing the doctrinal utterances of the Buddha; and the* Abhidhamma-piṭaka, *a repository of scholastic analyses of the doctrines. The* Sutta-piṭaka, *the heart of the canon, is subdivided into five collections. The criteria of division are the length of the discourses and their method of arrangement: the Long Discourses; the Middle-Length Discourses; the Connected Discourses; the Discourses Arranged by Numerical Progression; and the Minor Discourses.*

TRANSLATIONS

The entire Pāli Canon, along with much of the standard commentary, has been edited and translated into English by scholars affiliated with London's Pali Text Society. Also, there are many anthologies of canonical and paracanonical Theravāda literature, among which the following are the most useful:

Burlingame, Eugene Watson. *Buddhist Parables.* New Haven: Yale University Press, 1922.

A well-balanced anthology with original translations. A few texts from the Sanskrit and some European parallels are included.

Burtt, Edwin Arthur. *The Teachings of the Compassionate Buddha*. Pbk ed., New York: New American Library, Mentor, 1955.

A useful anthology of texts drawn from the works of various translators. Mahāyāna sources are also included. Emphasis is on the conceptual and devotional aspects of Buddhism.

Conze, Edward. *Buddhist Meditation*. London: Allen and Unwin, 1956; New York: Macmillan, 1956.

A good anthology dealing with devotion, mental training, and the concept of wisdom as represented in Buddhism.

—— *Buddhist Scriptures*. Harmondsworth and Baltimore, MD: Penguin, 1959. Pbk ed.

The translations are original and modern. Mahāyāna texts are also included.

Conze, Edward et al. *Buddhist Texts Through the Ages*. New York: Philosophical Library, 1954; Oxford: B. Cassirer, 1954.

Texts illustrating the basic concepts of Buddhism with emphasis on the Mahāyāna teachings.

de Bary, Wm. Theodore et al. *Sources of Indian Tradition*, pp. 93–202. New York: Columbia University Press, 1958; pbk ed., 2 vols., 1964; 2d ed., 1988.

The translations of Buddhist texts by A. L. Basham are short but representative of the principles of the Theravāda, Mahāyāna, and Vajrayāna forms of Buddhism.

—— *The Buddhist Tradition in India, China, and Japan*. New York: Modern Library, 1969. Pbk. ed., New York: Random House, Viking, 1972.

Hamilton, Clarence H. *Buddhism, a Religion of Infinite Compassion: Selections from Buddhist Literature*. New York: Liberal Arts, 1952.

A selection from Pāli, Sanskrit, Chinese, Japanese, and Tibetan texts.

Rhys-Davids, Thomas William. *Buddhist Suttas*. Sacred Books of the East, vol. 11. Oxford: Clarendon Press, 1881.

A very good translation of seven basic *suttas* (discourses) of

Theravāda Buddhism. The important First Sermon (*Dhammacakkappavaṭṭana Sutta*) is included.
Warren, Henry Clarke. *Buddhism in Translation*. Harvard Oriental Series, vol. 3. Cambridge: Harvard University Press, 1896, 1953. Reprint, New York: Atheneum, 1963.

Probably the best anthology of Pāli texts. Unfortunately the First Sermon is not included and there is some repetition of the basic concepts presented.

SECONDARY READINGS

Carrithers, Michael. *The Buddha*. Oxford and New York: Oxford University Press, 1983.

A brief biography of the Buddha.
Collins, Steven. *Selfless Persons: Imagery and Thought in Theravāda Buddhism*. Cambridge University Press, 1982.

A study of the Buddhist doctrine of "not-self."
Conze, Edward. *Buddhism: Its Essence and Development*. New York: Philosophical Library, 1951; Oxford: B. Cassirer, 1951. Pbk ed., New York: Harper, Torchbook, 1959.

Good survey of the major schools of Buddhism.
Coomaraswamy, Ananda K. *Buddha and the Gospel of Buddhism*. New York: Putnam, 1916; London: Harrap, 1916. Bombay: Asia Publishing House, 1956.

Discussion of the teachings of Buddhism, and of Buddhist art, sculpture, painting, and literature by an influential early writer.
Foucher, A. *The Life of the Buddha According to the Ancient Texts and Monuments of India*. Abridged translation by Simone Brangier Boas. Middletown, CT: Wesleyan University Press, 1963. (French ed., *La Vie du Bouddha*, Paris: Editions Payot, 1949.)
Horner, I. B. *Women under Primitive Buddhism: Laywomen and Almswomen*. New York: Dutton, 1930; London: Routledge, 1930.

A classic study.

Keith, Arthur Berriedale. *Buddhist Philosophy in India and Ceylon.* Oxford: Clarendon Press, 1923.

A single-volume analysis of Theravāda philosophy.

Oldenberg, Hermann. *Buddha; His Life, His Doctrine, His Order.* Translated from the German by William Hoey. London: Williams and Norgate, 1882. Calcutta: Book Co., 1927; London: Luzac, 1928.

An authoritative early account of Theravāda Buddhism.

Thomas, Edward J. *The History of Buddhist Thought.* London: Kegan Paul, Trench, Trübner, 1933; New York: Knopf, 1933. 2d ed., New York: Barnes and Noble, 1951; London: Routledge and Kegan Paul, 1951.

A good survey of the development of Buddhist thought from the earliest schools through Mahāyāna religion and philosophy.

—— *The Life of Buddha as Legend and History.* New York: Knopf, 1927; London: Kegan Paul, 1927. 3d ed., New York: Barnes and Noble, 1952.

Study of the historical and literary evidence pertinent to the life of Buddha.

Weiler, Royal. "The Buddhist Act of Compassion," in Ernest Bender, ed., *Indological Studies in Honor of W. Norman Brown.* New Haven: American Oriental Society, 1962.

Winternitz, Moriz. *A History of Indian Literature,* 2:1–226. Translated by S. Ketkar and H. Kohn. (See above, under General Works, for full bibliographic information.)

The best survey of Buddhist texts and literature. Mahāyāna materials are also included.

TOPICS FOR DISCUSSION

1. The Buddha as a religious teacher, philosopher, mystic, prophet, or savior. His life in the Indian context.
2. The Four Aryan or "Noble" Truths and the Eightfold Path

as both a diagnosis of the universal human predicament and a prescription for it.

3. The silence of the Buddha: types of questions that the Buddha considered irrelevant to the problem of suffering.
4. The doctrine of Dependent Origination as an answer to such questions as the creation of the world, the origin of suffering, and general causation.
5. The path to liberation: morality, meditation, and wisdom.
6. The role of monasticism in Buddhism and the relationship of monastic and lay communities.
7. Should Buddhism be considered pessimistic in view of its concepts of karma, rebirth, no-soul, the evanescence of life, and the extinction of desire (*nirvāṇa*)?
8. Is nirvana an object of desire?

THERAVĀDA BUDDHISM: THE DHAMMAPADA (*ca.* 300 B.C.)

A short work of 423 verses dealing with central themes of Buddhism, perhaps the most popular and influential Theravāda Buddhist text.

TRANSLATIONS

Max Müller, Friedrich. *The Dhammapada, A Collection of Verses.* Sacred Books of the East, vol. 10. Oxford: Clarendon Press, 1881.

Probably the best translation, but somewhat outdated. This translation is reproduced in Lin Yutang, *The Wisdom of China and India*, pp. 321–56 (New York: Random House, 1942); Clarence Hamilton, *Buddhism*, pp. 64–97 (New York: Liberal Arts Press, 1952); and E. Wilson, *Sacred Books of the East*, pp. 113–51 (New York: Willey, 1945).

Nārada Thera. *The Dhammapada.* London: John Murray, 1954.

A good translation by a Buddhist monk, with copious notes of a religious or philosophical rather than philological nature.

Radhakrishnan, Sarvepalli. *The Dhammapada.* London: Oxford University Press, 1950.

Translation, partially guided by Max Müller's, with an illuminating introductory essay. This translation is reproduced, almost completely, in Radhakrishnan and Charles A. Moore, eds., *A Source Book in Indian Philosophy*, pp. 292–325 (London: Oxford University Press, 1957; Princeton University Press, 1957).

SECONDARY READINGS

Beal, Samuel. *A Catena of Buddhist Scriptures from the Chinese*, pp. 188–203. London: Trübner, 1871.

—— *Texts from the Buddhist Canon, Commonly Known as Dhammapada, with Accompanying Narrative*. Boston: Houghton, 1878; London: Kegan Paul, Trench, Trübner, 1878; 2d ed., 1902. Reprint, Calcutta: Gupta, 1952.

Burlingame, Eugene W. *Buddhist Legends*. Harvard Oriental Series, vols. 28–30. Cambridge: Harvard University Press, 1921; London: Oxford University Press, 1922.

The traditional commentary on the *Dhammapada*, primarily a compilation of Buddhist legends and tales meant to illustrate the application and occasion for the Buddha's preaching the verses of the *Dhammapada*. Ascribed to Buddhaghosa.

Fausset, Hugh l'Anson. "Thoughts on the Dhammapada," in *Poets and Pundits: A Collection of Essays*, pp. 262–69. London: Cape, 1947; New Haven: Yale University Press, 1949.

TOPICS FOR DISCUSSION

1. The *Dhammapada* as wisdom literature: what kind of wisdom, prudence, practical guidance, is involved? How is poetic form and imagery suited to the message?

2. To what extent is the focus on the individual man and his moral cultivation? Is the aim to produce an ideal human type?

3. Moral behavior as a way of dealing with suffering. What has this to do with "enlightenment"?

4. Interpretation of traditional concepts, such as the Self, the Brahman-priest, and mind or thought, in moral terms. What kind of "ethics" is proposed here?

5. The relation of nirvana to consciousness, peace, bliss, and above all, the transcendence of good and evil.

THERAVĀDA BUDDHISM: THE
MILINDAPAÑHĀ (*ca.* first century C.E.)

One of the most important paracanonical prose works of Theravāda Buddhism in the form of a dialogue between the Greek king Milinda (Menander) and the Buddhist monk Nāgasena.

TRANSLATIONS

Horner, I. B. *King Milinda's Questions (Milindapaña).* Sacred Books of the Buddhists, vols. 22, 23. Vol. 1. London: Luzac, 1963.

Rhys-Davids, Thomas William. *The Questions of King Milinda.* Sacred Books of the East, vols. 35, 36. Oxford: Clarendon Press, 1890–94. Reprint, pbk ed., New York: Dover, 1963.
Translation, by competent scholars.

SECONDARY READINGS

Rhys-Davids, Caroline A. F. *The Milinda-Questions: An Inquiry into Its Place in the History of Buddhism.* London: George Routledge, 1930.
A scholarly study of the text with several original ideas regarding its composition, authorship, and interpretation.

Winternitz, Moriz. *A History of Indian Literature.* Translated by S. Ketkar and H. Kohn. Vols. 1–2, University of Calcutta, 1927–33; vol. 1, part 1, 2d ed., 1959. Vol. 3, part 1, Delhi: Motilal Banarsidass, 1963. Vol. 2, pp. 174–83.
An account of the work with emphasis on its composition and literary qualities.

TOPICS FOR DISCUSSION

1. What is the aim of the work? To what kind of audience is it addressed?
2. The composite nature of man and the doctrine of nonself.
3. If there is no transmigration, what is the nature of rebirth?
4. The relation of wisdom, faith, perseverance, mindfulness, and meditation to the attainment of nirvana.
5. The Chain of Causation: ignorance, "confections," phenomenal being, suffering.
6. Problems and dilemmas:
   a. why should a perfectly enlightened person, such as the Buddha, suffer and die?
   b. what is meant by Truth? What is an Act of Truth? How is this understanding related to the resolution of textual contradictions?
   c. what is wrong with philosophical discussion?
   d. if life is suffering, why is suicide not a way out?
   e. why do the virtuous suffer and the wicked prosper?
7. Reasons for joining the Buddhist Order.
8. Stylistic features of the work that contribute to the force of its argument; the use of analogy and metaphor.

THERAVĀDA BUDDHISM:
THE MAHĀSATIPAṬṬHANA SUTTA

The Greater Discourse on the Foundations of Mindfulness, one of the "larger discourses" of the Pāli canon, has long been a primary Theravāda text on the most essential of Buddhist practices—meditation.

TRANSLATIONS

Nyanaponika Thera. *The Heart of Buddhist Meditation.* New York: Samuel Weiser, 1970.

A fine translation with perceptive commentary and a useful introduction, by a European adherent of Theravāda.

Soma, Thera. *The Way of Mindfulness: The Satipaṭṭhana Sutta and Commentary.* Kandy, Sri Lanka: Buddhist Publication Society, 1967.

A literal translation incorporating the classical Pāli commentary.

SECONDARY READINGS

Buddhaghosa. *The Path of Purification (Visuddhimagga).* Translated by Bhikkhu Nyanamoli. Colombo: Gunasena, 1964.

The "Summa" of Theravāda meditation.

Conze, Edward. *Buddhist Meditation.* London: Allen and Unwin, 1956. Pbk ed., New York: Harper, Torchbooks, 1970.

A useful collection of texts on meditation.

Dhammasudhi, Sobhana. *Insight Meditation.* 2d ed., London: Committee for the Advancement of Buddhism, 1968.

A cogent explanation by a modern Thai meditation master.

King, Winston. *Theravāda Meditation: The Buddhist Transformation of Yōga.* University Park and London: Pennsylvania University Press, 1980.

Examines both classical and contemporary forms of Theravāda meditation.

Swearer, Donald K. *Secrets of the Lotus*. New York: Macmillan, 1971.

An original treatment of Buddhist meditation.

Upatissa. *The Path of Freedom (Vimuttimagga)*. Translated by Rev. N. R. M. Ehara et al. Colombo: Gunasena, 1961.

A translation from the Chinese of a shorter compendium of Theravāda meditation.

Vajirañāna, Paravahera Mahathera. *Buddhist Meditation in Theory and Practice*. Columbo: Gunasena, 1962.

An authoritative modern study of Theravāda meditation, based largely on Buddhaghosa.

TOPICS FOR DISCUSSION

1. What are the characteristics of the state of mindfulness outlined in this text?
2. What is the relation between the kind of meditation advocated here and the early Buddhist understanding of the nature of reality?
3. To whom is this text directed? (Compare with the *Dhammapada*.) What does this suggest about the early Buddhist conception of the appropriateness of certain Buddhist practices for the monks and nuns on the one hand, and for laymen and laywomen on the other?

MAHĀYĀNA BUDDHISM:
PRAJÑĀPĀRAMITĀ
(*ca.* 100 B.C.–A.D. 400)

The Buddhist texts that deal with the "Perfection of Wisdom" (Prajñāpāramitā) *are among the earliest of Mahāyāna scriptures. They are the foundation of much of later Buddhist thought and are especially associated with Nāgārjuna, one of India's greatest thinkers and founder of the Mādhyamika or "Middle Way" tradition. Despite their extraordinary influence on scholastic Buddhism, however, these texts are regarded by their adherents as scriptures rather than philosophical treatises.*

TRANSLATIONS

The term "Prajñāpāramitā" refers to a class of texts of varying length. For a detailed survey of the literature see Edward Conze, The Prajñā-pāramitā Literature *(The Hague: Mouton, 1960). See Moriz Winternitz,* A History of Indian Literature. *Translated by S. Ketkar and H. Kohn. Vols. 1–2, University of Calcutta, 1927–33; vol. 1, part 1, 2d ed., 1959. Vol. 3, part 1, Delhi: Motilal Banarsidass, 1963. Vol. 2, pp. 313–24 passim. For short selections, see the various anthologies cited under Theravāda Buddhism, above.*

Conze, Edward. *Aṣṭasāhasrikā Prajñāpāramitā.* Calcutta: Asiatic Society, 1958.

   An excellent translation of one of the oldest Prajñāpāramitā texts by a specialist on the subject.

—— *Buddhist Wisdom Books: Containing the Diamond Sutra and the Heart Sutra.* London: Allen and Unwin, 1958.

   Includes the "Heart" sūtra with the Sanskrit text and translator's commentary.

—— *The Large Sutra on Perfect Wisdom, with the Divisions of the Abhi Samayalankara.* London: Luzac, 1961.

—— *Selected Sayings from the Perfection of Wisdom.* London: Buddhist Society, 1955.

This volume of texts is probably the most useful introduction to this somewhat obscure literature.

—— *Vajracchedika Prajñāpāramitā.* Serie orientale Roma, vol. 13. Rome: Instituto Italiano per il Medio ed Estreme Oriente, 1957.

A critical edition of the text with translation, introduction, and glossary.

Cowell, E. B. and F. Max Müller, eds. *Buddhist Mahayana Texts.* Sacred Books of the East, vol. 49. London: Oxford University Press, 1894; reprint, New York: Dover, 1969; Berkeley: Asian Humanities Press, n.d.

This useful volume includes, in addition to the "Diamond" and "Heart" sūtras, the classic life of the Buddha *(Buddhacarita)* of Aśvaghosa and the larger and smaller *Sukhavativyūha* texts.

Thomas, Edward J. *The Perfection of Wisdom. The Career of the Predestined Buddhas: A Selection of Mahāyāna Scriptures.* London: John Murray, 1952.

Competent translation of Mahāyāna Buddhist texts that illustrate through parable and doctrine the superiority of Mahāyāna and the ideal of the Bodhisattva.

SECONDARY READINGS

See also Theravāda Buddhism, above.

Conze, Edward. "The Ontology of the Prajñāpāramitā," in *Philosophy East and West* 3 (July 1953)2:117–29.

A useful discussion of the metaphysical concepts of the Prajñāpāramitā texts, especially *dharmas* and emptiness, as well as psychological and religious factors.

—— *Thirty Years of Buddhist Studies.* Oxford: Cassirer, 1967.

A collection of several useful articles on Prajñāpāramitā and related topics by the expert in the field.

Dawamura, Leslie S., ed. *The Bodhisattva Doctrine in Buddhism.* Waterloo, ONT: Wilfrid University Press, 1981.

Essays by noted scholars on the Bodhisattva doctrine in India, Tibet, China, and Japan.

Dayal, Har. *The Bodhisattva Doctrine in Buddhist Sanskrit Literature.* Reprint of 1932 ed., Livingston, NJ: Orient Book Distributor, 1975. Pbk ed., New York: Samuel Weiser, 1978.

A classic critical study of the textual evidence dealing with the career of the Bodhisattva.

Murti, T. R. V. *The Central Philosophy of Buddhism: A Study of the Mādhyamika System.* London: Allen and Unwin, 1955.

A critical and comparative study of the *Mādhyamika* system of Mahāyāna Buddhist philosophy that derives from the Prajñāpāramitā texts.

Obermiller, Eugene. "A Study of the Twenty Aspects of Śūnyatā (Based on Haribhadra's *Abhisamayālaṃkārālokā* and the *Pañcaviṃśatisāhasrikā-prajñāpāramitāsūtra),*" in *Indian Historical Quarterly* 9 (1933):170–87.

—— "The Term *Śūnyatā* in Its Different Interpretations," in *Journal of Greater India Society* 1 (1934):105–17.

Robinson, Richard H. *Early Mādhyamika in India and China*, pp. 1–70. Madison: University of Wisconsin Press, 1967.

A systematic presentation of Nāgārjuna's thought using techniques of analysis derived from modern logic and linguistic philosophy.

Streng, Frederick J. *Emptiness: A Study in Religious Meaning.* New York: Abingdon Press, 1967.

An illuminating study of Nāgārjuna's use of the term *śūnya* (empty or void), which is basic Prajñāpāramitā. Streng treats the topic, in terms of modern philosophy, as a case study in the uses of religious language. He includes translations of two of Nāgārjuna's basic works and an exhaustive bibliography.

Suzuki, D. T. "The Philosophy and Religion of the Prajñāpāra-mitā," in *Essays in Zen Buddhism*, pp. 207–88. 3d Series. London: Luzac, 1934.

A treatment of the religious and devotional aspects of the Perfection of Wisdom.

TOPICS FOR DISCUSSION

1. The apparently "negative" nature of the method; its role as a *via negativa* to Perfect Wisdom (*prajñā*).
2. The ineffability of Perfect Wisdom; the paradoxical language of the Prajña texts.
3. Emptiness (*śūnyatā*) as a basis for enlightenment; enlightenment as "suchness."
4. Ethical implications of compassion and "skill in means."
5. The perfection of virtues, especially Wisdom, in the person of the Bodhisattva.
6. The relation of the Bodhisattva to the Buddha: the Perfection of Wisdom (*prajñāpāramitā*), and enlightenment as immanent and transcendent. The Bodhisattva as manifesting the immanence of the Perfection of Wisdom, and the Buddha as representing the transcendence of enlightenment.

MAHĀYĀNA BUDDHISM: THE ŚRĪMĀLĀDEVISIMHANĀDA SŪTRA

The Lion's Roar of Queen Śrīmālā is a basic Mahāyāna sūtra containing many of the common Mahāyāna teachings, but devoted especially to the notion of the Tathāgatagarbha or "Embryo of the Tathāgata"—Buddhism's most compelling metaphor for the immanence of absolute truth. This sūtra also attests to the theoretically prominent status of lay persons within Mahāyāna.

TRANSLATIONS

Wayman, Alex and Hideko Wayman. *The Lion's Roar of Queen Śrīmālā*. New York: Columbia University Press, 1973.

A translation based on the Tibetan and Chinese texts, extensively annotated and with a long, informative introduction.

SECONDARY READINGS

Paul, Diana Y. *Women in Buddhism: Images of the Feminine in the Mahāyāna Tradition*. Berkeley: Asian Humanities Press, 1979.

Considers Buddhist ideas of the feminine in several Mahāyāna texts, including *The Lion's Roar of Queen Śrīmālā*.

Ruegg, David Seyfort. *La Théorie du tathāgatagarbha et du gotra: études sur la sotériologie et la gnoséologie du Bouddhisme*, pp. 30–70, 245–408. Publications de l'École Française d'Extrême-Orient, 70. Paris: École Française d'Extrême Orient, 1969.

Suzuki, D. T. *Outlines of Mahāyāna Buddhism*. New York: Schocken Books, 1963.

A broad, interpretive introduction to Mahāyāna which places Tathāgatagarbha theory in its Mahāyāna context.

TOPICS FOR DISCUSSION

1. To what extent does the theory of Perfections—giving, etc.—apply to the layman?
2. What is the difference between the *Dharmakāya* and the *Tathāgatagarbha*?
3. The *Śrīmālā* as inspired utterance.
4. How does the saint (*arhat*) fare in the theory of the "One Vehicle"?
5. What is the *Śrīmālā*'s teaching concerning faith?

MAHĀYĀNA BUDDHISM:
THE LAŃKĀVATĀRA SŪTRA

The Sūtra of the Descent into Laṅka (Sri Lanka) is a rich but amorphous mixture of general Mahāyāna themes and discussions of the dynamics of consciousness. Its emphasis on interior experience testifies to the continuing importance of meditation in Mahāyāna Buddhism, while its "mind-only" teachings anticipate the "idealism" of the Yogācara tradition of Mahāyāna.

TRANSLATIONS

Suzuki, D. T. *The Laṅkāvatāra Sūtra: A Mahāyāna Text*. London: Routledge and Kegan Paul, 1932.

    An excellent translation of a very difficult text, based on the Sanskrit, Tibetan, and Chinese versions.

SECONDARY READINGS

Suzuki, D. T. *Studies in the Laṅkāvatāra Sūtra*. London: Routledge and Kegan Paul, 1930.

    A companion volume to Suzuki's translation and by far the most informative and authoritative treatment of the text.

Thomas, Edward J. *The History of Buddhist Thought*, pp. 230–48. London: Routledge and Kegan Paul, 1951.

Willis, Janet. *On Knowing Reality: A Translation of the Tattvārtha-patalam of Asanga's Bodhisattvabhūmi*. New York: Columbia University Press, 1979.

    An excellent study of a Yogācara text with important implications for our understanding of the *Laṅkāvatāra Sūtra*.

TOPICS FOR DISCUSSION

1. The relationship between the seventh consciousness and the eighth consciousness, the storehouse consciousness.
2. The *Laṅkāvatarā* as a map prepared by mediators and their systematizers.
3. In "turning over" or "revulsion," what turns over? What does it become?
4. Does the storehouse consciousness in any way resemble the "Self" of Brahmanism?
5. The storehouse consciousness and the unconscious of psychoanalysis.

MAHĀYĀNA BUDDHISM:
THE SUKHAVATIVYŪHA SŪTRAS

The longer and shorter Sukhavativyūha Sūtras concern the vision of Amitābha Buddha's "Land of Bliss" (Sukhavati), the Western Paradise. They are especially representative of the devotional aspects of Mahāyāna and yet they have their roots in Buddhist meditation. Together they bear eloquently affective witness to the universality of a spiritual tradition which promises salvation even to those who are incapable of the intellectual or meditative rigors of other strains in Mahāyāna.

TRANSLATIONS

Cowell, E. B. et al. *Buddhist Mahāyanā Texts*. Sacred Books of the East, vol. 49. Oxford: Clarendon Press, 1890. Reprint, New Delhi: Motilal Banarsidass, 1968. Pbk ed., New York: Dover, 1969; Berkeley, Asian Humanities Press, n.d.

Includes both the larger and smaller *Sukhavativyūha Sūtras* with a useful introduction.

Shinshu Seiten. Honolulu: Higashi Honpa Hongwanji, 1955; reprint, 1961, pp. 7–106.

Both sūtras are regarded as scriptural authorities in the Pure Land tradition of Japanese Buddhism and are thus included in this standard edition of the True Pure Land Sect's canon. The translations are from the Chinese versions which differ only slightly from the Sanskrit.

SECONDARY READINGS

Consult the relevant chapters in surveys of Indian Buddhism listed under Supplementary Readings on Indian Buddhism *and the works on Pure Land Buddhism listed under* Supplementary Readings on Japanese Buddhism.

TOPICS FOR DISCUSSION

1. Is faith alone sufficient for rebirth into the Land of Bliss? What is the place of repentance, good conduct, and meditation on Amitābha and his Land?
2. The delights of the Land of Bliss as an aid in reaching enlightenment rather than as an end in themselves.
3. The extremely lush, pictorial style of these sūtras.
4. What is Śākyamuni's place in the drama of Amitābha?
5. The teaching of rebirth into the Land of Bliss as an expedient (*upāya*).

MAHĀYĀNA BUDDHISM:
THE BODHICARYĀVATĀRA
OF SHĀNTIDEVA (*ca.* 650)

This primarily devotional work occupies a position in Mahāyāna Buddhism analogous to that of the Bhagavadgītā *in Hinduism, the* Dhammapada *in Theravāda Buddhism, and the* Imitatio Christi *of Thomas à Kempis in Christianity.*

TRANSLATIONS

Conze, Edward. *Buddhist Meditation*. London: Allen and Unwin, 1956; New York: Macmillan, 1956.
> Translation of only a very few verses.

Finot, Louis. *La march à la lumière*. Les Classiques de l'Orient 2. Paris: Éditions Bossard, 1920.
> One of the best complete translations in a Western language.

La Vallée Poussin, L. de. *Introduction à la pratique des futurs Bouddhas, poème de Çāntideva*. Paris: Bloud, 1907.
> French translation by an outstanding authority on Buddhism.

Matics, Marion L. *Entering the Path of Enlightenment: The Bodhicaryāvatāra of the Buddhist Poet Śāntideva*. New York: Macmillan, 1970.
> The first complete English translation, preceded by a long and useful introduction.

Schmidt, Richard. *Der Eintritt in den Wandel in Erleuchtung*. Paderborn: Ferdinance Schöningh, 1923.
> An excellent German translation.

SECONDARY READINGS

Bendall, Cecil and W. H. D. Rouse. *Śikshā-samuccaya: A Compendium of Buddhist Doctrine*. London: John Murray, 1922.

A fine translation of Shāntideva's longer work: an anthology, with comment, of Mahāyāna texts. The metrical epitome in twenty-seven stanzas of this "Compendium of Instruction" is provided by L. D. Barnett, *The Path of Light*, pp. 103–7.

Thomas, Edward J. *The Quest of Enlightenment: A Selection of the Buddhist Scriptures*. London: John Murray, 1950.

A short anthology of Mahāyāna texts in translation with particular reference to the career of the Bodhisattva.

Winternitz, Moriz. *A History of Indian Literature*, pp. 370–74. Translated from the German by S. Ketkar and H. Kohn. 2 vols. University of Calcutta, 1927–33.

Short summary of the work.

TOPICS FOR DISCUSSION

1. The Thought of Enlightenment: its nature and attainment. What significance does it have in a philosophy based on Emptiness (*śūnyatā*)?
2. The Bodhisattva as the ideal man.
3. The Perfection of the virtues of patience or long suffering, courage, and meditation, and their application to a world conceived as suffering.
4. The Perfection of Wisdom (*prajñāpāramitā*) as a philosophical basis for piety.
5. The Buddhist concept of compassion: its relation to the Bodhisattva's vow and the concept of Truth.
6. Conquest of evil through pious meditation and moral action.

SUPPLEMENTARY READINGS ON INDIAN BUDDHISM

Readers may wish to consult anthologies, surveys, and histories of Indian Buddhism. Among these the following should prove useful.

Agehananda Bharati, Swami. *The Tantric Tradition*. London: Rider, 1965.

A useful discussion of Hindu and Buddhist tantric teachings by a European adherent.

Bareau, André. *Bouddhisme*. Les religions de l'Inde, vol. 3. Paris: Payot, 1966.

Clearly organized short surveys.

Berry, Thomas M. *Buddhism*. New York: Hawthorn Books, 1967. Pbk ed., Chambersburg, PA: Anima, 1967.

A perceptive overview of the entire Buddhist tradition.

Conze, Edward. *Buddhist Thought in India*. London: Allen and Unwin, 1962; Ann Arbor: University of Michigan Press, 1967.

Especially good on Buddhist scholasticism.

Conze, Edward et al. *Buddhist Texts Through the Ages*. London: Cassirer, 1954. Reprint, New York: Harper, Torchbooks, 1964.

A fine selection of brief texts from all of Buddhism's canonical languages.

Dasgupta, Shashibhusan. *An Introduction to Tantric Buddhism*. University of Calcutta Press, 1950; Berkeley: Shambhala, 1974.

de Bary, Wm. Theodore et al. *The Buddhist Tradition in India, China, and Japan*. New York: Modern Library, 1969. Pbk ed., New York: Random House, Vintage, 1972.

The first third of this comprehensive anthology includes a judicious selection of well-translated texts from both the Theravāda and Mahāyāna traditions.

Dutt, Sukumar. *Buddhist Monks and Monasteries of India*. London: Allen and Unwin, 1962.

A good survey of the institutional development of Indian Buddhism.

Govinda, Lama Anagarika. *Foundations of Tibetan Mysticism*. New York: Samuel Weiser, 1969.

A discussion of Tibetan esoteric teachings.

Tucci, Giuseppe. *The Theory and Practice of the Mandala*. London: Rider, 1961.

A general discussion of mandala symbolism by a scholar of Indian and Tibetan Buddhism.

Warder, A. K. *Indian Buddhism*. Delhi: Motilal Banarsidass, 1970; rev. ed., 1980.

Contains a section on the great Buddhist universities and *mantrayāna*. Discusses the Kriyā, Caryā, Yoga, and Anuttara-yoga systems.

SHAKUNTALĀ (ABHIJÑĀNAŚAKUNTALĀ) OF KĀLIDĀSA (ca. 400)

Shakuntalā *is the major drama of Kālidāsa, the greatest poet and dramatist of classical India. The play, with its rich mythological layers and vast cosmic landscape, is the model of Indian "heroic romance."*

TRANSLATIONS

Coulson, Michael, trans. *Three Sanskrit Plays*. Harmondsworth: Penguin, 1981.

Emeneau, M. B. *Abhijñāna-śakuntalā*. Berkeley: University of California Press, 1962. Pbk ed.

An accurate literal translation from the Bengali (longer) recension.

Lal, P. *Great Sanskrit Plays in Modern Translation*. Norfolk, CT: New Directions, 1964. Pbk ed.

Translations of six plays, including *Shakuntalā* in vigorous English, by an Indian poet. There is a very useful introduction to Sanskrit drama in general, and a briefer one for each play. The translator has striven to recreate the effect of the Sanskrit play rather than to give a literal translation.

Miller, Barbara Stoler, trans., in *The Theater of Memory: Three Plays of Kalidasa*. New York: Columbia University Press, 1984. Pbk ed.

Best modern translation with excellent introduction.

Monier-Williams, M. *Śakoontalā; or, The Lost Ring*. Hertford: Madden, 1855; New York: Dodd, Mead, 1885. 5th ed., London: John Murray, 1887.

A competent translation of the Devanāgarī, or shorter,

recension of the drama, also available in an inexpensive anthology, John D. Yohannan, *A Treasury of Asian Literature*, pp. 131–272 (New York: New American Library, Mentor, 1960).

—— *Śakuntalā*. Hertford: Madden, 1853. 2d ed., Oxford: Clarendon Press, 1876.

A critical translation of all metrical passages from the Devanagari (shorter) recension of the text.

Ryder, Arthur W. *Kalidasa: Translations of Shakuntala and Other Works*. New York: Dutton, 1912; London: Dent, 1912. Also under the title *Shakuntala and Other Writings by Kalidasa*. Pbk ed., New York: Dutton, Everyman's Library, 1959.

Translation of the drama from the Bengali recension. The translation of the verse portions, while accurate, does not always preserve the dignified quality of the original text.

SECONDARY READINGS

Baumer, Rachel and James Brandon. *Sanskrit Drama in Performance*. Honolulu: University of Hawaii Press, 1981.

Essays on aspects of theory and practice.

Byrski, M. C. *Concept of Ancient Indian Theatre*. Delhi: Munshiram Manoharlal, 1974.

Emeneau, M. B. "Kālidāsa's Śakuntalā and the Mahābhārata," in *Journal of the American Oriental Society* 82 (March 1962)1:41–44.

An attempt to prove that Kālidāsa relied on the *Mahābhārata* for the story version of *Shakuntalā* rather than on the *Padma Purāṇa*, as maintained by Winternitz and Sarma.

Ghosh, Manomohan, ed. and trans. *Naṭyaśāstra of Bharata*. Calcutta: 1956–61; 2d rev. ed., Calcutta: Manisha Granthalaya, 1967.

Text and translation of the basic work on Indian dramaturgy.

Harris, Mary B. *Kalidasa, Poet of Nature*. Boston: Meador Press, 1936.

A general discussion of Kālidāsa's treatment of nature, animal life, etc.

Hillebrandt, Alfred. *Kālidāsa: Ein Versuch zu seiner literarischen Würdigung.* Breslau: Marcus, 1921.

An excellent scholarly study of the poet and his works, life, times, sources, etc., as well as his talent as an artist, humorist, and philosopher.

Jhala, G. C. *Kālidāsa, a Study.* Bombay: Padma Publications, 1943.

A study of the poet-dramatist and his works. *Shakuntalā* is discussed (pp. 130–59) in terms of the author's literary improvements of an old story. This book also contains a statement on Kālidāsa's conception of love (pp. 160–74).

Krisnamurthy, K. *Kalidasa.* New York: Twayne, 1972.

Good survey of poems and plays.

Levi, Sylvain. *Le Théâtre indien.* Paris: Bouillon, 1890.

A classical treatment of the Indian theater by an outstanding Indic scholar.

Misra, Vidya Niwas. "The Mango-Blossom Imagery in Kālidāsa," in *Journal of the American Oriental Society* 82 (March 1962)1:68–69.

A short note on the mango-blossom as an object of nature, an emblem of fruitful love, and a symbol of womanhood, in Kālidāsa's poems and the drama, *Shakuntalā.*

Mitchell, John D. "A Sanskrit Classic: Shakuntalā," in Wm. Theodore de Bary, ed., *Approaches to the Oriental Classics*, pp. 119–31. With comments by Royal W. Weiler, pp. 132–36. New York: Columbia University Press, 1959.

A primarily psychological study of the play and its characters, although the levels of "immediate appeal" (as a theater piece) and cultural significance are also treated. The comments point out the universal characteristics of this drama, and give some indication of available literature and translations.

Narang, S. P. *Kalidasa Bibliography.* New Delhi: Heritage, 1976; Columbia, MO: South Asia Books, 1976.

Wells, Henry Willis. *The Classical Drama of India: Studies in Its Value for the Literature and Theatre of the World*. Bombay: Asia Publishing House, 1963.

TOPICS FOR DISCUSSION

1. The stylization of characters: hero, heroine, confidant (*vidūṣhaka*), parasite (*viṭa*). Which of the persons of the drama really have character? How is characterization achieved? Can this be related to anything in the religious or philosophical background of India?

2. The understanding of love in the plays: the attempt to create a mood of tenderness, of girl's first love: the varieties of love.

3. The audience and the structure of the play.

4. The play's conception of nature as "human." The sense of intimacy with nature, of life as governed by the natural cycle.

5. Tragedy in the Indian drama: the rules governing the world of the play; the lack of mystery or ambiguity; the nature of destiny.

6. Does the drama have any of the overtones of a parable or allegory? What is the significance of Shakuntala's background?

7. Does one have any sense of participation in the drama through identification with any of the characters?

8. Specifically "traditional" notes: Brahman's curse; caste; obedience to parents; wife's duty to husband.

9. The reasons for the use of poetry.

10. Use of signs and symbols: throbbing arm, vine and mango, black bee, etc.

11. Two levels of working out of *karma*. Compare with *Rāmāyana*.

12. Compare the play with dramatic romances in Western literature, such as Aeschylus' *Oresteia*, Euripides' *Alcestis,* or Shakespeare's *The Tempest*.

THE LITTLE CLAY CART (MṚCCHAKAṬIKĀ) OF SHŪDRAKA (*ca.* 400)

The Little Clay Cart, attributed to King Shūdraka, with an impoverished Brahman merchant as the hero and a courtesan as the heroine, is the standard dramatic example of the Indian secular romance.

TRANSLATIONS

Lal, P. *Great Sanskrit Plays in Modern Translation.* Pbk ed., Norfolk, CT: New Directions, 1964.

Includes translation of *The Little Clay Cart* under the title *The Toy Cart.* See under *Shakuntalā*, above.

Oliver, Revilo Pendleton. *Mṛcchakatikā, the Little Clay Cart.* Urbana: University of Illinois Press, 1938.

A careful and meticulous translation with copious notes, an excellent introduction, and helpful appendices discussing the Indian context of the play.

Ryder, Arthur W. *The Little Clay Cart (Mṛcchakatikā).* Harvard Oriental series, vol. 9. Cambridge: Harvard University Press, 1905.

An accurate, highly literary translation, which attempts to reproduce many of the stylistic nuances of the original.

Van Buitenen, J. A. B. *Two Plays of Ancient India: The Little Clay Cart and The Minister's Seal.* New York: Columbia University Press, 1968.

Lively, scholarly English translations, enhanced by an excellent introduction to Indian drama.

Wilson, Horace Hayman. *The Mrichchhakati: or, The Toy Cart.* Calcutta: V. Holcroft, 1826. Reprint, with additional material, in *Hindu Dramatic Works*. Calcutta: Society for the Resuscitation of Indian Literature, 1901.

—— Same [excerpts], in *Select Specimens of the Theatre of the Hindus*. London: Parbury Allen, 1828. 3d ed., London: Trübner, 1871. Reprint, with additional material, under title *The Theatre of the Hindus*. Calcutta: Gupta, 1955.

Outdated but still interesting translations.

SECONDARY READINGS

Bhat, G. K. *Preface to Mṛcchakaṭikā*. Ahmedabad: New Order Book Co., 1953.

A critical study of this drama with special attention given to plot construction, characterization, humor, and background.

Faddegon, B. "Mṛcchakaṭikā and King Lear," in *India Antiqua, a Volume of Oriental Studies*, pp. 113–23. Leiden: Brill, 1947.

A provocative article by an excellent Indic scholar.

Keith, Arthur Berriedale. *The Sanskrit Drama: Its Origin, Development, Theory, and Practice*, pp. 128–42. Oxford: Clarendon Press, 1924.

A short account of the story, the authorship and age of the work, and the language and meters.

TOPICS FOR DISCUSSION

(See also topics under *Shakuntalā*, most of which are pertinent here.)

1. The cosmopolitan qualities of the drama: the minimal use of strictly Hindu imagery, theme, and symbol; the great appeal of the work to Western audiences.
2. The intricacy of the plot: a main plot with several subplots (Sharvilaka and Madanikā; the political revolt); the purpose of the interweaving of stories. How would removing one subplot effect the play?
3. The characterizations and the expression of human emotions.

Cārudatta as a real hero; Vasantasenā, a courtesan, as a real heroine, and Sansthānaka, the parasite (*viṭa*), as a villain. Maitreya's role as a confidante (*vidūṣaka*).

4. Didactic elements: the use of moral maxims and clichés as dramatic devices.
5. The expression of Indian humor and the question of satire in this drama.
6. Buddhist elements: compassion, charity, karma.
7. The realism (as opposed to the ephemeral atmosphere of *Shakuntalā*): the role of the monk; of the urban setting.

PAÑCATANTRA (ca. 200 B.C.)
ACCORDING TO PŪRṆABHADRA
(ca. 1199)

This collection of ancient Indian fables has exerted a greater influence on world literature than any other Indian work. It has been called the best collection of stories in the world.

TRANSLATIONS

Complete

Edgerton, Franklin. *The Panchatantra Reconstructed.* American Oriental Series, vol. 3. New Haven, CT: American Oriental Society, 1924.

An excellent translation of the reconstructed original text of the *Pañcatantra*. The translation is marred only by the author's idiosyncrasy in spelling. The volume includes a useful introduction discussing the origin, composition, and migration of the fables.

Ryder, Arthur W. *The Pañcatantra.* University of Chicago Press, 1925, reprint, 1956; Cambridge University Press, 1925, reprint, 1956. Bombay: Jaico Books. Pbk ed., University of Chicago Press, Phoenix, 1964.

Accurate translation with verse portions rendered in rhyme.

Selections

Yohannan, John D., ed. *A Treasury of Asian Literature,* pp. 15–20. New York: John Day, 1956; London: Phoenix House, 1958. Pbk ed., New York: New American Library, Mentor, 1960.

A translation by Charles R. Lanman of four short didactic fables.

SECONDARY READINGS

De, S. K. *A History of Sanskrit Literature*, pp. 86–92. University of Calcutta, 1947.

A brief general statement of the *Pañcatantra*, its composition, and recensions.

Keith, Arthur Berriedale. *A History of Sanskrit Literature*, pp. 242–65. Oxford: Clarendon Press, 1928.

An excellent short account and analysis of the origin of fable literature in India, the subject matter of the *Pañcatantra*, and its style and language. A short note on the genetically related *Hitopadeśa* is also included.

RELATED READINGS

Ryder, Arthur W. *Dandin: The Ten Princes*. University of Chicago Press, 1927.

Tawney, C. H. *The Ocean of Story* (A translation of Somadeva's *Kathāsaritsāgara*). 10 vols. London: C. J. Sawyer, 1924–28.

Van Buitenen, J. A. B. *Tales of Ancient India*. University of Chicago Press, 1959. Pbk ed., Phoenix, 1969.

TOPICS FOR DISCUSSION

1. The structure of the work: boxed fables (cf. *Arabian Nights*); the function of narrative prose and verse portions.
2. The concept of wise moral conduct; its importance in social and political relationships.
3. The use of didactic verse and moral maxims to justify or validate an action. Epigrammatic authority as a substitute for reason.
4. Worldly success and the problems of everyday life: security vs. poverty. Wit as means to resolve problems. The place of scholarship in human life. Human emotions and sentimentality.

5. The role of fate and the importance of human effort. The folly of hasty action.
6. The nature and importance of friendship in the face of adversity. The group ideal as opposed to the traditional emphasis on the spiritual wisdom of the individual ascetic.
7. The *Pañcatantra* as a practical guide for kings.
8. The use of stereotyped characters (e.g., the cat depicting hypocrisy; the jackal, craftiness; the heron, stupidity, etc.). The use of animal characters in preference to human ones.

SANSKRIT LYRIC POETRY

The extent of the Sanskrit lyric tradition is vast, extending over four millennia in various genres—rich in imagery of love, mystical experience, nature and society.

TRANSLATIONS

Works Attributed to Single Authors
Kālidāsa's Meghadūta (The Cloud Messenger)—a long love lyric (*ca.* A.D. 400)

Edgerton, Franklin and Eleanor Edgerton, trans. *Kālidāsa: The Cloud Messenger*. Ann Arbor: University of Michigan Press, 1964.
   A bilingual edition; the translation is readable, but the language is often archaic.
Nathan, Leonard, trans. *The Transport of Love: The Meghadūta of Kālidāsa*. Berkeley: University of California Press, 1976. Pbk ed.
   A good translation with perceptive introductory notes and commentary on sections of the poem.

Bhartṛihari's Śatakatraya: Nīti, Śṛṅgāra, Vairāgya (Centuries of Worldly Life, Passion, and Renunciation)—lyric and epigrammatic verses expressive of life's conflicting concerns (*ca.* 400–450).

Miller, Barbara Stoler. *Bhartṛihari: Poems*. New York: Columbia University Press, 1967. Reprinted in *The Hermit and the Love-Thief*. New York: Columbia University Press, 1978. Pbk ed.
   A bilingual edition based on D. D. Kosambi's definitive edition. The verse translation is excellent.

136

Ryder, Arthur W. *Women's Eyes*. San Francisco: A. M. Robertson, 1917, 1927.

Eighty-five verses from various *śataka*s (poetic works containing 100 verses) plus fifteen poems from other sources, are rendered in metrical versions that have both flaws and merits. Ryder's style is best suited to the gnomic verses.

Bilhaṇa's Caurapañcāśikā (Fifty Lyrics of a Thief)—a series of verses of remembered love (*ca.* 1070–1100).

Mathers, E. Powys. *Black Marigolds* (A free interpretation of the *Chaurapañchāśikā*). Reprinted in its entirety in Mark Van Doren, ed., *An Anthology of World Poetry*, pp. 66–77. New York: Harcourt, Brace, 1936.

Miller, Barbara Stoler. *Phantasies of a Love-Thief: The Caurapancasika Attributed to Bilhana*. New York: Columbia University Press, 1971. Reprinted in *The Hermit and the Love-Thief.* New York: Columbia University Press, 1978. Pbk ed.

A bilingual edition, including the critically edited texts of two versions of the work, an introduction, notes, and illustrations. The verse translation is excellent.

Anthologies

Brough, John. *Poems from the Sanskrit*. Baltimore: Penguin, 1968.

Translations of verses from various Sanskrit sources, with an excellent introduction.

Ingalls, Daniel H. H. *An Anthology of Sanskrit Court Poetry*. Cambridge: Harvard University Press, 1965.

Almost two thousand verses from various sources, as presented in Vidyākara's "Subhāṣitaratnakoṣa." The introduction, translations, and notes all attest to Ingall's great sensitivity for Sanskrit poetry.

—— *Sanskrit Poetry from Vidyākara's Treasury*. Cambridge: Harvard University Press, 1968.

A brief version of the above, aimed at a general audience.

Merwin, W. S. and J. Moussaiff Masson, trans. *Classical San-*

skrit Love Poetry. New York: Columbia University Press, 1977.

A fine version of stray verses, based on a collaboration of poet and scholar.

SECONDARY READINGS

De, S. K. *A History of Sanskrit Literature*, pp. 132–34, 161–65, and 364–69. University of Calcutta, 1947.

Dimock, Edward C. et al. *The Literatures of India: An Introduction*. University of Chicago Press, 1974. Pbk ed., 1978.

Ingalls, Daniel H. H. Introduction to *An Anthology of Sanskrit Court Poetry*. Cambridge: Harvard University Press, 1965.

Keith, Arthur Berriedale. *A History of Sanskrit Literature*, pp. 175–90. Oxford: Clarendon Press, 1928.

Siegel, Lee. *Fires of Love—Waters of Peace*. Honolulu: University of Hawaii Press, 1983.

Sensitive essay including good translations of poems of Amaru.

RELATED READINGS

Ramanujan, A. K., trans. *The Interior Landscape: Love Poems from a Classical Tamil Anthology*. Bloomington: Indiana University Press, 1967.

—— *Poems of Love and War: From the Eight Anthologies and the Ten Songs of Classical Tamil*. New York: Columbia University Press, 1985.

Superb translations of Tamil lyric poetry, which has much in common with this Sanskrit poetry.

TOPICS FOR DISCUSSION

1. What particular qualities of this poetry qualify it as "lyric?"
2. How are the compressed miniature molds of the poems ex-

panded? Consider the highly inflected Sanskrit language, the extensive use of long compound words, figures of speech, conventions, and suggestive overtones of words and images.

3. The environment of the poems—what is the role of nature? What is the relation between nature and love? How are elements of poetry used to create a particular mood or atmosphere (*rasa*)? Consider the interplay of conventions and descriptive details. (Compare *Shakuntalā* verses.)

4. What do the verses require of the reader? How does the educated reader enrich the poems? Is this possible through translation?

5. The themes of Sanskrit poetry: love-in-enjoyment and love-in-separation; the seasons; the poet's plight; the world of villains and kings; the pursuit of peace and liberation.

6. Compare the aesthetic world of Sanskrit poetry with that of classical Indian painting, sculpture, and music.

GĪTAGOVINDA OF JAYADEVA
(*ca.* twelfth century)

"Krishna Praised in Song" is a unique operatic lyric in Sanskrit, regarded both as a great poem and as a major work of medieval devotionalism.

TRANSLATIONS

Arnold, Edwin. *The Indian Song of Songs.* 6th ed. London: Kegan Paul, Trench, Trübner, 1891 (1st ed., 1875; Bombay: Jaico, 1949).

    A fairly accurate poetical translation, slightly bowdlerized.

Keyt, George. *Gita Govinda.* Bombay: Kutub, 1947.

    A good translation, but now superseded by that of Miller, below.

Miller, Barbara Stoler. *Love Song of the Dark Lord: Jayadeva's Gitagovinda.* New York: Columbia University Press, 1977. Pbk ed.

    Splendid translation in modern verse based on the translator's critical edition. Detailed introduction, notes, and glossary.

Rückert, Friedrich. *Gita Gowinda oder die Liebe des Krischna und der Radha.* Berlin: Schnabel, 1920.

    A translation by a gifted German poet.

SECONDARY READINGS

Archer, William George. *The Loves of Krishna in Indian Painting and Poetry.* London: Allen and Unwin, 1957; New York: Macmillan, 1957. Pbk ed., New York: Grove, Evergreen, 1958.

    A very fine survey of the Krishna-Rādhā legend as reflected in Indian painting.

De, S. K. *A History of Sanskrit Literature*, pp. 388–98. University of Calcutta, 1947.

A critical evaluation of Jayadeva's poem with reference to religious influences on the work and its position in Indian literature.

Keith, Arthur Berriedale. *A History of Sanskrit Literature*, pp. 190–98. Oxford: Clarendon Press, 1928.

A short discussion of the poet and his work.

Mukerjee, Radhakamal. *The Lord of the Autumn Moons.* Bombay: Asia Publishing House, 1957.

A good translation, with comment and introduction, of chapters 29–33 of Book 10 of the *Bhāgavata Purāṇa*, on which the *Gītagovinda* of Jayadeva is based.

Siegel, Lee. *Sacred and Profane Dimensions of Love in Indian Traditions as Exemplified in the Gītagovinda of Jayadeva.* New York and Dehli: Oxford University Press, 1978.

Stimulating essay.

Vaudeville, Charlotte. "Evolution of Love-Symbolism in Bhagavatism," in *Journal of the American Oriental Society* 82 (March 1962)1:31–40.

An illuminating article on the philosophical background of devotional Hinduism. Although the references are primarily to the *Bhagavadgītā* (see above) and Tamil poetry, this is a good article on the role of devotion (*bhakti*) in the Hindu thought basic to the *Gītagovinda*.

TOPICS FOR DISCUSSION

1. The *Gītagovinda* as an erotic and religious lyric; as an epic poem; as a dramatic lyric or a pastoral drama.
2. The ornate and artificial form; its melodic quality; its sensuous descriptions and mood (*rasa*). The function of recitative verses following each song to portray simple action.
3. The sensuous quality of Indian love songs (see *Shakuntalā*, above), and its dependence on form for dramatic effect.

4. The characters: Krishna (see *Mahābhārata, Bhagavadgītā,* above), Rādhā, and her friend (see *Shakuntalā*). Do their personalities emerge in the poem?
5. Why is Lord Krishna portrayed as having human passions? What is the reason for vivid imagery describing his erotic behavior?
6. The mood and atmosphere of the poem; Jayadeva's feelings for nature.
7. The *Gītagovinda* as an allegory (cf. *Song of Songs*) or mystery play, with mystical meaning expressed in terms of devotion (*bhakti*); love of the human soul, Rādhā, for a god, Krishna.
8. Are there any distinctions made between kinds of sensuality in the poem? Is there any religious element in the sexual imagery?

INDIAN DEVOTIONAL POETRY

Bhakti *poetry in three representative literary traditions—Tamil and Kannada, Hindi, and Bengali—exploring the human-divine relationship in concrete imagery of love in separation and union.*

TRANSLATIONS

Tamil and Kannada (ca. 200–1000)

Hooper, J. S. M., trans. *Hymns of the Ālvārs.* Calcutta: Association Press, 1929.

Somewhat old-fashioned, but readable selections.

Kingsbury, F. and G. E. Phillips, trans. *Hymns of the Tamil Śaivite Saints.* Calcutta: Association Press, 1921 (reissued).

As in the case of the above, a translation which serves as an introduction.

Ramanujan, A. K., trans. *Hymns for the Drowning: Poems for Vishnu by Nammalvar.* Princeton University Press, 1981.

Fine translations.

—— *Speaking of Śiva.* Harmondsworth: Penguin, 1973.

Fine, wide-ranging translations.

Zvelebil, K. V., trans. *The Lord of the Meeting Rivers.* Delhi: Motilal Banardidass, 1984.

Hindi (Kabīr, ca. 1440–1518; Tulasīdās, ca. 1532–1623)

Allchin, F. R., ed. and trans. *Tulasī Dās: Kavitāvāli.* New York: A. S. Barnes, 1964, 1965.

A readable verse translation of the work of Tulasīdās' old age, in two parts, including episodes from the Rāma legend and highly personal expressions of devotion. Excellent introduction to the poet and his poetry.

Allchin, F. R., trans. *The Petition to Rām: Hindi Devotional*

Hymns of the Seventeenth Century. London: Allen and Unwin, 1966.

Translation of another of the important works of Tulasīdās, the *Vinayapatrikā*.

Alston, A. J., trans. *The Devotional Poems of Mīrābāi*. Delhi: Motilal Banarsidass, 1980.

Useful, although the translations are somewhat stilted.

Atkins, A. G., trans. *The Rāmāyana of Tulsīdās, with Hindi Text*. 3 vols. New Delhi: Hindustan Times, Introduction dated 1954; Calcutta: Birla Academy of Art and Culture, 1966.

While the attempt to reproduce in English verse the prosody of the original is not very successful, the translation is reasonably accurate and gives something of the devotional flavor of Tulasīdās.

Hawley, John Stratton. *Sūr Dās: Poet, Singer, Saint*. Seattle: University of Washington Press; Delhi: Oxford University Press, 1984.

Scholarly study with excellent translations.

Hawley, John Stratton and Mark Juergensmeyer. *Songs of the Saints of India*. New York: Oxford University Press, 1988.

Hess, Linda, ed. and trans. *The Bījak of Kabīr*. San Francisco: North Point, 1983.

Vigorous, accurate translation.

Hill, W. Douglas P., trans. *The Holy Lake of the Acts of Rāma*. Bombay: Oxford University Press, 1952.

A fairly literal translation with a good introduction.

Vaudeville, Charlotte, ed. *Kabīr*. Vol. 1. Oxford: Clarendon Press, 1974.

Scholarly study, but less readable translations than Hess, above.

Bengali (ca. 1400–1700)

Bhattracarya, Deben, trans. *Love Songs of Chandidas: The Rebel Poet-Priest of Bengal*. London: Allen and Unwin, 1967.

Readable translations, with introduction and notes.

—— *Love Songs of Vidyapati*. London: Allen and Unwin, 1961.
The Introduction is by W. G. Archer.

Dimock, Edward C., Jr. and Denise Levertov, trans. *In Praise of Krishna: Songs from the Bengali*. Garden City, NY: Doubleday, Anchor Books, 1967.
Superb translations.

Nathan, Leonard and Clinton Seely, trans. *Grace and Mercy in Her Wild Hair: Selected Poems to the Mother Goddess*. Boulder, CO: Great Eastern, 1982.
These are translations from Rāmprasād Sen.

SECONDARY READINGS

Archer, W. G. *The Loves of Krishna in Indian Painting and Poetry*. New York: Grove, 1958.

Bhanadarkar, R. G. *Vaiṣṇavism, Śaivism and Minor Religious Systems*. Strassburg: Trübner, 1913.

Bryant, Kenneth E. *Poems to the Child-God: Structures and Strategies in the Poetry of Sūrdās*. Berkeley and Los Angeles: University of California Press, 1978.

Chatterji, Suniti Kumar. *Languages and Literatures of Modern India*, Part B. Calcutta: Prakash Bhavan, 1963.

Dimock, Edward C., Jr. *The Place of the Hidden Moon: Erotic Mysticism in Vaishnava Sahajiyā Cult of Bengal*. University of Chicago Press, 1966.
Includes an excellent discussion of the role of poetic imagery and esthetics in devotionalism, orthodox and heterodox.

Feldhaus, Anne, ed., with a chapter by Eleanor Zelliot. *The Deeds of God in Ṛddhipur*. New York: Oxford University Press, 1984.

Hardy, Friedhelm. *Viraha-Bhakti: The Early History of Krana Devotion in South India*. Delhi: Oxford, 1983.
A major study touching on the Alvars.

Hawley, John Stratton. *Krishna, the Butter Thief*. Princeton University Press, 1983.

145

Has a long section, with translations, on the poet Sūr Dās on this theme, and another on its treatment in the *rās līlās*.

Hawley, John Stratton, in association with Shrivatsa Goswami. *At Play with Krishna: Pilgrimage Dramas from Brindavan.* Princeton University Press, 1981. Pbk ed., 1985.

Translates four plays from the *rās līlā* genre, "celebrating the life of Krishna."

Hein, Norvin. *The Miracle Plays of Mathurā.* New Haven: Yale University Press, 1972. Pbk ed.

The standard source on the dramatic traditions centering in the Mathura area.

Singer, Milton B., ed. *Krishna: Myths, Rites, and Attitudes.* Honolulu: East-West Center, 1966.

Scholarly studies.

Thiel-Horstmann, Monika. *Crossing the Ocean of Existence: Braj Bhāsā Religious Poetry from Rajashan.* Weisbaden: Harrassowitz, 1983.

Contains translations from the Hindi poet Dādū.

Yocum, Glenn. *Hymns to the Dancing Śiva.* Columbia, MO: South Asia Books, 1982.

On Manikkavacakar.

TOPICS FOR DISCUSSION

1. The nature of devotion (*bhakti*) in these poems. Cf. *Bhagavadgītā, Gītagovinda*. What elements are drawn from previous religious traditions? What elements are drawn from literary traditions?

2. The language of the poetry. The effects of the vernacular languages versus Sanskrit.

3. Stylistic use of hyperbole and exaggerated imagery to create moods of heightened love, wonder, and awe.

4. Resolution of the conflict between a worldly life of love (*kāma*) and the duties of religion (*dharma*); how is it achieved?

The quality of love and religious duty in relation to Krishna, Rāma, Śiva, in the various poems.

5. The characters of Krishna and Rāma: cf. Krishna of poetry with Krishna of *Mahābhārata* and *Bhagavadgītā*; cf. Tulasīdāsa's and Kabīr's Rāma with Vālmīki's. The significance of various aspects of these characters: as incarnate gods in the Vedantic tradition of pantheism, as personal supreme God.

6. What is the relationship between the god and his devotee? What is the effect of love suffered in separation from the beloved? Cf. Shakuntalā, Vālmīki's Rāmāyana, Caurapañcā-śika, Gītagovinda.

INDO-ISLAMIC POETRY

Poetry written in Urdu and Persian comprises a distinct genre in Indian writing. The beauty and power of this poetry has led its admirers to rank it among the world's great literary achievements.

TRANSLATIONS

Eighteenth and Nineteenth Century Poets

Ahmad, Aijaz, ed. *Ghazals of Ghalib*. New York: Columbia University Press, 1971.

Versions of Urdu poems of Ghālib, generally regarded as the greatest of Urdu poets, by a number of American poets, including W. S. Merwin, Adrienne Rich, and William Stafford, based on translations by Aijaz Ahmad, a Pakistani poet.

Ali, Ahmed, ed. *The Golden Tradition: An Anthology of Urdu Poetry*. New York: Columbia University Press, 1973.

Translations, with excellent introductory essays, of the poetry of fifteen of the most important Urdu poets.

Ali, Ahmed, trans. *Ghalib: Selected Poems*. Rome: Is. M. E. O., 1969.

Careful, sensitive translations of both Urdu and Persian poetry.

Matthews, D. J. and C. Shackle. eds. *An Anthology of Classical Urdu Love Lyrics*. London: Oxford University Press, 1972.

Translations of representative works of twenty-two poets, with notes on prosody, grammar, and vocabulary.

Russell, Ralph and Khurshidul Islam, eds. and trans. *Three Mughal Poets: Mir, Sauda, Mir Hasan*. Cambridge: Harvard University Press, 1968.

Contains a valuable introductory essay on the eighteenth century background, with translations and critical interpretations of the work of three outstanding poets.

Sir Muhammad Iqbal (1876–1938)

Arberry, A. J., trans. *The Mysteries of Selflessness (Rumūz-i-Bekhudī)*. London: John Murray, 1953.

This long Persian poem is a passionate expression of the bases of an ideal Islamic society.

Nicholson, R. A., trans. *The Secrets of the Self (Asrār-i-Khudī)*. London: Macmillan, 1920. Rev. ed., Lahore: Ashraf, 1940.

Iqbal's most famous work, this poem asserts the role of the individual over what seemed to Iqbal to be the false emphasis of the Sufis on mystical communion with the Divine.

SECONDARY READINGS

Iqbal, Muhammad. *The Reconstruction of Religious Thought in Islam*. London: Oxford University Press, 1934; Lahore: Ashraf, 1944.

Perhaps the clearest and best statement of Iqbal's attitude toward Islam.

Malik, Hafeez, ed. *Iqbal, Poet-Philosopher of Pakistan*. New York: Columbia University Press, 1971.

Collection of essays on many aspects of Iqbal's thought.

Matthews, D. J., C. Shackle, and Shahrukh Husain, eds. and trans. *Urdu Literature*. London: Urdu Markaz, 1985.

A lively summary of the history of Urdu as a language and a literature. Contains a number of vivid, energetic translations. An entertaining overview for the general reader.

Matthews, D. J. and C. Shackle, eds. and trans. *An Anthology of Classical Urdu Love Lyrics*. London: Oxford University Press, 1972.

Contains text, translations, notes, glossary; translations are literal (although sometimes erroneous). A reader for the serious student of language and literature.

Pritchett, Frances W. *Urdu Literature: A Bibliography of English*

Language Sources. New Delhi: Manohar, 1979; Columbia, MO: South Asia Books, 1979.

Russell, Ralph, ed. *Ghalib: The Poet and His Age.* London: Allen and Unwin, 1972; New York: Barnes and Noble, 1972.

Russell, Ralph and Khurshidul Islam, trans. *Ghalib, 1797–1869.* Vol. I: *Life and Letters.* Cambridge: Harvard University Press, 1969; London: Allen and Unwin, 1969.

Sadiq, Muhammad. *A History of Urdu Literature.* London: Oxford University Press, 1964. 2d rev. ed., Delhi and New York: Oxford University Press, 1984.

> Comprehensive, scholarly study.

Schimmel, Annemarie. *A Dance of Sparks: Imagery of Fire in Ghalib's Poetry.* New Delhi: Vikas, 1979.

> General overview.

—— *As Through a Veil: Mystical Poetry in Islam.* New York: Columbia University Press, 1982.

—— *Gabriel's Wing: A Study of the Religious Ideas of Sir Muhammad Iqbal.* Leiden: Brill, 1963.

> Authoritative analysis.

Singh, Iqbal. *The Ardent Pilgrim.* London and New York: Longman's, 1951.

> Well-written study of Iqbal's life and ideas.

Vahid, S. A. *Iqbal, His Art and Thought.* Lahore: Ashraf, 1944; London: John Murray, 1959.

> A useful study of Iqbal's poetry and ideas.

TOPICS FOR DISCUSSION

1. The Lover and the Beloved in Urdu poetry: how are they to be understood?
2. What is the relationship between the use of conventional imagery and originality in this kind of poetry? How does adherence to a rigid convention affect poetry?
3. In the *ghazal*s, is each couplet a separate poem, or are there relationships to the main setting?

4. What is the significance of urban imagery in the Urdu poets?
5. The poetry of Iqbal: the significance of Iqbal's exaltation of the individual self; his understanding of love as "the desire to assimilate, to absorb. . . . Love individualizes the lover as well as the beloved"; his rejection of nationalism as an evil; the resolution of the contradiction between the self and the community; the concept of the "superman" in his poetry.

POEMS AND PLAYS OF
RABINDRANATH TAGORE (1861–1941)

The greatest literary figure of the Indian national revival in the twentieth century.

TRANSLATIONS

Chakravarty, Amiya, ed. and trans. *A Tagore Reader.* New York and London: Macmillan, 1961.

Selections with an introduction by a close associate of Tagore.

Radice, William, trans. *Selected Poems.* New York: Viking, 1985. Pbk ed., Harmondsworth: Penguin, 1985.

This recent selection and fresh translation by a British scholar far surpasses previous efforts at bringing Tagore's poetry to a Western audience. It has a brief introduction to his life and extensive literary and linguistic notes on the translations, all of which are carefully and intelligently done.

Tagore, Rabindranath. *Collected Poems and Plays of Rabindranath Tagore.* London: Macmillan, 1936; New York: Macmillan, 1937; reissued, 1952, 1956.

Many of the translations in this collection are by the author. While they are at times quite different in mood and style from the original Bengali, they indicate the poet's sensitivity to nature and his deep kinship with the traditional poetry of Bengal.

SECONDARY READINGS

Dimock, Edward C. "Rabindranath Tagore—'The Greatest of the Bāuls of Bengal,'" in *Journal of Asian Studies* 19 (1959)1:33–51.

A valuable study of the sources of Tagore's inspiration and imagery.

Ghose, S. K. *The Later Poems of Tagore*. London: Asia Publishing House, 1961.

Literary criticism with a number of translations.

Hay, Stephen N. *Asian Ideas of East and West: Tagore and His Critics in Japan, China, and India*. East Asian Series, No. 40. Cambridge: Harvard University Press, 1970.

A useful study of Tagore's cultural and political ideas and responses to them throughout Asia.

Kripalani, Krishna. *Rabindranath Tagore: A Biography*. New York: Grove, 1962; New York and London: Oxford University Press, 1962.

One of the best studies of the poet's life and works, by a close associate.

Tagore Society under the direction of Humayun Kabil, ed. *Towards Universal Man*. Bombay and New York: Asia Publishing House, 1961; reprinted 1967.

Excellent translations of eighteen of Tagore's most important essays on education, Indian culture, social problems, and the "Crisis in Civilization," done by some leading Bengali writers on the occasion of the Tagore centenary.

TOPICS FOR DISCUSSION

1. Tagore's relationship to his own tradition and to that of the West.
2. The pain and joy of religious experience as a theme of Tagore's poetry; time and death in the poems.
3. Tagore's emphasis on nature mysticism in contrast to customary Hindu attitudes; his concept of nature as *māyā* (illusion).
4. The significance of Tagore's imagery drawn from the *bhakti* (devotional) tradition: birds and flute music for the elusiveness of true joy; the market place, thieves, for man's blurred

153

sense of reality; fire for self-concern and passion; the river and boats for man's loneliness and danger.

5. The plays as expressions of ideas rather than as dramatic works; in sacrifice, the conflict between human feeling and the bonds of tradition, liberal humanism and religious authority. Are the issues acted out on even terms and fairly resolved?

6. The relation between Tagore's poetic vision and his criticism of nationalism; his understanding of the West.

7. Tagore's poetry as an aid in relating Indian art to Hindu metaphysical concepts; the mingling of human and divine love.

8. What were Tagore's ideals for education and why did he devote so much of his life to the effort of education as teacher and fund-raiser?

9. What is the significance of what Tagore called his *jīban-debatā* ("the goddess of my life"; an idealized female figure) in his poetry and in his life?

10. How did Tagore reconcile his poetical approach to the world and his keen interest in modern science?

AUTOBIOGRAPHY OF MOHANDAS KARAMCHAND GANDHI (1869–1948)

Episodic in style and lacking in narrative content, this is, nevertheless, one of the world's great autobiographies, providing insights into the motivations and actions of one of the most extraordinary men of our time.

TRANSLATIONS

Gandhi, Mohandas Karamchand. *An Autobiography: The Story of My Experiments with Truth. Translated from the Gujarati by Mahadev Desai.* Washington: Public Affairs Press, 1954. Pbk ed., Boston: Beacon Press, 1957. (First published under the title *The Story of My Experiments with Truth.* 2 vols. Ahmedabad: Navajivan Press, 1927–29; 2d ed., 1940; London: Phoenix Press, 1949.)

The translation, which is excellent, was revised by Gandhi himself.

Gandhi, Mohandas Karamchand. *All Men Are Brothers: Life and Thoughts of Mahatma Gandhi as Told in his Own Words.* Edited by Krishna Kripalani. 1st ed., New York: Columbia University Press, 1959. 2d ed., New York: Columbia University Press, 1969. Also, *All Men are Brothers: Autobiographical Reflections of Mahatma Gandhi,* compiled and edited by Krishna Kripalani. New York: Continuum, 1980.

A representative brief collection of Gandhi's thought, including a fine segment from his autobiography.

—— *Satyagraha: Non-violent Resistance.* Edited by Bharatan Kumarappa. New York: Schocken, 1951, 1961, 1968. Pbk ed., 1983.

Focuses on Gandhi's theory of nonviolent action, distinguishing among terms like passive resistance and civil disobedience.

SECONDARY READINGS

Ashe, Geoffrey. *Gandhi: A Study in Revolution*. London: Heinemann, 1968.

Informative especially on Gandhi's early period in London.

Bondurant, Joan. *The Conquest of Violence*. Princeton University Press, 1958; London: Oxford University Press, 1958; Bombay: Oxford University Press, 1959. Rev. ed., Berkeley: University of California Press, 1965.

An analysis of Gandhi's political philosophy.

Brown, Judith M. *Gandhi and Civil Disobedience: The Mahatma in Indian Politics, 1928–34*. New York: Cambridge University Press, 1977.

—— *Gandhi's Rise to Power: Indian Politics, 1915–1922*. New York: Cambridge University Press, 1972.

Two volumes by a careful historian of India that offer a thorough study of Gandhi's emergence and experience as the leader of the nationalist movement from 1919–1934.

Duncan, Ronald, ed. *Selected Writings of Mahatma Gandhi*. Boston: Beacon, 1951; London: Faber, 1951.

A good introductory essay, and a number of interesting selections.

Erikson, Erik H. *Gandhi's Truth: On the Origins of Militant Nonviolence*. New York: Norton, 1969. Pbk ed.

A psychoanalyst's view.

Fischer, Louis. *The Life of Mahatma Gandhi*. New York: Harper, 1950; London: Cape, 1951. Pbk ed., New York: Collier, 1962.

A detailed sympathetic study.

Gandhi, M. K. *Collected Works*. Vols. 1–90. Delhi: Publications Division of the Ministry of Information and Broadcasting, 1958–82.

—— *Constructive Programme: Its Meaning and Place*. Ahmedabad: Navajivan, 1941; 2d ed., rev. and enl., 1945.

Outlines Gandhi's views on economics and education.

—— *Key to Health*. Ahmedabad: Navajivan, 1948.

Gives Gandhi's views on food, medicine, sex, etc.

—— *Non-Violence in Peace and War*. 2 vols. 2d ed., Ahmedabad: Navajivan, 1944.

Collection of Gandhi's speeches and writings.

Nanda, B. R. *Mahatma Gandhi: A Biography*. Boston: Beacon, 1958; London: Allen and Unwin, 1958.

Useful narrative account, with good bibliography.

Nehru, Jawaharlal. *Towards Freedom*. New York: John Day, 1941. Boston: Beacon, 1958. Toronto: S. J. R. Saunders, 1958. (First published under the title *Jawaharlal Nehru: An Autobiography*. London: John Lane, 1936.)

Aside from its importance in its own right, this autobiography gives Nehru's interpretation of Gandhi's actions.

Sharma, J. S. *Mahatma Gandhi: A Descriptive Biography*. New Delhi: S. Chand, 1955.

Classified references to the vast literature on Gandhi.

TOPICS FOR DISCUSSION

1. The *Experiments* in comparison with other autobiographies or apologetic works, e.g., Augustine's *Confessions* or al-Ghazālī's *Deliverance from Error*. The significance of the title; Gandhi's attempts to simplify life and experience.
2. Is there a common background for Gandhi's characteristic concerns, e.g., vegetarianism, continence, attitude toward Western medicine, economic theories, etc.
3. The nature of *ahiṃsa* and *satyāgraha*: the conquest of violence.
4. The importance of fasting as purification, not as a weapon.
5. What is the significance of Gandhi's saying "Mind is the root of all sensuality"? "All restraint is wholesome for man"? "Man is man because he is capable of self-restraint"?

6. The sources of Gandhi's ideas: the transformation of Indian concepts under Western influence.
7. Gandhi's economic ideas as a valid alternative to industrialism.
8. The nature of Gandhi's toleration of other religions and of those who disagreed with him.
9. Gandhi's attitude to caste as exemplifying his attitude toward social reform.
10. The translation of Gandhi's ideas into a political program; *swarāj* (self-rule) as an expression of truth.
11. Gandhi's autobiography as an illumination of the Indian tradition.

III. Classics of the Chinese Tradition

GENERAL WORKS

Bibliographies

Chan, Wing-tsit. *An Outline and an Annotated Bibliography of Chinese Philosophy.* Rev. ed., New Haven: Yale University, Far Eastern Publications, 1961; supplement, 1965.

Hucker, Charles O. *China: A Critical Bibliography.* Tucson: University of Arizona Press, 1962.

Chinese Literature

Birch, Cyril, ed. *Anthology of Chinese Literature.* New York: Grove, vol. 1, 1965; vol. 2, 1972. Pbk ed., Evergreen, vol. 1, 1965; vol. 2, 1972.

Representative works of poetry, prose, fiction, and drama from early times to the present century, competently translated by a variety of experts.

—— *Studies in Chinese Literary Genres.* Berkeley: University of California Press, 1975.

Seminal essays on the key generic forms of classical Chinese literature.

Bishop, John L., ed. *Studies in Chinese Literature.* Cambridge: Harvard University Press, 1965.

Chai Ch'u and Winberg Chai. *A Treasury of Chinese Literature.* New York: Appleton-Century, 1965.

An anthology of Chinese prose with generous excerpts from major traditional novels as well as modern fiction.

Chang, H. C., trans. *Chinese Literature: Popular Fiction and Drama.* Edinburgh University Press, 1973. Pbk ed., New York: Columbia University Press, 1982.

An anthology of short stories and excerpts from the best-known plays and novels, including *The Water Margin* and *Dream of the Red Chamber.* Each selection is impeccably translated and fully annotated.

—— *Chinese Literature: Nature Poetry*. Vol. 2. Chinese Literature Series. New York: Columbia University Press, 1977.

Includes translations of important prose texts.

Chaves, Jonathan. *The Columbia Book of Later Chinese Poetry: Yüan, Ming, and Ch'ing Dynasties*. New York: Columbia University Press, 1986.

A representative selection of a hitherto neglected, yet very large, body of poetry.

Ch'en Shou-yi. *Chinese Literature: A Historical Introduction*. New York: Ronald Press, 1961.

A general survey with much useful information but with serious deficiencies from the scholarly point of view.

Chow Tse-tsung, ed. *Wen-lin: Studies in the Chinese Humanities*. Madison: University of Wisconsin Press, 1968.

Important papers by thirteen scholars, mainly on literature.

de Bary, Wm. Theodore, ed. *Approaches to the Oriental Classics: Asian Literature and Thought in General Education*. New York: Columbia University Press, 1959; 2d rev. ed., 1989.

Giles, Herbert A. *A History of Chinese Literature*. With a Continuation by Liu Wu-chi. New York: F. Ungar, 1967.

First published in 1901, this pioneer survey is quite out of date, but the continuation by Liu Wu-chi provides a succinct introduction to twentieth-century literature.

Hanan, Patrick. "The Development of Fiction and Drama," in Raymond Dawson, ed., *The Legacy of China*. Oxford: Clarendon Press, 1964.

A succinct account, especially good on the beginnings of Chinese fiction and drama.

Hawkes, David. "Chinese Poetry and the English Reader," in Raymond Dawson, ed., *The Legacy of China*. Oxford: Clarendon Press, 1964.

Excellent introduction to the problems of reading Chinese poetry in translation.

Hightower, J. R. *Topics in Chinese Literature: Outlines and Bibli-*

ographies. Rev. ed., Cambridge: Harvard University Press, 1962.

A concise and authoritative guide with bibliographic aids.

Hsia, C. T. *The Classic Chinese Novel: A Critical Introduction.* New York: Columbia University Press, 1968; pbk ed., 1972. Bloomington: Indiana University Press, 1981. Pbk ed.

An indispensable guide to six major novels, including *The Water Margin, Journey to the West, The Golden Lotus,* and *Dream of the Red Chamber,* with a valuable appendix on the colloquial short story.

Liu, James J. Y. *Essentials of Chinese Literary Art.* North Scituate, MA: Duxbury, 1979.

A good concise introduction.

Liu Wu-chi. *An Introduction to Chinese Literature.* Bloomington: Indiana University Press, 1966. Pbk ed., 1969.

A general survey which, though weak in spots, provides the best introduction to the subject.

Lynn, Richard John. *Chinese Literature: A Draft Bibliography in Western European Languages.* Oriental Monograph Series, no. 24. Canberra: Australian National University Press, 1979.

Munro, Donald. *The Concept of Man in Early China.* Stanford University Press, 1969.

A stimulating and perceptive analysis of early Chinese thought.

Nienhauser, William H., ed. *Critical Essays in Chinese Literature.* Honolulu: University of Hawaii Press, 1976.

Articles of varying interest and value, on topics ranging from classical poetry to modern fiction.

—— *The Indiana Companion to Traditional Chinese Literature.* Bloomington: University of Indiana Press, 1985.

An invaluable reference for information on major and minor figures, forms, and movements in Chinese literary history, with introductory essays on the main literary genres.

Watson, Burton. *Columbia Book of Chinese Poetry: From Early*

Times to the Thirteenth Century. New York: Columbia University Press, 1984.

A good representative selection of major poetic works.

—— *Early Chinese Literature*. New York: Columbia University Press, 1962; pbk ed., 1971.

Discusses the literary aspects of Chinese poetry, history, and philosophy in the period ending A.D. 200.

Chinese Thought and Religion

Chan Wing-tsit. *A Source Book in Chinese Philosophy*. Princeton University Press, 1963.

Extensive translations of the highest quality with commentary emphasizing the significance of each new concept to the development of later Chinese thought.

Creel, Herrlee G. *Chinese Thought from Confucius to Mao Tsetung*. University of Chicago Press, 1953; London: Eyre and Spottiswoode, 1954.

A clear, concise account by a scholar especially conversant with classical thought.

de Bary, Wm. Theodore et al. *Sources of Chinese Tradition*. New York: Columbia University Press, 1960. Pbk ed., 2 vols., 1964.

Source readings in Chinese intellectual history, with introductory essays and commentary.

—— *The Buddhist Tradition in India, China, and Japan*. New York: Modern Library, 1969. Pbk. ed., New York: Random House, Viking, 1972.

Eliade, Mircea, ed. *The Encyclopedia of Religion*. 16 vols. New York: Macmillan, 1986.

Eber, Irene, ed. *Confucianism: The Dynamics of Tradition*. New York: Macmillan, 1986.

Fung Yu-lan. *A History of Chinese Philosophy*. Translated by Derk Bodde. 2 vols. Princeton University Press, 1952–53.

A standard work by a leading contemporary Chinese philosopher. The careful and scholarly translation is a great contribution in itself.

Hsiao Kung-ch'üan. *A History of Chinese Political Thought*. Vol. 1. Translated by F. W. Mote. Princeton University Press, 1979.

A masterful characterization of China's political development and insightful discussion of individual thinkers of the pre-imperial and early imperial periods, to the fifth century.

Hughes, Ernest R., ed. and trans. *Chinese Philosophy in Classical Times*. London: Dent, 1942; New York: Dutton, 1942; rev. ed., 1954.

A representative selection of source readings, carefully translated and explained.

Mote, F. W. *Intellectual Foundations of China*. New York: Knopf, 1971.

Rubin, Vitaly A. *Individual and State in Ancient China: Essays on Four Chinese Philosophers*. Translated by Steven I. Levine. New York: Columbia University Press, 1976.

Essays on Confucius, Mo Tzu, Shang Yang, and Chuang Tzu.

Schwartz, Benjamin I. *The World of Thought in Ancient China*. Cambridge: Harvard University Press, Belknap Press, 1985.

A mature and stimulating discussion of early Chinese thought, rich with comparisons with Western philosophy.

Chinese History

Creel, Herrlee G. *The Origins of Statecraft in China*. Vol. 1. University of Chicago Press, 1970.

A study of political organization in the Western Chou dynasty, with comparisons to Western historical experience.

de Bary, Wm. Theodore. *East Asian Civilizations: A Dialogue in Five Stages*. Cambridge, MA: Harvard University Press, 1987.

An overview of Chinese history and thought in the East Asian context.

Ebrey, Patricia B., ed. *Chinese Civilization and Society: A Sourcebook.* New York: Free Press, 1981. Pbk ed.

Selected primary documents from earliest times to the modern era, with focus on "little" traditions as well as the "great."

Fairbank, John K., Edwin O. Reischauer, and Albert M. Craig. *East Asia: The Great Tradition, New Impression.* Boston: Houghton Mifflin, 1973. See also Edwin O. Reischauer, John K. Fairbank, and Albert M. Craig. *East Asia: The Great Tradition.* Vol. 1 of *A History of East Asian Civilization.* Boston: Houghton Mifflin, 1960; London: Allen and Unwin, 1961.

The best available survey of institutional developments.

Gentzler, J. Mason. *A Syllabus of Chinese Civilization.* 2d ed., New York: Columbia University Press, 1972. Pbk ed.

Gernet, Jacques. *A History of Chinese Civilization.* Translated from the French by J. R. Foster. Cambridge: Westview, 1980. Pbk ed., New York: Cambridge University Press, 1982.

The best overall survey.

Goodrich, L. Carrington. *A Short History of the Chinese People.* 2d ed., London: Allen and Unwin, 1958; 3d ed., New York: Harper, 1959; London: Allen and Unwin, 1969. Pbk reprint, Harper, Torchbook, 1969. Pbk ed.

—— *China to 1850: A Short History.* Stanford University Press, 1978.

A concise, factual, and up-to-date survey.

Grousset, Rene. *The Rise and Splendour of the Chinese Empire.* Translated by Anthony Watson-Gancy and Terence Gordon. London: Geoffrey Books, 1952; Berkeley: University of California Press, 1953. Pbk ed., 1962.

A general cultural history. No longer wholly up to date, but still recommended for its balanced treatment and sensitivity of interpretation.

Hucker, Charles O. *China's Imperial Past: An Introduction to Chinese History and Culture.* Stanford University Press, 1975.

A good, comprehensive textbook covering political, social,

economic, intellectual, and cultural history from the beginings to 1850.

Latourette, Kenneth Scott. *The Chinese, Their History and Culture.* 2 vols. London and New York: Macmillan, 1934. 3d ed., rev. (2 vols in 1), New York: Macmillan, 1946.

A standard work.

Meskill, John, ed. *Introduction to Chinese Civilization.* New York: Columbia University Press, 1973.

An excellent general survey with specialized essays by various scholars.

Michael, Franz. *China Through the Ages: History of a Civilization.* Boulder, CO: Westview Press, 1986.

Morton, W. Scott. *China: Its History and Culture.* New York: Harper and Row, 1981.

Focus on the modern period.

Schirokauer, Conrad. *A Brief History of Chinese and Japanese Civilizations.* New York: Harcourt, Brace, 1978, 2d rev. ed., 1988. Pbk ed.

THE ANALECTS (LUN-YÜ) OF CONFUCIUS (551–479 B.C.)

The best single source for the ideas of Confucius, which have shaped and influenced East Asian thought into modern times.

TRANSLATIONS

Complete

Lau, D. C., trans. *Confucius: The Analects.* Pbk ed., Harmondsworth: Penguin, 1979.

    Readable and reliable.

Legge, James, trans. *The Confucian Analects,* in *The Chinese Classics,* vol. 1. 2d ed., 5 vols. Oxford: Clarendon Press, 1893. Reprinted, with minor corrections, notes, and concordance tables, Hong Kong University Press, 1960. Also in *The Four Books.* Shanghai: Chinese Book Company, 1933.

    This standard work by a pioneer translator of the Chinese classics into English is still one of the best. Interprets the *Analects* generally as it was understood in later Confucian tradition.

Pound, Ezra, trans. *Confucian Analects.* New York: Kasper and Horton, 1956. Reprinted in *Confucius: The Great Digest, The Unwobbling Pivot, The Analects.* Pbk ed., New Yor New Directions, 1969.

    A poetic interpretation of more value for Pound's unique insights and choice of language than for its fidelity to the original text. Recommended only for use alongside other, more scholarly translations.

Soothill, W. E., trans. *The Analects; or, The Conversations of Confucius.* London: Oxford University Press, 1937. New York: Oxford University Press, 1941. (Originally published as

The Analects of Confucius, Yokohama: The Author, 1910.)
A dependable translation, with a helpful introduction.

Waley, Arthur, trans. *The Analects of Confucius.* London: Allen and Unwin, 1938; New York: Random House, 1938; reprinted as *Analects.* Pbk ed., New York: Random House, 1966.

The translation is recommended for its literary qualities and its attempt to present the work in its historical context rather than in its traditional interpretation. Especially valuable for its introduction explaining the basic terms and concepts appearing in the text.

Selections

Chan Wing-tsit, ed. *A Source Book in Chinese Philosophy*, Chapter 2. Princeton University Press, 1963. Pbk ed.

An extremely useful selection, reliably translated, which retains the order of the original text and includes helpful comments on interpretation.

Hughes, Ernest R., ed. and trans. *Chinese Philosophy in Classical Times,* Chapter 2. London: Dent, 1942; New York: Dutton, 1942; rev. ed., 1954.

McNeill, William H. and Jean W. Sedlar, eds. *Classical China.* New York: Oxford University Press, 1970.

A selection arranged topically under the headings "Ethics," "Politics," and "Religion."

Mei, Y. P. Selections in Wm. Theodore de Bary et al., *Sources of Chinese Tradition,* pp. 17–35. New York: Columbia University Press, 1960; pbk ed., 2 vols., 1964.

SECONDARY READINGS

Boodberg, Peter A. "The Semasiology of Some Primary Confucian Concepts," in *Philosophy East and West* 2 (January 1953)4:317–32.

Creel, Herrlee G. *Confucius, the Man and the Myth.* New York:

John Day, 1949; London: Routledge and Kegan Paul, 1951. Also under title *Confucius and the Chinese Way*. New York: Harper, Torchbooks, 1960. Pbk ed.

The most extensive study in English, by a specialist in the field.

Fingarette, Herbert. *Confucius: The Secular as Sacred*. New York: Harper and Row, Torchbooks, 1972. Pbk ed.

A controversial and suggestive essay, from the point of view of modern philosophy, on the place of ritual in the thought of Confucius.

Hamburger, Max. "Aristotle and Confucius: A Comparison," in *Journal of the History of Ideas* 20 (1959):236–49.

Hsiao Kung-ch'üan. *A History of Chinese Political Thought*, chapter 2. Translated by F. W. Mote. Princeton University Press, 1979.

A study of the background to Confucian thought and major concepts and categories by a leading Chinese scholar.

Kaizuka Shigeki. *Confucius*. Translated from the Japanese by Geoffrey Bownas. London: Allen and Unwin, 1956; New York: Macmillan, 1956.

The life of Confucius against the political and social background of his times, as seen by a Japanese specialist in the period.

Kupperman, Joel. "Confucius and the Nature of Religious Ethics," in *Philosophy East and West* 21 (April 1971)2:189–94.

Liu Wu-chi. *Confucius, His Life and Time*. New York: Philosophical Library, 1955.

A popular introduction.

Munro, Donald. *The Concept of Man in Early China*. Stanford University Press, 1969.

A stimulating and perceptive analysis of early Chinese thought.

Schwartz, Benjamin. *The World of Thought in Ancient China*, chapter 3. Cambridge: Harvard University Press, Belknap, 1985.

Sinaiko, Herman L. "The Analects of Confucius," in Wm. Theodore de Bary, ed., *Approaches to the Oriental Classics,* pp. 142–52. New York: Columbia University Press, 1959.

An essay which identifies the values in the *Analects* for humanistic general education. The author is sympathetic to his subject and sophisticated in his evaluation.

Smith, D. H. "The Significance of Confucius for Religion," in *History of Religions* 2 (Winter 1963)2:242–55.

Tu Wei-ming. "Jen as a Living Metaphor in the Confucian *Analects,*" in *Philosophy East and West* 31 (January 1981)1:45–54. Reprinted in his *Confucian Thought: Selfhood as Creative Transformation,* pp. 81–92. Albany: State University of New York Press, 1985.

TOPICS FOR DISCUSSION

1. What kind of text is the *Analects*?
2. What kind of authority does Confucius invoke? Do you find him authoritarian in his attitude toward learning and ritual (or decorum)? Why do we accept what he says? If it is through reason, how does this reason manifest itself, given that Confucius does not engage in systematic argument?
3. Confucius' central theme: man in society. His ideal of harmony. How does Confucius handle the tension between personal moral feeling and society's claims upon him, self-development and social obligation?
4. What kind of virtue is humaneness (Chinese, *jen* or *ren),* or Goodness (Waley), or benevolence (D. C. Lau)? What is Confucius' commitment to reciprocity or empathy (Chinese, *shu*)?
5. The immediate problem: how to govern men and how to govern oneself; Confucius' answer in the noble man or gentleman *(chün-tzu).* The power of political and moral example. The functions of the ruling class.
6. How do the categories of morality and religion figure into

the analysis of Confucian humanism? What is Confucius' concept of Heaven? Of ritual (or decorum)? Is there a clear distinction between the sacred and the secular?

7. What insights does Confucius have concerning the role of the family in personality development and social relations? What is his view of filial piety in the conduct of personal relations and in the ordering of society?

8. What is the intellectual or moral significance of the rectification of names?

9. Should Confucius be seen as traditionalist or as reformer, as idealist or realist, as optimistic or pessimistic, as "feudal" or "democratic"?

10. Is there any place for the individual in the philosophy of Confucius?

MO TZU, OR MO TI

A sharp critic of Confucianism in the late fifth and early fourth centuries B.C., and a major alternative voice in politics and religion.

TRANSLATIONS

Complete

Mei, Y. P., trans. *The Ethical and Political Works of Motse*. London: Probsthain, 1929.

Selections

Chan, Wing-tsit, ed. *A Source Book in Chinese Philosophy*, chapter 9. Princeton University Press, 1963.

Hughes, Ernest R. *Chinese Philosophy in Classical Times*, pp. 43–67. London: Dent, 1942; New York: Dutton, 1942; rev. ed., 1954.

Mei, Y. P., trans. Selections in Wm. Theodore de Bary et al., *Sources of Chinese Tradition*. New York: Columbia University Press, 1960; pbk ed., 2 vols, 1964.

Watson, Burton, trans. *Basic Writings of Mo Tzu, Hsün Tzu, and Han Fei Tzu*. New York: Columbia University Press, 1967.

　　Contains a translation of selected chapters representing Mo Tzu's essential ideas.

—— *Mo Tzu: Basic Writings*. New York: Columbia University Press, 1963. Pbk ed.

　　Same selection of the Mo Tzu text as appears in the larger collection listed above.

SECONDARY READINGS

"Chuang Tzu" (judgment of Mo Tzu in the T'ien Hsia [World of Thought] chapter of the *Chuang Tzu*), in Wm. Theodore de Bary et al., *Sources of Chinese Tradition*, pp. 80–83. New York: Columbia University Press, 1960; pbk ed., 2 vols., 1964; 1:78–81.

Creel, Herrlee G. *Chinese Thought,* pp. 46–66. University of Chicago Press, 1953.

Dobson, W. A. C. H. "Micius," in Douglas Grant and Millar MacLure, eds., *The Far East: China and Japan*, pp. 299–310. University of Toronto Press, 1961.

Fung Yu-lan. *History of Chinese Philosophy*, 1:76–105. 2 vols. Princeton University Press, 1952–53.

Graham, A. C. *Later Mohist Logic, Ethics and Science.* Hong Kong: Chinese University Press, 1978; School of Oriental and African Studies, University of London, 1978.

    An extremely careful scholarly account of the background to Mohist thought, its philosophical range and major concepts, as well as textual problems in the later tradition. The introductory account on pp. 1–22 is helpful for general readers.

Hsiao Kung-chuan. *A History of Chinese Political Thought*, chapter 4. Translated by F. W. Mote. Princeton University Press, 1979.

Hu Shih. *The Development of the Logical Method in Ancient China*, pp. 63–82. Shanghai: Oriental Book Co., 1922; reprint ed., New York: Krishna Press, n.d.

Mei, Y. P. *Motse, the Neglected Rival of Confucius.* London: Probsthain, 1934.

Needham, Joseph. *Science and Civilisation in China*, Vol. 2 (1956), pp. 165–84. Cambridge University Press, 1954– .

Rubin, Vitaly A. *Individual and State in Ancient China: Essays on Four Chinese Philosophers*, chapter 2. Translated by Steven I. Levine. New York: Columbia University Press, 1976.

Schwartz, Benjamin. *The World of Thought in Ancient China*, chapter 4. Cambridge: Harvard University Press, Belknap, 1985.

Waley, Arthur. *Three Ways of Thought in Ancient China*, pp. 163–81. London: Allen and Unwin, 1939; New York: Macmillan, 1940. New York: Doubleday, Anchor, 1956, pp. 121–35.

TOPICS FOR DISCUSSION

1. Mo Tzu's utilitarianism and its social basis. Is it rooted in any "class" outlook?
2. Mo Tzu's religious activity and zeal. Does his rigor or puritanism derive from his religious views, from moral idealism, from a particular view of human nature?
3. Mo Tzu's concept of universal love versus the differentiated love of the Confucianists. How is this related to their differing views of Heaven? How does this affect Mo's view of the individual vis-à-vis the state?
4. Mo Tzu's methods of argumentation and criteria of proof or value. His emphasis on certainty, and the question of authoritarianism.
5. Idealism and totalitarianism in Mo Tzu's political philosophy and in Moism as an organized movement. How does this reflect Mo's view of the common standard (uniformity) as compared to Confucian accommodation of difference?
6. Mo Tzu as an intellectual and as a reformer. The *Chuang Tzu*'s judgment of him as an individual.
7. Mo Tzu and Mao Tse-tung: resemblances and differences.
8. Mo Tzu as an observer and critic of Confucianism.

LAO TZU, OR TAO-TE CHING

A basic text of Taóism that has become a world classic because of its radical challenge to basic assumptions of both traditional and modern civilizations. Its date and provenance are still much disputed.

TRANSLATIONS

Bynner, Witter. *The Way of Life According to Lao Tzu.* New York: John Day, 1944. London: Editions Poetry, 1946.

More a stimulating poetic interpretation than a translation.

Chan Wing-tsit. *The Way of Lao Tzu.* Indianapolis: Bobbs-Merrill, 1963.

A careful translation based on extensive study of Chinese commentaries.

Duyvendak, J. J. L. *Tao Te Ching: The Book of the Way and Its Virtue.* London: John Murray, 1954.

This translation by an eminent sinologue rearranges the text and offers an unusual naturalistic interpretation of it.

Lau, D. C. *Lao Tzu Tao Te Ching.* Baltimore: Penguin Books, 1963.

A competent translation by a knowledgeable scholar, with a useful introduction and appendices which include a discussion of authorship, an analysis of the nature of the work, and a useful glossary.

Waley, Arthur. *The Way and Its Power: A Study of the Tao Te Ching and Its Place in Chinese Thought.* London: Allen and Unwin, 1934; Boston: Houghton, 1935. Pbk ed., New York: Grove, Evergreen, 1958.

An original translation with a lengthy introduction, both reflecting the astute scholarship and literary finish that are characteristic of Waley. His rigorous method of reconstructing the historical and linguistic context as a basis for interpre-

176

tation, rather than accepting the traditional or "scriptural" view, has its own difficulties, however. In this case there is sometimes a tendency to interpret the *Tao-te ching* perhaps too narrowly as a dialogue between quietists and realists (legalists) in the third century B.C.

Wu, John C. H. *Tao Teh Ching.* Jamaica, NY: St. John's University Press, 1961.

A graceful and poetic translation of the text by one for whom it represents a living tradition, not a philological exercise.

SECONDARY READINGS

Boodberg, Peter A. "Philological notes on Chapter One of the Lao Tzu," in *Harvard Journal of Asiatic Studies* 30 (1957)3–4:598–618.

Ch'en, Ellen M. "Is There a Doctrine of Physical Immortality in the *Tao Te Ching*?" in *History of Religions* 12 (1973)3:231–47.

Creel, Herrlee G. *Chinese Thought*, chapter 6. University of Chicago Press, 1953.

Fung Yu-lan. *History of Chinese Philosophy*, 1:170–91. 2 vols. Princeton University Press, 1952–53.

Kaltenmark, Max. *Lao Tzu and Taoism.* Stanford University Press, 1969.

Kimura Eiichi. "A New Study on Lao-tzu," in *Philosophical Studies of Japan* 1 (1959):85–104.

Lagerwey, John. *Taoist Ritual in Chinese Society and History.* New York: Macmillan, 1987.

Maspero, Henri. *Le Taoïsm* (vol. 2 of *Mélanges Posthumes sur les Religions et l'Histoire de la Chine*), pp. 227–42. Paris: Musée Guimet, 1950.

Needham, Joseph. *Science and Civilisation in China*, Vol. 2 (1956), pp. 33–127. Cambridge University Press, 1954– .

Saso, Michael. "Buddhist and Taoist Notions of Transcendence: A Study in Philosophical Contrast," in Michael Saso and David W. Chappell, eds., *Buddhist and Taoist Studies,* no. 1, pp. 3–22. Honolulu: University of Hawaii Press, 1977. Pbk ed.

Schwartz, Benjamin. *The World of Thought in Ancient China*, chapter 6. Cambridge: Harvard University Press, Belknap, 1985

Tu Wei-ming. "The 'Thought of Huang-Lao': A Reflection on the Lao Tzu and Huang Ti Texts in the Silk Manuscripts of Ma-wang-tui," in *Journal of Asian Studies* 39 (November 1979)1:95–110.

Waley, Arthur. *The Way and Its Power: A Study of the Tao Te Ching and Its Place in Chinese Thought.* London: Allen and Unwin, 1934; Boston: Houghton, 1935. Pbk ed., New York, Grove, Evergreen, 1958, pp. 17–137.

Welch, Holmes. *The Parting of the Way: Lao Tzu and the Taoist Movement,* pp. 18–87. Boston: Beacon, 1957; London: Methuen, 1958. Pbk ed., Beacon, 1966.

Welch, Holmes and Anna Seidel, eds. *Facets of Taoism: Essays in Chinese Religion.* New Haven: Yale University Press, 1979. Pbk ed.

TOPICS FOR DISCUSSION

1. The multiple meanings of the term "Way" (*Tao*): as a way of life in the everyday world; as the Way of Nature or Cosmic Process; as the One, the First Principle or Source; as the Transcendent, Absolute; as Nothing; as knowable and unknowable.

2. The "natural" and "artificial," feminine and masculine, in Taoism and Confucianism.

3. *Wu-wei* (doing nothing, nonstriving, effortlessness) as a guide to life; as a way of government. Individual life and human values in relation to the Way.

4. Practicality and impracticality in relation to the Way. Lao Tzu as a critic of civilization, of humanism.
5. Lao Tzu as social reformer and "antihero."
6. Lao Tzu "has insight into what is crooked (bent) but not what is straight" (Hsün Tzu).

CHUANG TZU

*A philosophical work of the Taoist school, attributed to Chuang Chou,
ca. 369–286 B.C., characterized by speculative ramblings, at once
delightful and utterly serious, philosophical parodies, and amusing
parables.*

TRANSLATIONS

Complete

Giles, Herbert A., trans. *Chuang Tzu: Mystic, Moralist and Social
Reformer.* 2d ed., London: B. Quaritch, 1926. Shanghai: Kelly
and Walsh, 1926. London: Allen and Unwin, 1961.

A free translation into a Victorian English style, somewhat
incongruous with Chuang Tzu.

Legge, James, trans. *The Writings of Kwang-tsze.* Sacred Books
of the East, vol. 40. Oxford: Clarendon Press, 1891. Also
published under title *The Texts of Taoism.* New York: Julian
Press, 1959.

A pioneering effort, this rather literal-minded rendering
loses much of the wit and fancy of the original.

Watson, Burton, trans. *The Complete Works of Chuang Tzu.*
New York: Columbia University Press, 1968.

An excellent translation, especially valuable for its literary
quality.

Selections

Fung Yu-lan, trans. *Chuang Tzu: A New Selected Translation
with an Exposition of the Philosophy of Kuo Hsiang.* Shanghai:
Commercial Press, 1931. Reprint, New York: Paragon, 1964.

The first seven chapters of the *Chuang Tzu* translated with extensive commentary by the philosopher Kuo Hsiang (3d century) by a leading contemporary Chinese authority. Out of print and difficult to obtain, but still a valuable source.

Giles, Lionel, ed. *Musings of a Chinese Mystic: Selections from the Philosophy of Chuang Tzu.* Wisdom of the East series. London: John Murray, 1906, 1927.

Representative selections drawn from the translation of Herbert A. Giles and arranged topically, with a helpful introduction by the editor.

Hughes, Ernest R. *Chinese Philosophy in Classical Times*, pp. 165–211. London: Dent, 1942; New York: Dutton, 1941; rev. ed., 1954.

Graham, A. C., trans. *Chuang Tzu: The Inner Chapters.* London: Allen and Unwin, 1981.

Proposes some rearrangement of the traditional text and emphasizes philosophical rigor and consistency. Virtually a complete translation and excellent for philosophically oriented readers.

Lin Yutang, ed. "The Book of Tao," in *The Wisdom of Laotse.* New York: Random House, Modern Library, 1948.

—— *The Wisdom of China and India*, pp. 625–91. New York: Random House, 1942. (For other editions, see below, under *Mencius.*)

Substantial selections from eleven of the thirty-three chapters of Chuang Tzu.

Waley, Arthur. *Three Ways of Thought in Ancient China*, pp. 17–112. London: Allen and Unwin, 1939; New York: Doubleday, Anchor, 1956, pp. 5–79.

Watson, Burton, trans. *Chuang Tzu: Basic Writings.* New York: Columbia University Press, 1964. Pbk ed.

Selected chapters for the general reader (see *Complete Works* above).

SECONDARY READINGS

Creel, Herrlee G. *Chinese Thought*, pp. 94–114. University of Chicago Press, 1953.

—— "The Great Clod: A Taoist Conception of the Universe," in Chow Tse-tsung, ed., *Wen-lin: Studies in the Chinese Humanities*, pp. 157–68. Madison: University of Wisconsin Press, 1968.

—— *What Is Taoism? and Other Studies in Chinese Cultural History*. University of Chicago Press, 1970.

Fung Yu-lan. *History of Chinese Philosophy*, 1:221–45. 2 vols. Princeton University Press, 1952–53.

Graham, A. C., trans. *Chuang Tzu: The Inner Chapters*. London: Allen and Unwin, 1981.

> Translator's Introduction, pp. 3–39, is excellent both for background and an approach to the world of thought of Chuang Tzu.

—— "Chuang Tzu's Essay on Seeing Things as Equal," in *History of Religions* 9 (November and February 1969–70)2–3:137–59.

—— "Taoist Spontaneity and the Dichotomy of 'Is' and 'Ought,'" in Victor H. Mair, ed., *Experimental Essays in Chuang Tzu*. Honolulu: University of Hawaii Press, 1983.

Hu Shih. *The Development of the Logical Method in Ancient China*, pp. 140–48. Shanghai: Oriental Book Co., 1922; Krishna Press, n.d.

Schwartz, Benjamin. *The World of Thought in Ancient China*, chapter 6. Cambridge: Harvard University Press, Belknap, 1985.

Wu, John C. H. "The Wisdom of Chuang Tzu: A New Appraisal," in *International Philosophical Quarterly* 3 (February 1963)1:5–36.

TOPICS FOR DISCUSSION

1. The Way (*Tao*) as conceived by Lao Tzu and Chuang Tzu.
2. Skepticism and mysticism in Chuang Tzu.
3. Chuang Tzu's radical individualism. His conception of the sage.
4. The meaning of Chuang Tzu's "sitting in forgetfulness," and its implications for learning.
5. Chuang Tzu and Lao Tzu as social reformers.
6. Romanticism and realism in Chuang Tzu's approach to the conduct of life.
7. Creativity and vitalism as basic themes in Taoism.
8. "Chuang Tzu was prejudiced in favor of nature and did not know man." (Hsün Tzu)

MENCIUS (MENG TZU, 372–289 B.C.)

A leading Confucian thinker, second in importance only to Confucius, Mencius addressed a broad range of practical and philosophical problems. With the Analects *of Confucius, the* Great Learning, *and the* Doctrine of the Mean, *the* Mencius *came to be canonized as one of the "Four Books."*

TRANSLATIONS

Complete

Dobson, W. A. C. H., trans. *Mencius.* University of Toronto Press, 1963.

 Literary translation rearranged topically, by a specialist in ancient Chinese language and literature.

Lau, D. C., trans. *Mencius.* Harmondsworth: Penguin, 1970.

 A readable and reliable translation, with helpful appendices on several topics, including the life of Mencius, and a glossary of names and places.

Legge, James, trans. *The Works of Mencius,* in *The Chinese Classics,* vol. 2. 5 vols. Oxford: Clarendon Press, 1895; reprint with minor corrections, notes, and concordance tables, Hong Kong University Press, 1960. Also in *The Four Books.* Shanghai: Chinese Book Company, 1933. Pbk ed., New York: Dover, 1970.

 Still the standard scholarly translation.

Selections

Chan Wing-tsit, ed. *A Source Book in Chinese Philosophy*, chapter 3. Princeton University Press, 1963.

Giles, Lionel, trans. *The Book of Mencius*. Wisdom of the East series. London: John Murray, 1942; Reprint, Westport, CT: Greenwood, 1983.

An extensive selection in a readable translation by a noted Sinologue.

Legge, James, trans. Selections in Lin Yutang, ed., *The Wisdom of China and India*, pp. 747–84. New York: Random House, 1942; reprint, Modern Library edition, 1945. Also published in England in separate volumes as *The Wisdom of China* and *The Wisdom of India*. London: Michael Joseph, 1944.

SECONDARY READINGS

Creel, Herrlee G. *Chinese Thought*, pp. 68–93. University of Chicago Press, 1953.

Fung Yu-lan. *History of Chinese Philosophy*, 1:106–31. 2 vols. Princeton University Press, 1952–53.

Graham, A. C. "The Background of the Mencian Theory of Human Nature," in *Tsing Hua Journal of Chinese Studies* NS 6 (December 1967)1–2:215–71.

Hsiao Kung-ch'üan. *A History of Chinese Political Thought*. Vol. 1, chapter 3. Translated by F. W. Mote. Princeton University Press, 1979.

An analysis of the relation between Mencius and his successor, Hsün Tzu, on major topics.

Lau, D. C. "Theories of Human Nature in Mencius and Shyun-Tzy," in *Bulletin of the School of Oriental and African Studies* (University of London), 15 (1953):541–65.

Munro, Donald. *The Concept of Man in Early China*. Stanford University Press, 1969.

A stimulating and perceptive analysis of early Chinese thought.

Richards, I. A. *Mencius on the Mind: Experiments in Multiple Definition*. London: Routledge and Kegan Paul, 1932; New York: Harcourt, Brace, 1932.

Schwartz, Benjamin. *The World of Thought in Ancient China*, chapter 7. Cambridge: Harvard University Press, Belknap, 1985.

Shih, Vincent. "Metaphysical Tendencies in Mencius," in *Philosophy East and West*, 12 (January 1963)4:319–41.

Waley, Arthur. *Three Ways of Thought in Ancient China*, pp. 115–95. London: Allen and Unwin, 1939. New York: Macmillan, 1940. Pbk ed., New York: Doubleday, Anchor, 1956, pp. 83–147.

TOPICS FOR DISCUSSION

1. Mencius' juxtaposition of virtue and profit in government, and his valuation of the former over the latter. His idealism in an age of power politics and brutality.
2. The kingly way versus the way of the overlord or despot. Ethical cultivation and social action. Mencius' awareness of institutional problems; his utopian vision.
3. The relation between Mencius' view of humane government and the virtue of humaneness or humanity in personal life.
4. Mencius' definition of the problem of human nature; its implications for his political and economic philosophy.
5. The question of the acuity of Mencius' psychological insights.
6. Democratic and aristocratic tendencies in Mencius. Significance to him of "the people," of the person or individual as a participant in government.
7. Mencius as a defender and definer of Confucianism against the attacks of others.
8. The wide scope of Mencius' thought; his contributions to the development of Confucian thought.
9. The personality of Mencius as it appears in the text.

THE GREAT LEARNING (TA-HSÜEH)

A basic text of the early Confucian school, later canonized in the "Four Books."

TRANSLATIONS

Chan Wing-tsit, ed. *A Source Book in Chinese Philosophy*, pp. 85–94. Princeton University Press, 1963. Pbk ed.

A clear and accurate translation, reflecting the translator's thorough grounding in both the Confucian and Neo-Confucian traditions.

Legge, James, trans. "The Great Learning," in *The Chinese Classics*, Vol. 1. 2d ed., 5 vols. Oxford: Clarendon Press, 1893. Reprint with minor corrections, notes, and concordance tables, Hong Kong University Press, 1960. Also in *The Four Books*. Shanghai: Chinese Book Company, 1933.

A faithful translation of the text as edited by Chu Hsi.

Lin Yutang. "Ethics and Politics," in *The Wisdom of Confucius*. London: H. Hamilton, 1938; New York: Modern Library, 1938. New York: Peter Pauper, 1965.

An accurate and readable translation of the Chu Hsi text.

Pound, Ezra. *Confucius: The Great Digest & Unwobbling Pivot.* New York: New Directions, 1951; London, Owen, 1952. Reprint: *Confucius: The Great Digest, The Unwobbling Pivot, The Analects.* New York: New Directions, 1969. Pbk ed.

A stimulating interpretation rather than an actual translation.

SECONDARY READINGS

Fung Yu-lan. *History of Chinese Philosophy*, 1:361–69. 2 vols. Princeton University Press, 1952–53.

Gardner, Daniel K. *Chu Hsi and the Ta-hsüeh: Neo-Confucian*

Reflection on the Confucian Canon. Cambridge: Harvard University Press, 1985.

A study of the text of *The Great Learning*, its background, and its interpretation by the major twelfth-century philosopher Chu Hsi.

Hughes, Ernest R., ed. and trans. Introduction. *Chinese Philosophy in Classical Times*. London: Dent, 1942; New York: Dutton, 1942.

TOPICS FOR DISCUSSION

1. The *Great Learning* as a guide to self-examination and self-cultivation. The so-called Eight Steps.
2. The relation of the self and the world at large, according to the *Great Learning*.
3. The *Great Learning* as a political primer. Its idealism and optimism.
4. Why should the *Great Learning* have merited a place alongside the *Analects* and *Mencius* in the "Four Books" of Confucianism?

THE MEAN (CHUNG-YUNG)

A Confucian text of the late Chou period (ca. fourth century B.C.), traditionally attributed to Tzu Ssu, Confucius' grandson, and also one of the "Four Books."

TRANSLATIONS

Chan Wing-tsit, ed. *A Source Book in Chinese Philosophy*, pp. 97–114. Princeton University Press, 1963.

A clear and well-documented translation which places the *Mean* in the context of both classical Confucian and Neo-Confucian thought.

Hughes, Ernest R., trans. *The Great Learning and The Mean in Action.* London: Dent, 1942; New York: Dutton, 1943.

A careful translation of the older (pre-Chu Hsi) text, emphasizing its metaphysical aspects. There is an extensive introduction.

Ku Hung-ming, trans. "The Central Harmony," in Lin Yu-tang, *The Wisdom of Confucius.* London: H. Hamilton, 1938; New York: Modern Library, 1938. New York: Peter Pauper, 1965.

A favorite among Chinese readers of English, who consider that Ku captures well the spirit of the text as it has been known to and appreciated by Chinese in the later tradition.

Legge, James, trans. "The Doctrine of the Mean," in *The Chinese Classics,* vol. 1. 2d ed., 5 vols. Oxford: Clarendon Press, 1893. Reprint with minor corrections, notes, and concordance tables, Hong Kong University Press, 1960. Also in *The Four Books.* Shanghai: Chinese Book Company, 1933.

A standard version of the text as edited by Chu Hsi.

SECONDARY READINGS

Tu Wei-ming. *Centrality and Commonality: An Essay on Chung-yung.* Monograph no. 3 of the Society for Asian and Comparative Philosophy. Honolulu: University of Hawaii Press, 1976.
See also above under *The Great Learning.*

TOPICS FOR DISCUSSION

1. Multiple meanings of the term "Mean." Does it correspond to Aristotle's "Mean"?
2. The ethical and metaphysical significance of "sincerity" (*ch'eng*).
3. The evolution of Confucian thought from the *Analects* to the *Mean;* its relation to Taoism.

HSÜN TZU, OR HSÜN CH'ING

Writings of the third great formulator of Confucian teaching, in the third century B.C., who gave special attention to the basis of learning and rites.

TRANSLATIONS

Dubs, Homer H., trans. *The Works of Hsün Tze*. Probsthain's Oriental Series, vol 16. London: Probsthain, 1928; reprint, New York: AMS, n.d.

A scholarly translation of the greater part of the *Hsün Tzu* text, affording a good overall view of his philosophy. There are a number of errors of translation, however.

Duyvendak, J. J. L., trans. "Hsün-tzu on the Rectification of Names," in *T'oung Pao* 21 (1924):221–54.

A translation of chapter 22 of the *Hsün Tzu*.

Hughes, Ernest R. *Chinese Philosophy in Classical Times,* chapter 16. London: Dent, 1942; New York: Dutton, 1942; rev. ed., 1954.

Mei, Y. P., trans. "Hsün-tzu on Terminology." *Philosophy East and West* 1 (1951):51–66.

A translation of chapter 22 of the *Hsün Tzu*.

—— Selections from chapters 17, 19, 22, and 23 in Wm. Theodore de Bary et al., *Sources of Chinese Tradition*. New York: Columbia University Press, 1960. Pbk ed., 2 vols., 1964.

Watson, Burton, trans. *Basic Writings of Mo Tzu, Hsün Tzu, and Han Fei Tzu*. New York: Columbia University Press, 1967.

Contains a substantial selection from the Hsün Tzu translated in an accurate, readable manner for college and general use.

—— *Hsün Tzu: Basic Writings*. New York: Columbia University Press, 1963. Pbk ed.

Identical to the *Hsün Tzu* section of the above.

SECONDARY READINGS

Creel, Herrlee G. *Chinese Thought*, pp. 114–34. University of Chicago Press, 1953.

Cua, A. S. *Ethical Argumentation: A Study in Hsün Tzu's Moral Epistemology*. Honolulu: University of Hawaii Press, 1985.

Dubs, Homer H. *Hsüntze, the Moulder of Ancient Confucianism*. Probsthain's Oriental series, no. 15. London: Probsthain, 1927; Milwaukee: Caspar, Crueger, Dory, 1930.

Remains the fullest study of Hsün Tzu in a Western language.

Duyvendak, J. J. L. "The Chronology of Hsün Tzu," in *T'oung Pao* 26 (1929):73–95.

—— "Notes on Dubs' Translation of Hsün Tzu," in *T'oung Pao* 29 (1932):1–42.

Hsiao Kung-chuan. *A History of Chinese Political Thought*, chapter 3. Vol. 1. Translated by F. W. Mote. Princeton University Press, 1979.

An analysis of the differences between Mencius and Hsün Tzu on major topics.

Lau, D. C. "Theories of Human Nature in Mencius and Shyuntzy," in *Bulletin of the School of Oriental and African Studies* (University of London), 15 (1953):541–65.

Schwartz, Benjamin. *The World of Thought in Ancient China*, chapter 7. Cambridge: Harvard University Press, Belknap, 1985.

Shih, Vincent Y. C. "Hsüntzu's Positivism," in *Tsing Hua Journal* 4 (February 1964)2:162–73.

TOPICS FOR DISCUSSION

1. Hsün Tzu's defense of scholarship and the intellectual life as opposed to mysticism. His conception of the sage.
2. Hsün Tzu's view of Heaven and man's relation to it, in comparison to Mo Tzu and Lao Tzu.
3. Hsün Tzu's concept of "human nature." To what extent does his teaching as a whole reflect a view of human nature as evil; the issue between him and Mencius.
4. The importance of individual autonomy vis-à-vis discipline in the social order; the nature of learning and cultivation of individual desires.
5. Rites or decorum (*li*): varied functions and profound, even cosmic, significance for Hsün Tzu.
6. Hsün Tzu's political and social philosophy. To what extent is it authoritarian or liberal? To what extent does it derive from his view of human nature?
7. Hsün Tzu and how much he has learned from, or reacted against, Taoism.

HAN FEI TZU

The fullest theoretical statement and synthesis of the ancient Chinese school known as Legalism (fa-chia), *which exerted a major influence on the Chinese political tradition.*

TRANSLATIONS

Complete

Liao, W. K., trans. *The Complete Works of Han Fei Tzu.* 2 vols. London: Probsthain, 1939–59.

A complete translation of the text, though the attribution of much of it to the historical figure of Han Fei Tzu is doubtful. The rendering is smooth and generally accurate. Note should be taken, however, of the translator's procedure as explained in the methodological introduction to vol. 1.

Selections

Hughes, Ernest R., ed. and trans. *Chinese Philosophy in Classical Times,* pp. 254–68. London: Dent, 1942; New York: Dutton, 1942; rev. ed., 1954.

Mei, Y. P., trans. Selections from chapters 49 and 50 in Wm. Theodore de Bary et al., *Sources of Chinese Tradition.* New York: Columbia University Press, 1960. Pbk ed., 2 vols., 1964.

Watson, Burton, trans. *Basic Writings of Mo Tzu, Hsün Tzu, and Han Fei Tzu.* New York: Columbia University Press, 1967.

Contains an accurate, readable translation of sections 5–10, 12, 13, 17, 18, 49, and 50.

—— *Han Fei Tzu: Basic Writings.* New York: Columbia University Press, 1964. Pbk ed.

Identical to the section on Han Fei Tzu in the above.

SECONDARY READINGS

Creel, Herrlee G. *Chinese Thought*, pp. 135–38. University of Chicago Press, 1953.

—— "The Fa-chia: Legalists or Administrators?" in *Bulletin of the Institute of History and Philology* (Academica Sinica, Taipei, Taiwan), Extra volume no. IV (1961). Reprinted in *What Is Taoism? And Other Studies in Chinese Cultural History*, pp. 92–120. University of Chicago Press, 1970.

Duyvendak, J. J. L. *The Book of Lord Shang . . . a Classic of the Chinese School of Law*. Probsthain's Oriental series, no. 17. London: Probsthain, 1928.

Fung Yu-lan. *History of Chinese Philosophy*, 1:312–36. 2 vols. Princeton University Press, 1952–53.

Hsiao Kung-chuan. *A History of Chinese Political Thought*, vol. 1, chapter 7. Translated by F. W. Mote. Princeton University Press, 1979.

—— "Legalism and Autocracy in Traditional China," in *Tsing Hua Journal* 4 (February 1964)2:108–21.

Rubin, Vitaly A. *Individual and State in Ancient China: Essays on Four Chinese Philosophers*. Translated by Steven I. Levine. Columbia University Press, 1976.

Schwartz, Benjamin. *The World of Thought in Ancient China*, chapter 8. Cambridge: Harvard University Press, Belknap, 1985.

Waley, Arthur. *Three Ways of Thought in Ancient China*, pp. 199–255. London: Allen and Unwin, 1939. Pbk ed., New York: Doubleday, Anchor, 1956, pp. 151–96.

TOPICS FOR DISCUSSION

1. The essence and scope of law (*fa*) in Han Fei Tzu. Its relation to punishments and the definition of social functions.
2. Government by laws (legalism) versus government by men (Confucianism), as a basic dichotomy of traditional Chinese thought.

3. Can we assume that Han Fei Tzu, once a pupil of Hsün Tzu, holds the same view of human nature? How could they have arrived at such different conclusions politically?
4. Does Han Fei Tzu repudiate morality in government, or only Confucian morality?
5. The Legalist view of history and tradition; critique of Confucianism.
6. Effortless (*wu-wei*) government, quietism and activism in Legalist political thought. Science and art in Han Fei Tzu's conception of rulership.
7. The relation between Han Fei Tzu's Legalism and Taoism, totalitarianism and anarchism.

RECORDS OF THE HISTORIAN:
THE SHIH CHI OF SSU-MA CH'IEN
(*ca.* 145 – *ca.* 90 B.C.)

The masterpiece of Chinese histories, this monumental attempt to record the entire known past became a standard for future historians, and is notable for its combination of chronicles, tables, topical treatises, and biographies.

TRANSLATIONS

Extensive

Chavannes, Edouard, trans. *Les mémoires historiques de Se-ma Ts'ien*. 6 vols. Paris: E. Leroux, 1895–1905.

A translation of the first 47 chapters of the 130 which make up the book, with a lengthy introduction to the historian and his times.

Watson, Burton, trans. *Records of the Grand Historian of China. Translated from the "Shih Chi" of Ssu-ma Ch'ien*. 2 vols. New York: Columbia University Press, 1961. Pbk ed.

Excellent translations of 65 chapters, most of them complete, pertaining mainly to the early Han dynasty.

—— *Records of the Historian: Chapters from the "Shih Chi" of Ssu-ma Ch'ien*. Translations for the Oriental Classics. New York: Columbia University Press, 1970. Pbk ed.

Thirteen chapters from the preceding book plus five chapters relating to the times of the earlier Chou and Ch'in dynasties.

Selections

Birch, Cyril, ed. *Anthology of Chinese Literature,* 1:93–133. New York: Grove Press, 1965.

Contains an important letter by Ssu-man Ch'ien, translated by J. R. Hightower, and four biographies from the *Shih chi,* translated by Burton Watson.

Bodde, Derk, trans. *Statesman, Patriot, and General in Ancient China.* New Haven: American Oriental Society, 1940.

Three biographies of men of the Ch'in dynasty, taken from the work of Ssu-ma Ch'ien. Two of the three biographies are also translated by Watson in the works above.

Hervouet, Yves, trans. *Le chapitre 117 du Che-ki (biographie de Sseu-ma Siang-jou).* Paris: Presses Universitaires de France, 1972.

The biography of a famous poet and statesman. Also translated by Watson in the first of his works above.

Swann, Nancy Lee. *Food and Money in Ancient China.* Princeton University Press, 1950.

This study includes a translation of Ssu-ma Ch'ien's chapter on economic life. Also translated in Watson's works above.

SECONDARY READINGS

Kierman, Frank Algernon. *Ssu-ma Ch'ien's Historiographical Attitude as Reflected in Four Warring States Biographies.* Studies on Asia, Far Eastern and Russian Institute, University of Washington, Seattle. Weisbaden: Harrassowitz, 1962.

Watson, Burton. *Early Chinese Literature.* Companions to Asian Studies. New York: Columbia University Press, 1962; pbk ed., 1971.

Although the discussion of Ssu-ma Ch'ien's work in this book is not as full as that in the following entry, it is placed in the context of early Chinese historical writing generally and includes comments comparing Chinese historiography with that of ancient Greece and Rome.

—— *Ssu-ma Ch'ien, Grand Historian of China.* New York: Columbia University Press, 1958. Pbk ed.

TOPICS FOR DISCUSSION

1. Ssu-ma Ch'ien's view of the values of history: as a mirror of human successes and failures, as proof of the lasting power of goodness, as a tool of rhetoric, and as a basis of fame and immortality.
2. The power of human will and the power of Heaven or fate in the pattern of history.
3. Ssu-ma Ch'ien's style of biography: paradigmatic anecdotes and telling dialogues.
4. The qualities of great men: ambition and will, respect for learning and moral conduct, skill in leadership.
5. The rewards of power.
6. Ssu-ma Ch'ien's sympathy for human feelings.
7. The importance of the individual in Ssu-ma Ch'ien's conception of history.

TEXTS OF CHINESE BUDDHISM

The important texts of Chinese Buddhism are of two kinds. There are, first, those from India and other Buddhist lands, which were translated into Chinese and widely accepted as basic scriptures or treatises of the religion in China. Second, there are native Chinese writings, frequently commentaries on the original scriptures, which interpreted Buddhist thought in Chinese terms and in some cases became the basis of characteristically Chinese schools. The two together represent a vast body of literature still inadequately represented in translation. The Lotus *and* Vimalakīrtinirdésa Sūtras *are of the former type. Written originally in Sanskrit and expressive of fundamental Mahāyāna ideas, they were translated into Chinese and became especially important in the development of Buddhism in East Asia. The* Awakening of Faith in Mahāyāna, *though attributed to an Indian author, was probably written in China during the sixth century. The* Platform Sūtra of the Sixth Patriarch *and the* Record of Lin-chi *are authentically Chinese, and are products of the Ch'an (Zen) tradition. Though not without their special difficulties, these texts have been found satisfactory for use in general education.*

THE LOTUS SŪTRA
(SADDHARMA PUNDARĪKA SŪTRA, OR MIAO-FA LIEN-HUA CHING)

One of the most influential of all Mahāyāna texts throughout East Asia.

TRANSLATIONS

From the Sanskrit

Kern, H., trans. *The Saddhama-pundarīka; or, The Lotus of the True Law.* Sacred Books of the East, vol. 21. Oxford: Clarendon Press, 1884. Reprint, New York: Dover, 1963.

From the Chinese

Hurvitz, Leon, trans. *The Scripture of the Lotus Blossom of the Fine Dharma, translated from the Chinese of Kumārajīva.* New York: Columbia University Press, 1976. Pbk ed.

   The most reliable and accurate version; includes comparison with the Sanskrit text.

Katō Bunnō, Yoshirō Tamura, and Kōjirō Miyasaka, trans. *The Threefold Lotus Sutra.* New York: Weatherhill, 1975.

Murano Senchin, trans. *The Sutra of the Lotus Flower of the Wonderful Law.* Tokyo: Nichiren Shu Headquarters, 1974.

Soothill, W. E., trans. *The Lotus of the Wonderful Law; or, The Lotus Gospel.* Oxford: Clarendon Press, 1930.

   An abridged rendering into translation and paraphrase by a Sinologue known for his contributions to the study of Chinese thought.

SECONDARY READINGS

Chan Wing-tsit. "The Lotus Sūtra," in Wm. Theodore de Bary, ed., *Approaches to the Oriental Classics*, pp. 153–65. New York: Columbia University Press, 1959.

Davidson, J. Leroy. *The Lotus Sūtra in Chinese Art: A Study in Buddhist Art to the Year 1000*. New Haven: Yale University Press, 1954.

Hurvitz, Leon. *Chih-i (538–97): An Introduction to the Life and Ideas of a Chinese Buddhist Monk*. Mélanges chinois et bouddhiques, 12. Brussels: L'Institut Belge des Hautes Études Chinoises, 1962.

A thorough study of the use made of the Lotus Sūtra by the founder of the T'ien-t'ai tradition in China. The Lotus is the primary scripture of T'ien-t'ai.

TOPICS FOR DISCUSSION

1. The *Lotus*: cosmic religious drama or philosophical discourse? The dramatic scope and style of the work: supernatural setting expressed in concrete but extravagant images. Countless Buddha-worlds and endless world-ages give new dimensions of space and time to Buddhism.
2. The doctrine that one ultimate vehicle (*yāna*) replaces earlier and, necessarily, limited revelations of truth. The use of parables (e.g., the Burning House, the Lost Heir) to illustrate this new concept.
3. The teaching of "expedient means" or "devices" and its relation to the seldom-mentioned but central concept of emptiness. Can there be any real distinction of means and ends?
4. The eternality of the Buddha's teaching. The overshadowing of the historical Buddha, Shakyamuni, as teacher by the eternal Buddha. Buddhist docetism.
5. Buddhism in the *Lotus* as theistic or atheistic. The Bodhi-

sattvas (especially Avalokiteshvara) as saviors and helpers of humanity.

6. Salvation for all through devotion (to Buddhas and Bodhi-sattvas), simple acts of faith, worship of stupas, copying the text, etc. The tendency for Buddhahood to supersede *nirvāna* as the goal of enlightenment. Buddhahood as the realization of the sameness of all phenomena (*dharma*).

7. Spells, miracles, jeweled stupas, etc., embodied in art as stimuli to the religious imagination and practice.

8. Compare the use of parables in the *Lotus Sūtra* with biblical parables, such as similarities and differences between the stories of the Lost Heir and the Prodigal Son.

THE VIMALAKĪRTINIRDEŚA SŪTRA (WEI-MO-CHIEH SO-SHUO CHING)

An originally Indian scripture that struck a responsive chord in the minds of Chinese Buddhists and that has always been one of the most cherished texts in the Chinese Buddhist tradition. Coming from the mouth of the sagely, humane layman Vimalakīrti, alien notions such as "emptiness," "nonduality," and "inconceivable liberation" seemed more accessible to the Chinese.

TRANSLATIONS

Lamotte, Etienne, trans. *L'enseignement de Vimalakīrti*. Bibliotheque du Meséon, 51. Louvain: Publications Universitaires, 1962.

An excellent translation from the Chinese and Tibetan, but more concerned with reconstituting the original Sanskrit than with seeing the text through Chinese eyes.

Luk, Charles (Lu K'uan-yü), trans. *The Vimalakīrti Nirdeśa Sūtra*. Berkeley: Shambala Publications, 1972.

Thurman, Robert A. F. *The Holy Teaching of Vimalakīrti, a Mahāyāna Scripture*. University Park and London: Pennsylvania State University Press, 1976.

A first-rate translation from the Tibetan.

SECONDARY READINGS

Bunker, Emma C. "Early Chinese Representations of Vimalakīrti," in *Artibus Asiae* 30 (1968)1:28–52.

An interesting study of the artistic repercussions of Chinese fascination with Vimalakīrti.

Demiéville, Paul. "Vimalakīrti en Chine," appended to Lamotte translation (see above), pp. 438–55; also in Demiéville, *Choix d'études Buddhiques*, pp. 347–64. Leiden: Brill, 1973.

Mather, Richard B. "Vimalakīrti and Gentry Buddhism," in *History of Religions* 8 (1968)1:60–74.

An excellent treatment of the early years of Vimalakīrti's popularity in China.

See also the appropriate chapters in secondary readings listed in *Supplementary Readings on Chinese Buddhism*.

TOPICS FOR DISCUSSION

1. The significance of the Buddha's major disciples declaring themselves unworthy to go and inquire after the health of a layman. The object of Vimalakīrti's criticism of the disciples: their practice or attitude?
2. Vimalakīrti as a holy layman or as living embodiment of the sūtra's teachings regarding the importance of transcending dualities.
3. Word-play as a dramatic technique in the initial exchange between Vimalakīrti and Mañjusrā, and as a formal device that evokes nondualism.
4. The nature and importance of "expedient means" or "liberative technique" (*upāya*). The difference between Buddhist and Confucian views of what is practical.
5. The significance of Vimalakīrti's "thunderous silence." How does it compare to Taoist "namelessness" (*wu-ming*), "forgetting" or "doing nothing" (*wu-wei*)?
6. Buddhist "liberation" as compared to the freedoms sought by Confucianism and Taoism.

THE AWAKENING
OF FAITH IN MAHĀYĀNA
(TA-CH'ENG CH'I-HSIN LUN)

A brief but seminal treatise of uncertain provenance that came to have profound influence on many of the traditions of East Asian Buddhist thought.

TRANSLATIONS

Hakeda Yoshito, trans. *The Awakening of Faith in Mahāyāna, Attributed to Aśvaghosha.* New York: Columbia University Press, 1967. Pbk ed., 1974.

The best English translation, with a useful commentary by the translator based on traditional exegesis.

Suzuki, D. T., trans. *Açvaghosha's Discourse on the Awakening of Faith in the Mahāyāna.* Chicago: Open Court, 1900.

SECONDARY READINGS

Demiéville, Paul. "Sur l'authenticité du Ta Tch'eng K'i Sin louen," in *Bulletin de la Maison Franco-Japonaise* 2 (1929)2:1–78.

A learned treatment of the origins of the text.

Liebenthal, Walter. "New Light on the *Mahāyāna-Śraddhotpāda Śāstra,*" in *T'oung Pao* 46 (1959)3–5:155–216.

Suzuki, D. T. *Outlines of Mahayana Buddhism.* New York: Schocken, 1963.

A good general treatment of many of the key ideas of the *Awakening of Faith.*

TOPICS FOR DISCUSSION

1. What is the relationship between the One Mind and the two aspects?
2. How is the arising of ignorance explained?
3. Since the *dharmakāya* (the body of *dharma*; truth body) is one and the same everywhere, what is the need of the five practices (charity, precepts, patience, zeal, and cessation)?
4. The *Awakening of Faith* as a synthesis of the major trends of Mahāyāna thought.
5. The extremely concise, outline style of the text.

PLATFORM SŪTRA OF THE SIXTH PATRIARCH (LIU-TSU T'AN CHING)

An original Chinese work and early statement of Ch'an (Zen) thought, which assumed the status of both classic and scripture because of its unique claim to religious enlightenment.

TRANSLATIONS

Complete

Chan Wing-tsit, trans. *The Platform Scripture: The Basic Classic of Zen Buddhism.* Jamaica, NY: St. John's University Press, 1963.

Luk, Charles (Lu K'uan-yü), trans. "The Altar Sutra of the Sixth Patriarch," in *Ch'an and Zen Teaching,* series 3, pp. 15–102. London: Rider, 1962.

An accurate translation of the greatly enlarged Yüan version.

Yampolsky, Philip, trans. *The Platform Sutra of the Sixth Patriarch.* New York: Columbia University Press, 1967; pbk ed., 1978.

A precise and annotated translation of the earliest manuscripts, with a thorough historical and philological introduction.

Selections

Chan Wing-tsit, trans. Selections in Wm. Theodore de Bary et al., *Sources of Chinese Tradition.* New York: Columbia University Press, 1960. Pbk ed., 2 vols., 1964.

SECONDARY READINGS

Hu Shih. "Ch'an (Zen) Buddhism in China: Its History and Method," in *Philosophy East and West* 3 (April 1953):3–24.

Also in Sidney Ratner, ed., *Vision and Action: Essays in Honor of Horace M. Kallen on His 70th Birthday*, pp. 223–50. New Brunswick: Rutgers University Press, 1953.

An influential interpretation of the early history of Ch'an in China.

TOPICS FOR DISCUSSION

1. The "myth" of Hui-neng; what does it say about the nature of enlightenment and Buddhahood?
2. Sudden and gradual methods of enlightenment. Do they imply different views of the nature of man; of Buddhahood?
3. Ch'an and the Sixth Patriarch as representative of a new "this-worldly," "Chinese" Buddhism. Does Ch'an still seek to reach the "Other Shore?"
4. The concept of no-thought and the identity of *prajñā* (wisdom) and *dhyāna* (meditation).
5. The problem of religious authority and authentic transmission. Does Ch'an carry on or break with Buddhist tradition? What are the criteria of authentic transmission? What is the status of either teacher or text in the transmission?
6. Is there a Ch'an ethic? Isn't the competition to "succeed" a rather sordid business?
7. The early history of Ch'an in China: historical fact and mythology as seen in the *Platform Sutra*.

THE RECORD OF LIN-CHI (*d.* 866)

The recorded sayings of the late T'ang Buddhist master, Lin-chi Hui-chao, founder of the Lin-chi (Rinzai) school of Ch'an, which spread throughout East Asia. It contains many stories used later as subjects of meditation.

TRANSLATIONS

Demiéville, Paul, trans. *Entretiens de Lin-Tsi*. Documents Spirituels, 6. Paris: Fayard, 1972. Pbk ed.

An authoritative version by the great French Sinologist and Buddologist.

Sasaki, Ruth Fuller, trans. *The Recorded Sayings of Ch'an Master Lin-chi Hui-chao of Chen Prefecture*. Kyoto: Institute for Zen Studies, Hanazono College, 1975.

The best available translation in English.

SECONDARY READINGS

Chang Chung-yuan, trans. *Original Teachings of Ch'an Buddhism: Selected from The Transmission of the Lamp*. New York: Pantheon, 1969. Pbk ed., New York: Vintage Books, 1971.

An anthology of texts from the Ch'an tradition, though not the "original" teachings.

Sasaki, Ruth Fuller et al., trans. *The Recorded Sayings of Layman P'ang: A Ninth-Century Zen Classic*. New York: Weatherhill, 1971.

Yanagida Seizan. "The Life of Lin-chi I-hsüan." Translated by Ruth Fuller Sasaki, in *Eastern Buddhist,* n.s. 5 (October 1972)2:70–94.

TOPICS FOR DISCUSSION

1. Lin-chi's spiritual quest before turning to Ch'an.
2. The major emphases of Lin-chi's teachings: the Buddha-nature within, no reliance on externals.
3. Is there a rationale behind Lin-chi's often bizarre behavior: the sharp language, shouts and slaps?
4. The role of the Ch'an master.
5. Life after enlightenment.

SUPPLEMENTARY READINGS ON CHINESE BUDDHISM

Readers may wish to consult other texts, surveys, and histories of Chinese Buddhism. Among these the following should prove useful.

Chang Ch'eng-chi. *The Buddhist Teaching of Totality: The Philosophy of Hua-yen Buddhism.* University Park: Pennsylvania State University Press, 1971.

    The first survey in English of the intricate field of Hua-yen.

Chappell, David, ed. *T'ien-t'ai Buddhism: An Outline of the Fourfold Teaching.* Tokyo: Daiichi Shobō, 1983. Distributed by the University of Hawaii Press.

    A translation of the influential guide to T'ien-t'ai teachings, compiled by the tenth-century Korean Buddhist master, Chegwan.

Ch'en, Kenneth K. S. *Buddhism in China: A Historical Survey.* Princeton University Press, 1963. Pbk ed., 1972.

    The only survey of the entire history of Chinese Buddhism, including a good bibliography.

—— *The Chinese Transformation of Buddhism.* Princeton University Press, 1973.

Cleary, Thomas, trans. *Flower Ornament Scripture: A Translation of the Avatamsaka Sutra.* Vol. 1. Boulder, CO: Shambala Publications, 1984.

Cook, Francis. *Hua-yen Buddhism: The Jewel Net of Indra.* University Park and London: Pennsylvania State University Press, 1977.

    Examines the philosophy of Hua-yen as systematized by the third patriarch of the school, Fa-tsang.

de Bary, Wm. Theodore et al. *The Buddhist Tradition in India,*

China, and Japan. New York: Modern Library, 1969. Pbk ed., New York: Random House, Viking, 1972.

Contains a number of important selections from Chinese Buddhist literature.

Gimello, Robert M. and Peter Gregory, eds. *Studies in Ch'an and Hua-yen.* Honolulu: University of Hawaii Press, 1983.

Essays by five specialists on the Ch'an and Hua-yen traditions, emphasizing both religion and its social contexts.

Hsu, Sung-peng. *A Buddhist Leader in Ming China: The Life and Thought of Han-shan Te-ch'ing, 1546–1623.* University Park and London: Pennsylvania State University Press, 1979.

Treats a major Buddhist figure of the Ming dynasty.

Lancaster, Lewis R. and Whalen Lai, eds. *Early Ch'an in China and Tibet.* Berkeley, CA: Asian Humanities Press, 1983.

Paul, Diana Y. *Philosophy of Mind in Sixth-Century China: Paramārtha's "Evolution of Consciousness."* Stanford University Press, 1984.

Robinson, Richard H. *Early Mādyamika in India and China.* Madison: University of Wisconsin Press, 1967.

Robinson, Richard H. and W. Johnson. *The Buddhist Religion.* The Religious Life of Man Series. 1st ed., Belmont, CA: Dickensen, 1970; 2d ed., Encino, CA: Dickensen, 1977. 3d ed., Belmont, CA: Wadsworth, 1982.

Takakusu Junjirō. *The Essentials of Buddhist Philosophy.* 3d ed. Honolulu: University of Hawaii Press, 1956.

A survey of the development of the scholastic traditions of East Asian Buddhism.

Thompson, Lawrence. *Chinese Religion: An Introduction.* 2d ed., Encino, CA: Dickensen, 1975. 3d ed., Belmont, CA: Wadsworth, 1979.

Wright, Arthur F. *Buddhism in Chinese History.* Stanford University Press, 1959. Pbk ed., 1970.

Yü, Chün-fang. *The Renewal of Buddhism in China: Chu-hung*

and the Late Ming Synthesis. New York: Columbia University Press, 1981.

Examines the life, work, and teachings of an important Ming dynasty Buddhist leader.

Zürcher, Eric. *The Buddhist Conquest of China*. 2d ed., 2 vols. Leiden: Brill, 1972.

The standard work on the early history of Buddhism in China, including several translations.

WORKS OF CHU HSI (1130–1200)

Leading exponent and synthesizer of Neo-Confucianism in the twelfth century, which became orthodox state teaching in later centuries and spread throughout East Asia.

TRANSLATIONS

Complete

Chan Wing-tsit, trans. *Reflections on Things at Hand: The Neo-Confucian Anthology Compiled by Chu Hsi and Lü Tsu-ch'ien.* New York: Columbia University Press, 1967. Pbk ed., 1984.

    An accurate, complete translation of the *Chin-ssu lu* with an exhaustive scholarly apparatus.

Graf, Olaf, trans. *Djin-Si lu.* 3 vols. Tokyo: Sophia University Press, 1953.

    A massive work, providing a German translation of Chu Hsi's classic anthology of four Neo-Confucian masters *(Chin-ssu lu).* It is extensively annotated and includes a substantial introduction.

Selections

Chan Wing-tsit, trans. Selections, in *A Source Book in Chinese Philosophy*, pp. 593–653. Princeton University Press, 1963.

—— Selections, in Wm. Theodore de Bary et al., *Sources of Chinese Tradition.* New York: Columbia University Press, 1960; pbk ed., 2 vols., 1964.

SECONDARY READINGS

Abe Yoshio. "Development of Neo-Confucianism in Japan, Korea, and China: A Comparative Study," in *Acta Asiatica* 17–19 (1969–70):16–39.

Chang, Carsun. *The Development of Neo-Confucian Thought*. New York: Bookman Associates, vol. 1, 1957, pp. 243–331.

Chan Wing-tsit, ed. *Chu Hsi and Neo-Confucianism*. Honolulu: University of Hawaii Press, 1986.

Essays by leading scholars on major topics in Chu Hsi's thought.

de Bary, Wm. Theodore. *The Liberal Tradition in China*, chapters 2 and 3. New York: Columbia University Press, 1983.

—— *The Message of the Mind in Neo-Confucianism*. New York: Columbia University Press, 1988.

—— *Neo-Confucian Orthodoxy and the Learning of the Mind-and-Heart*. New York: Columbia University Press, 1981.

An account of the development of Chu Hsi's philosophy from the thirteenth century onward in China and its adoption in seventeenth-century Japan.

—— "A Reappraisal of Neo-Confucianism," in Arthur F. Wright, ed., *Studies in Chinese Thought*, pp. 81–111. Comparative Studies of Cultures and Civilizations. University of Chicago Press, 1953.

—— "Some Common Tendencies in Neo-Confucianism," in Davis S. Nivison and Arthur F. Wright, eds., *Confucianism in Action*, pp. 25–49. Stanford Studies in the Civilizations of Eastern Asia. Stanford University Press, 1959.

Fung Yu-lan. *History of Chinese Philosophy*, 2:533–71. 2 vols. Princeton University Press, 1952–53.

Gardner, Daniel K. *Chu Hsi and the Ta-hsüeh: Neo-Confucian Reflection on the Confucian Canon*. Cambridge: Harvard University Press, 1985.

Graham, A. C. *Two Chinese Philosophers: Ch'eng Ming-tao and Ch'eng Yi-ch'uan*. London: Lund Humphries, 1958.

An excellent study of Chu Hsi's predecessors.

Hughes, Ernest R. *The Great Learning and The Mean-in-Action*, pp. 167–71. London: Dent, 1942; New York: Dutton, 1943.

Shirokauer, Conrad. "Chu Hsi's Political Career: A Study in

Ambivalence," in Arthur F. Wright and D. Twitchett, eds., *Confucian Personalities*. Stanford University Press, 1962.

Tomoeda Ryūtarō. "The Characteristics of Chu Hsi's Thought," in *Acta Asiatica* 20–21 (1971):52–72.

TOPICS FOR DISCUSSION

1. The ideal of sagehood as compared to the ideal of the bodhisattva; as a human ideal.
2. The *Reflections on Things at Hand* as a manual of sagehood and its practice.
3. Neo-Confucianism as a philosophy of human nature; as "learning for the sake of one's self."
4. Humanity (*jen*) as both a cosmic and an ethical force.
5. The Neo-Confucian reaffirmation of the goodness of human nature vis-à-vis Buddhist skepticism concerning any substantial nature or self. Chu Hsi's handling of the problem through such concepts as the original or essential nature and the physical nature; the moral mind and the human mind.
6. Political implications of Chu Hsi's philosophy: self-cultivation as the key to government.
7. Basic concepts in Neo-Confucian metaphysics: the Supreme Ultimate (*t'ai-chi*); Principle (*li*), and ether or material force (*ch'i*). The significance of these in relation to Taoism and Buddhism.

WORKS OF WANG YANG-MING
(1472–1529)

The principal Neo-Confucian philosopher of the fifteenth-sixteenth centuries, his philosophy of the mind drew on that of Chu Hsi, yet also provided the principal alternative to Chu Hsi's intellectualism in later Chinese thought, in regard to the role of moral intuition versus cognitive learning.

TRANSLATIONS

Complete

Chan Wing-tsit, trans. *Instructions for Practical Living and Other Neo-Confucian Writings by Wang Yang-ming.* New York: Columbia University Press, 1963. Pbk ed., 1984.

Includes complete translations of "Instructions for Practical Living," "Inquiry on the *Great Learning,*" etc., by a leading contemporary scholar of Neo-Confucianism.

Henke, Frederick Goodrich, trans. *The Philosophy of Wang Yang-ming.* Introduction by James H. Tufts. Chicago: Open Court, 1916. 2d ed., New York: Paragon, 1964; Gordon Press, 1976.

A pioneer study of Wang's basic works, now superseded.

Selections

Chan Wing-tsit, trans. Selections, in Wm. Theodore de Bary et al., *Sources of Chinese Tradition.* New York: Columbia University Press, 1960. Pbk ed., 2 vols, 1964.

Ching, Julia Chia-yi, trans. *The Philosophical Letters of Wang Yang-ming.* Canberra: Australia National University Press, 1972; Columbia: University of South Carolina Press, 1973.

—— "Wang Yang-ming in Translations: Some Selected Letters," in *Chinese Culture* 11 (June 1970)2:62–68.

SECONDARY READINGS

Cady, Lyman V. *Wang Yang-ming's "Intuitive Knowledge."* Peiping, 1936.

Chang, Carsun. *The Development of Neo-Confucian Thought,* 2:30–97. 2 vols. New York: Bookman, 1963.

—— *Wang Yang-ming: Idealist Philosopher of Sixteenth Century China.* Jamaica, NY: St. John's University Press, 1962.

—— "Wang Yang-ming's Philosophy," in *Philosophy East and West* 5 (1955)1:3–18.

Ching, Julia. *To Acquire Wisdom: The Way of Wang Yang-ming.* New York: Columbia University Press, 1976.

Cua, A. S. *The Unity of Knowledge and Action: A Study in Wang Yang-ming's Moral Psychology.* Honolulu: University of Hawaii Press, 1982.

Attempts to compare Wang's assumptions and ideas with some of those of modern Western philosophy.

de Bary, Wm. Theodore, ed. *Self and Society in Ming Thought.* New York: Columbia University Press, 1970.

See de Bary's essay "Individualism and Humanitarianism in Late Ming Thought" and T'ang Chün-i's "The Development of the Concept of Moral Mind from Wang Yang-ming to Wang Chi."

—— *The Unfolding of Neo-Confucianism.* New York: Columbia University Press, 1975.

Fung Yu-lan. *History of Chinese Philosophy,* 2:596–620. 2 vols. Princeton University Press, 1952–53.

Nivison, David S. "The Problem of 'Knowledge' and 'Action' in Chinese Thought since Wang Yang-ming," in Arthur F. Wright, ed., *Studies in Chinese Thought,* pp. 112–45. University of Chicago Press, 1953.

T'ang Chün-i. "The Development of Ideas of Spiritual Value in Chinese Philosophy," in Charles A. Moore, ed., *The Chinese Mind,* pp. 188–212. Honolulu: East-West Center Press, 1967.

Tu Wei-ming, *Neo-Confucian Thought in Action: Wang Yang-*

ming's Youth (1472–1509). Berkeley: University of California Press, 1976.

TOPICS FOR DISCUSSION

1. Wang Yang-ming and the ideal of sagehood. Sagehood and human nature; the identity of mind and principle.
2. Wang's experience in trying to practice Chu Hsi's "investigation of things"; his belief that he was only carrying Chu's teachings to their logical conclusion.
3. Innate knowledge (*liang-chih*) and the goodness of human nature; "Humaneness as forming one body with Heaven, Earth, and all things."
4. Wang's philosophy and the tension between knowledge and action in Confucian self-cultivation; his doctrine of the unity of knowledge and action. Comparison to Hui-neng's identity of wisdom and meditation.
5. Wang's teaching as quietistic or activistic. Wang's own life and character as reflected in his teachings.
6. Is Wang Yang-ming Buddhistic? His criticisms of Buddhism.
7. Wang Yang-ming as a reformer; as a traditionalist; his social views.
8. Wang's attitude toward learning, scholarship, culture. Is Wang anti-intellectual?

GENERAL READINGS IN CHINESE FICTION

The following studies provide background information and contain as well sections applicable to each of the topics in the following sections on Chinese fiction.

Bishop, John L. *The Colloquial Short Story in China: A Study of the San-Yen Collections.* Harvard-Yenching Institute Studies, vol. 14. Cambridge: Harvard University Press, 1956. Pbk ed.

—— "Some Limitations of Chinese Fiction," in John L. Bishop, ed., *Studies in Chinese Literature,* pp. 237–45. Cambridge: Harvard University Press, 1965. Pbk ed.

Hanan, Patrick. *The Chinese Short Story: Studies in Dating, Authorship, and Composition.* Cambridge: Harvard University Press, 1973.

   An important contribution to scholarship, but too technical for the beginner.

—— *The Chinese Vernacular Story.* Cambridge: Harvard University Press, 1981.

—— "The Early Chinese Short Story: A Critical Theory in Outline," in *Harvard Journal of Asiatic Studies* 27 (1967):168–207.

   Presents a theory that is of great value for our understanding of the genre as a whole.

Hegel, Robert. *The Novel in Seventeenth Century China.* New York: Columbia University Press, 1981.

   A study of six novels in their historical and critical contexts.

Hsia, C. T. *The Classic Chinese Novel: A Critical Introduction.* New York: Columbia University Press, 1968; pbk ed., 1972. Pbk ed., Bloomington: Indiana University Press, 1981.

Idema, W. L. *Chinese Vernacular Fiction: The Formative Period.* Leiden: Brill, 1974.

Li Tien-yi, ed. *Chinese Fiction: A Bibliography of Books and Articles in Chinese and English*. New Haven: Yale University Press, 1968.

Lu Hsün (Chou Shu-jen). *A Brief History of Chinese Fiction*. Translated by Yang Hsien-yi and Gladys Yang. Peking: Foreign Languages Press, 1959.

A standard reference.

Ma, Y. W. and Joseph S. M. Lau, eds. *Traditional Chinese Stories: Themes and Variations*. New York: Columbia University Press, 1978. Pbk ed.

Includes translations by various scholars of a number of short stories.

Mair, Victor. "The Narrative Revolution in Chinese Literature: Ontological Presuppositions," in *Chinese Literature: Essays, Articles, Reviews (CLEAR)* 5 (July 1983)1 and 2:1–28.

Controversial article that appears in a symposium on "The Origin of Chinese Fiction," along with responses from Kenneth J. Dewoskin, "On Narrative Revolutions," pp. 29–45, and W. L. Idema, "The Illusion of Fiction," pp. 47–51.

Plaks, Andrew, ed. *Chinese Narrative: Critical and Theoretical Essays*. Princeton University Press, 1977.

Essays covering the *Tso chuan* through Ch'ing novels.

Průšek, Jaroslav. *Chinese History and Literature: Collection of Studies*. Dordrecht, Holland: Reidel, 1970.

Contains many valuable studies of traditional fiction. The colloquial short story is examined in depth in relation to the oral storytelling tradition.

Yang, Winston L. Y., Peter Li, and Nathan K. Mao. *Classical Chinese Fiction: A Guide to Its Study and Appreciation, Essays and Bibliographies*. Boston: G. K. Hall, 1978; London: George Prior, 1978.

THE WATER MARGIN, OR, ALL MEN ARE BROTHERS (SHUI-HU CHUAN)

A classic of Chinese popular fiction, narrating the adventures of a band of outlaws in the Sung dynasty.

TRANSLATIONS

Birch, Cyril, trans. "The Plot Against the Birthday Convoy (*Shui hu chuan*, 14–16)," in Cyril Birch, ed., *Anthology of Chinese Literature,* 1:451–87. New York: Grove, 1965. Pbk ed.

Buck, Pearl S., trans. *All Men Are Brothers.* 2 vols. New York: John Day, 1933. New York: Grove, 1957; London: Methuen, 1957. 1 vol. ed., New York: Reynal and Hitchcock, 1937, and several other reprint editions.

A complete translation of the 70–chapter version, done in a style that does not suggest the colloquial of the original.

Jackson, J. H., trans. *Water Margin.* 2 vols. Shanghai: Commercial Press, 1937. Reprint, New York: Paragon, 1968. Pbk ed., Cheng and Tsui, n.d.

A somewhat abridged translation in language which misses the spirit of the original.

Shapiro, Sidney, trans. *Outlaws of the Marsh.* 2 vols. Bloomington: Indiana University Press, 1981; Peking: Foreign Language Press, 1981.

A complete translation of *Shui-hu chuan,* done in a simple and idiomatic style that is far closer to the original than Buck's stilted over-literalness.

SECONDARY READINGS

Alber, Charles. "A Survey of English Language Criticism of the *Shui-hu chuan*," in *Tsing Hua Journal of Chinese Studies* 7 (1969)2:102–18.

Demiéville, Paul. "Au bord de l'eau," in *T'oung Pao* 46 (1956):242–65.

   A review of Richard G. Irwin's book, listed below.

Hsia, C. T. Chapter 3, "The Water Margin," in *The Classic Chinese Novel: A Critical Introduction*. New York: Columbia University Press, 1968; pbk ed., 1972. Bloomington: Indiana University Press, 1981.

Irwin, Richard G. *The Evolution of a Chinese Novel: Shui-hu-chuan*. Harvard-Yenching Institute Studies, vol. 10. Cambridge: Harvard University Press, 1953.

—— "Water Margin Revisited," in *T'oung Pao* 48 (1960):393–415.

   Modifies the author's earlier conclusions in regard to the filiation of the *Shui-hu chuan* texts.

Li Hsi-fan. "A Great Novel of Peasant Revolt," in *Chinese Literature* (December 1959)12:62–71.

   An orthodox Marxist appraisal.

Liu, James J. Y. *The Chinese Knight-Errant*. London: Routledge and Kegan Paul, 1967; University of Chicago Press, 1967.

   Discusses, among other works of fiction and drama glorifying the knight-errant, the *Shui-hu chuan,* and plays drawing upon the Liangshan legend.

Lu Hsün (Chou Shu-jen). Chapter 15, "All Men are Brothers," in *A Brief History of Chinese Fiction*. Translated by Yang Hsien-yi and Gladys Yang. Peking: Foreign Languages Press, 1959.

Plaks, Andrew. "*Shui-hu Chuan* and the Sixteenth Century Novel Form: An Interpretive Reappraisal," in *Chinese Literature: Essays, Articles, Reviews (CLEAR)* 2 (January 1980)1:3–53.

Ruhlmann, Robert. "Traditional Heroes in Chinese Popular

Fiction," in Arthur F. Wright, ed., *The Confucian Persuasion*, pp. 141–76. Stanford University Press, 1960.

TOPICS FOR DISCUSSION

1. The composition of the book as episodes of adventure; the inventiveness of the "storyteller."
2. The historical and literary evolution of the basic story.
3. Characteristics of the novel reflecting its popular origins. Common literary devices.
4. Structure and unity in the novel. Is there any unifying theme or outlook on life? Is there anything characteristically Chinese about the world these figures move in?
5. The *Shui-hu chuan* as a panorama of human types. Effectiveness and depth of characterization.
6. What is the significance of the supernatural framework in which the novel is set? The *Shui-hu chuan* as a secular novel.
7. The *Shui-hu chuan* as social protest or revolutionary literature. What are the basic social or political values embodied here?
8. The code of behavior implicitly followed by the heroes of the Liangshan band. Their attitudes toward food, drink, and sex. Instances of savagery and sadism. Punishment of licentious women.
9. Vengeance as a motive. The band's collective adventures: do they indicate lust for aggression or a desire to carry out the will of Heaven? Is the band as corrupt and unjust in its own way as the hated officialdom?

JOURNEY TO THE WEST, OR MONKEY (HSI YU CHI), BY WU CH'ENG-EN (*ca.* 1506–1581)

A highly imaginative fictional account of the epic pilgrimage to India of the Buddhist monk Hsüan-tsang, by the sixteenth-century novelist Wu Ch'eng-en.

TRANSLATIONS

Complete

Yü, Anthony C., trans. *Journey to the West*. 4 vols. University of Chicago Press, 1977–84. Pbk ed.

A highly literate and graceful as well as complete and accurate translation. Its length may make it unsuitable for general education purposes, but samples may be used with great profit.

Selections

Hsia, C. T. and Cyril Birch, trans. "The Temptation of Saint Pigsy *(Hsi yu chi,* 23)," in Cyril Birch, ed., *Anthology of Chinese Literature,* 2:67–85. New York: Grove, 1972. Pbk ed.

An episode of comic allegory.

Hsien-yi Yang and Gladys Yang, trans. "Pilgrimage to the West: Chapter 27," in *Chinese Literature* (1966)5:100–117.

An important chapter translated in its entirety.

Waley, Arthur, trans. *Monkey*. New York: John Day, 1944. Pbk eds., New York: Grove, Evergreen, 1958. Harmondsworth: Penguin, 1961.

Though much abridged (omits the poetry in the original) and containing occasional minor errors, a delightful translation.

SECONDARY READINGS

Ch'en Shou-yi. *Chinese Literature; A Historical Introduction*, pp. 483–87. New York: Ronald Press, 1961.

Dudbridge, Glen. *The Hsi-yu Chi: A Study of Antecedents to the Sixteenth-Century Novel*. Cambridge University Press, 1970.
    Traces the sources and early versions of the novel, with particular reference to the oral tradition.

—— "The Hundred-Chapter *Hsi-yu Chi* and Its Early Versions," in *Asia Major* 14 (1969)2:141–91.

Feuerwerker, Yi-tse Mei. "The Chinese Novel," in Wm. Theodore de Bary, ed., *Approaches to the Oriental Classics*, pp. 177–79. New York: Columbia University Press, 1959.

Hsia, C. T. Chapter 4, "Journey to the West," in *The Classic Chinese Novel: A Critical Introduction*. New York: Columbia University Press, 1968. Pbk ed., 1972; Bloomington: Indiana University Press, 1981.

Hsia, C. T. and T. A. Hsia. "New Perspectives on Two Ming Novels: *Hsi Yu Chi* and *Hsi Yu Pu*," in Chow Tse-tsung, ed., *Wen-lin: Studies in the Chinese Humanities*, pp. 229–45. Madison: University of Wisconsin Press, 1968.

Liu Ts'un-yan. "The Prototypes of *Monkey (Hsi Yu Chi)*," in *T'oung Pao* 51 (1964)1:55–71.
    A scholarly article linking Wu Ch'eng-en's novel to its more primitive versions.

—— "Wu Ch'eng-en: His Life and Career," in *T'oung Pao* 53 (1967)1:1–97.
    An impeccably researched biography of the putative author of the *Hsi yu chi*.

Lu Hsün (Chou Shu-jen). *A Brief History of Chinese Fiction*, chapters 16 and 17. Translated by Yang Hsien-yi and Gladys Yang. Peking: Foreign Languages Press, 1959.

Ou Itaï. "Chinese Mythology," in *Larousse Encyclopedia of Mythology*. New York: Prometheus Press, 1959; London: Batchworth Press, 1959.

Useful information about the Chinese pantheon, which figures importantly in this novel.

Waley, Arthur. *The Real Tripitaka, and Other Pieces*. New York: Macmillan, 1952; London: Allen and Unwin, 1952.

The title essay, a biography of Hsüan-tsang, provides an illuminating historical perspective to his legendary counterpart in the novel.

Yü, Anthony C. "Heroic Verse and Heroic Mission: Dimensions of the Epic in the *Hsi-yu Chi*," in *Journal of Asian Studies* 31 (August 1972)4:879–97.

—— "Narrative Structure and the Problems of Chapter Nine in the *Hsi-Yu Chi*," in *Journal of Asian Studies* 34 (February 1975)2:295–311.

TOPICS FOR DISCUSSION

1. The vernacular novel: its social origins and relations to the classical tradition.
2. The author's role in bridging the great (elite) and little (popular) traditions. Does any class affiliation of his, or status as an artist or intellectual, have any bearing on our understanding of the work?
3. The form of the work. Its episodic character and unifying themes.
4. The legend of Hsüan-tsang. Its historical and popular significance.
5. The *Journey* as allegory, satire, or farce; as a quest for spiritual fulfillment.
6. The major characters as complementary allegorical figures. Do they represent different aspects of human nature or different philosophical positions (Confucian, Taoist, Buddhist)?
7. The *Journey* as a expression of the "unity of the Three Religions." Attitudes toward early religions, their adherents, and their institutions. What is being satirized: religion

in general, particular religions, human institutions or foibles? Religious syncretism in Chinese life and literature.

8. What light does this novel shed on the characterization of the Chinese as "this-worldly?"

9. Satire of social organizations and practices. Is this social protest?

10. Compare the Monkey King with Abu Zayd in the *Assemblies of al-Ḥarīrī* as heroic or comic figures.

11. The Chinese mode of imagination compared with the Western, as seen in similar fantastic episodes in *The Odyssey, Don Quixote, The Faerie Queene, Paradise Lost,* and *Faust.*

12. The novel seen in the light of anthropology. Cannibalism: Hsüan-tsang coveted as food. The sick or impotent king and the blighted land. Fertility rites. Primitive religious motifs in Chinese folklore.

THE GOLDEN LOTUS
(CHIN P'ING MEI)

The first Chinese novel to depict urban domestic life in naturalistic terms, by an unidentified sixteenth-century author.

TRANSLATIONS

Egerton, Clement, trans. *The Golden Lotus.* 4 vols. London: Routledge, 1939. New York: Paragon, 1962. Rev. ed., London: Routledge and Kegan Paul, 1972.

This translation, a labor of love, preserves the prose text in its entirety. Done with the "untiring and generously given help" of C. C. Shu (Lau Shaw). The revised edition is the first complete, unexpurgated edition.

Kuhn, Franz, trans. *Kin Ping Meh, oder, Die Abenteuerliche Geschichte von Hsi Men und seinen sechs Frauen.* Leipzig: Insel-Verlag, 1930. Wiesbaden: Insel-Verlag, 1955, 1970.

An admirable abridgement that retains intact the power and the main incidents of the novel.

Miall, Bernard, trans. *Chin P'ing Mei: The Adventurous History of Hsi Men and His Six Wives.* London: John Lane, 1939; New York: Putnam, 1940. Reprint, Capricorn Books, 1962; New York: Putnam, 1982.

A translation of the Kuhn version. Recommended for the general reader. Mistranslations, inherited from the German text, are minor and inconsequential.

SECONDARY READINGS

Bishop, John L. "A Colloquial Short Story in the Novel *Chin P'ing Mei,*" in John L. Bishop, ed., *Studies in Chinese Literature*, pp. 226–34. Cambridge: Harvard University Press, 1965.

Carlitz, Katherine. "Allusion to Drama in the *Chin P'ing Mei*," in *Ming Studies* (Spring 1978)6:30–35.

—— "The Conclusion of the *Jin Ping Mei*," in *Ming Studies* (Spring 1980)10:23–29.

—— *The Rhetoric of Ch'in Ping Mei*. Studies in Chinese Literature and Society. Bloomington: Indiana University Press, 1986.

Cass, Victoria. "Revels of a Gaudy Night," in *Chinese Literature: Essays, Articles, Reviews (CLEAR)* 4 (1982)2:213–231.

Feuerwerker, Yi-tse Mei. "The Chinese Novel," in Wm. Theodore de Bary, ed., *Approaches to the Oriental Classics*, pp. 179–81. New York: Columbia University Press, 1959.

Hanan, P. D. "A Landmark of the Chinese Novel," in Douglas Grant and Millar MacLure, eds., *The Far East: China and Japan*, pp. 325–35. University of Toronto Press, 1961.

A perceptive critique of the *Chin P'ing Mei*.

—— "Sources of the Chin P'ing Mei," in *Asia Major* (n.s.) 10 (July 1963)1:23–67.

A thorough study of the sources.

—— "The Text of the Chin P'ing Mei," in *Asia Major* (n.s.) 9 (April 1961)1:1–57.

A detailed examination of the extant early editions and of a few spurious chapters in these editions. Of general interest to the student who wants to know something of the intellectual excitement the novel created when its manuscripts were being circulated.

Hsia, C. T. Chapter 5, "Chin P'ing Mei," in *The Classic Chinese Novel: A Critical Introduction*. New York: Columbia University Press, 1968. Pbk ed., 1972. Bloomington: Indiana University Press, 1981. Pbk ed.

Lu Hsün (Chou Shu-jen). *A Brief History of Chinese Fiction*, chapter 19. Translated by Yang Hsien-yi and Gladys Yang. Peking: Foreign Languages Press, 1959.

Martinson, Paul V. "The *Chin P'ing Mei* as Wisdom Literature: A Methodological Essay," in *Ming Studies* (Fall 1977)5:44–56.

TOPICS FOR DISCUSSION

1. The novel's single authorship and its lesser dependence on the repertoire of professional storytellers. Compare the story of P'an Chin-lien's seduction as found in this novel and in *Shui-hu chuan*. The novelist's use of episodes drawn from popular tales of his time.

2. The philosophical implications of the novel. *Chin P'ing Mei* as a study of man's uninhibited enjoyment of sensual pleasure and power over fellow men in a hypothetical state of freedom. Kinship of this theme to the Faust and Don Juan themes in Western literature.

3. Life in a polygamous and promiscuous household: the frank acceptance of sexual pleasure as the only reality in life; the submission of women to Hsi-men's despotism; their contention for his favors; their contempt for men unable to satisfy their sexual demands.

4. Hsi-men's gruesome death. In what sense is P'an Chin-lien a more frightening character than Hsi-men?

5. The conflict between decent human feelings versus lust and greed. The role of specific characters: contrast Li P'ing-erh with P'an Chin-lien; is Hsi-men's grief over P'ing-erh's death out of character? Moon Lady as an upholder of Confucian duty.

6. Hsi-men's household as a microcosm of political disorder and corruption in the author's time.

7. The novel as a Buddhist allegory: moral retribution and reincarnation as the primary facts of human existence; the emptiness of the mundane world. The necessity for redemption: compare the novel in this respect with the works of Aeschylus, O'Neill, and Faulkner.

DREAM OF THE RED CHAMBER (HUNG LOU MENG), BY TS'AO HSÜEH-CH'IN (TS'AO CHAN, *d.* 1763)

An eighteenth-century realistic-allegorical novel of the decline of a great family and its young heir's involvement in the world of passion and depravity.

TRANSLATIONS

Complete

Hawkes, David, trans. *The Story of the Stone,* Vol. 1, *The Golden Days*; Vol. 2, *The Crab-Flower Club*; Vol. 3, *The Warning Voice*; and John Minford, trans., Vol. 4, *The Debt of Tears*; Vol. 5, *The Dreamer Wakes,* edited by Gao E. Pbk eds., Harmondsworth and Baltimore: Penguin, 1973–86.

A complete translation of the 120–chapter novel *Hung lou meng.* Faithful to the original in content and tone, in most readable English, with a scholarly introduction to the work for the general reader.

Selections

Birch, Cyril, trans. "How To Be Rid of a Rival (*Hung-lou-meng,* 63–69, extracts)," in Cyril Birch, ed., *Anthology of Chinese Literature,* 2:203–58. Pbk ed., New York: Grove, Evergreen, 1972.

McHugh, Florence, trans. *The Dream of the Red Chamber,* trans. from the German text of Franz Kuhn. New York: Pantheon, 1958; London: Routledge and Kegan Paul, 1958; reprint, Greenwood, 1975.

A fuller and more powerful version than Chi-chen Wang's, though much less accurate.

Wang Chi-chen, trans. *Dream of the Red Chamber*. New York: Twayne, 1958; London: Vision, 1959.

An incomplete but readable translation. The last forty chapters much abridged.

—— *Dream of the Red Chamber*. Pbk ed., New York: Doubleday, Anchor, 1958.

An abridgment of the clothbound edition.

Yang Hsien-yi and Gladys Yang, trans. *A Dream of Red Mansions*. 2 vols. Peking: Foreign Languages Press, 1978.

Translation of chapters 1–80.

—— "Dream of the Red Chamber (An Excerpt from the Novel)," in *Chinese Literature* (1964)6:38–82, 7:43–75, 8:41–95.

Translation of chapters 18–20, 32–34, 74–77.

SECONDARY READINGS

Ch'en Shou-yi. *Chinese Literature: A Historical Introduction*, pp. 584–89. New York: Ronald Press, 1961.

Ho Ch'i-fang. "On 'The Dream of the Red Chamber,'" in *Chinese Literature* (1963)1:65–86.

A standard Marxist interpretation.

Hsia, C. T. Chapter 7, "Dream of the Red Chamber," in *The Classic Chinese Novel: A Critical Introduction*. New York: Columbia University Press, 1968. Pbk ed., 1972. Bloomington: Indiana University Press, 1981.

Knoerle, Jeanne S. P. *The Dream of the Red Chamber: A Critical Study*. Bloomington: Indiana University Press, 1972.

Liu Ts'un-yan. *Buddhist and Taoist Influence on Chinese Novels*. Weisbaden: Harrassowitz, 1962.

Liu Ts'un-yan, ed. *Chinese Middlebrow Fiction*. Chinese University of Hong Kong and Seattle: University of Washington Press (Renditions), 1983.

Lu Hsün (Chou Shu-jen). *A Brief History of Chinese Fiction*,

chapter 24, pp. 298–316. Translated by Yang Hsien-yi and
Gladys Yang. Peking: Foreign Languages Press, 1959.

Miller, Lucien. *Masks of Fiction in Dream of the Red Chamber:
Myth, Mimesis, and Persona*. Tucson: University of Arizona
Press, 1975.

Plaks, Andrew. *Archetype and Allegory in the Dream of the Red
Chamber*. Princeton University Press, 1975.

Spence, Jonathan D. *Ts'ao Yin and the K'ang-hsi Emperor, Bond-
servant and Master*. New Haven: Yale University Press, 1966.

   This historical study casts valuable biographical light on the
author of *Dream of the Red Chamber*.

West, Anthony. "Through a Glass, Darkly," in *The New Yorker*,
November 22, 1958, pp. 223–32.

   A review of the Wang and Kuhn-McHugh versions, re-
freshingly astute and original in its comments on the novel's
greatness. An excellent guide for a beginning student.

Westbrook, Francis A. "On Dreams, Saints, and Fallen Angels:
Reality and Illusion in *Dream of the Red Chamber* and *The
Idiot*," in *Literature East and West* 15 (1971)3:371–91.

   A valuable comparative study of two world masterpieces.

Wu Shih-ch'ang. "History of 'The Red Chamber Dream,'" in
Chinese Literature (1963)1:87–100.

—— *On the Red Chamber Dream: A Critical Study of Two Annotated Manuscripts of the XVIIIth Century*. Oxford: Clarendon
Press, 1961.

   The interested student may want to read chapter 20, "Summaries and Conclusions," to get a notion of the complex
problems attending the novel's authorship and texts.

Yü, Anthony C. "Self and Family in the *Hung-lou Meng*: A
New Look at Lin Tai-yü as Tragic Heroine," in *Chinese
Literature: Essays, Articles, Reviews (CLEAR)* 2 (July
1980)2:199–223.

TOPICS FOR DISCUSSION

1. The novel as autobiography. Compared with *Chin P'ing Mei*, *Journey to the West*, and *The Water Margin*, why is *Hung lou meng* the far subtler and more complex novelistic structure? Is the autobiographical experience completely objectified as fiction?

2. To what extent is the household here a typical or ideal Chinese family? Is the portrayal of the family sympathetic or critical?

3. The novel as tragedy. What constitutes the major tragic conflict in the novel? Is the hero's final action—forsaking the world—understandable? How are the immense amount of suffering depicted in the novel and the hero's determined quest for personal liberation reconciled?

4. The novel of manners vs. allegory. Are the allegorical portions as successful as the realistic portions? Is there a basic ambiguity in the author's attitude toward sexual love? The novel was originally titled *Shih t'ou chi* or *The Story of the Stone*. Discuss the stone motif.

5. The novel is especially admired in China for its gallery of heroines. Which of the heroines strikes you as the most memorable? How would you characterize Black Jade?

6. Many Chinese scholars maintain that the last forty chapters of *Dream of the Red Chamber*, a 120–chapter novel, were "completed" by one Kao É, a total stranger to the author. Do you get the impression that the last third of the novel (chapters 39–50 in the Kuhn-McHugh version; Books 4 and 5 of the Hawkes) differ stylistically from the first two thirds?

7. Philosophical and religious themes in the novel: what roles do Confucianism, Taoism, and Buddhism play in the overall structure of the novel and in depiction of individual characters and scenes? How do you understand the stone's desire to live in the Red Dust—in Buddhist, Taoist, or Confucian terms?

CHINESE DRAMA

Chinese drama developed during the Yüan dynasty, drawing on earlier traditions of poetry written to set tunes, oral storytelling, and variety shows for its methods and subjects. It is highly stylized and symbolic, and its appeal lay primarily in the beauty of the poetic arias sung by the performers. New and distinctive regional types of theater flourished during the Ming and Ch'ing dynasties.

TRANSLATIONS

Crump, James I. *Chinese Theater in the Days of Kublai Khan.* Tucson: University of Arizona Press, 1980.

Complete translations of three Yüan plays, plus information on social and historical backgrounds and details of performance.

Dolby, William A., trans. *Eight Chinese Plays from the Thirteenth Century to the Present.* New York: Columbia University Press, 1978.

Includes three plays from the Yüan, two from the Ming, one from the Ch'ing, and two traditional pieces arranged in the twentieth century.

Hayden, George, trans. *Crime and Punishment in Medieval Chinese Drama: Three Judge Pao Plays.* Harvard East Asian Monographs, no. 82. Cambridge: Council on East Asian Studies, Harvard University, 1978.

Hsiung, S. I., trans. *The Romance of the Western Chamber.* New York: Columbia University Press, 1978.

Translation of Wang Shih-fu's masterpiece of Yüan drama.

Kao Ming. *The Lute.* Translated by Jean Mulligan. New York: Columbia University Press, 1980.

Translation of a fourteenth-century Ming *ch'uan-ch'i* drama.

K'ung Shang-jen. *The Peach Blossom Fan.* Translated by Chen

Shih-hsiang, Harold Acton, and Cyril Birch. Berkeley: University of California Press, 1976. Pbk ed.

Translation of an important Ming *k'un-ch'ü* drama.

Liu, Jung-en, trans. *Six Yüan Plays*. Harmondsworth: Penguin, 1972.

Contains a long, though not particularly scholarly, introduction and lively translations in a convenient paperback edition.

Scott, A. C., ed. and trans. *Traditional Chinese Plays*. 3 vols. Madison: University of Wisconsin Press, 1967, 1969, 1975.

Translations of Peking operas with valuable technical information on staging.

Shih, Cheng-wen, trans. *Injustice to Tou O*. Cambridge University Press, 1972. Pbk ed.

Scholarly translation with much background material and original text.

Tang Xianzu. *The Peony Pavilion*. Translated by Cyril Birch. Bloomington: Indiana University Press, 1980.

Great attention paid to the language in this translation of the 1598 famous love story.

Yang, Hsien-yi and Gladys Yang, trans. *Selected Plays of Kuan Han-ch'ing* (Guan Hanqing). Shanghai: New Art and Literature Publishing House, 1958; Peking: Foreign Language Press, 1979.

Works of the major Yüan dramatist.

SECONDARY READINGS

Dolby, William A. *A History of Chinese Drama*. London: Paul Elek Press, 1976; New York: Harper and Row, 1976.

Survey from putative historical origins of the drama to the present.

Johnson, Dale. *Yuarn Music Dramas: Study in Prosody and Catalogue of Northern Arias in the Dramatic Style*. Michigan Papers on Chinese Studies, vol. 40. Ann Arbor: University of Michigan Press, 1980.

Mackerras, Colin, ed. *Chinese Theater: From Its Origins to the Present Day*. Honolulu: University of Hawaii Press, 1983.

Scholarly essays and good annotated bibliographies.

Shih, Chung-wen. *The Golden Age of Chinese Drama: Yüan Tsa-chü*. Princeton University Press, 1976.

Good attention to literary aspects of the *tsa-chü*, the main form of drama during the Yüan.

Schlepp, Wayne. *San-ch'ü: Its Technique and Imagery*. Madison: University of Wisconsin Press, 1970.

The only full-length study of the poetry of the drama, its most important element.

Strassberg, Richard E. *The World of K'ung Shang-jen: A Man of Letters in Early Ch'ing China*. Studies in Oriental Culture, no. 17. New York: Columbia University Press, 1983.

West, Stephen and Wilt Idema. *Chinese Theater, 1100–1450: A Source Book*. Wiesbaden: Franz Steiner, 1982.

Includes translations of several plays and much background information on performance.

TOPICS FOR DISCUSSION

1. What are the conventions of Chinese drama, and how do they differ from those with which you are familiar? What does the playwright seem to assume the audience will know and expect?
2. How are characters presented and developed? Do they change within individual dramas, and if so, how?
3. Can Western concepts of tragedy and comedy be applied fruitfully to Chinese drama? How are central conflicts set up within an individual play?
4. Discuss the relevance of the poems to the action within an individual play.
5. How is the context of a play (especially its historical context, but also, social, religious, and literary contexts) important to an understanding of its meaning?

CHINESE POETRY

Chinese poetry was traditionally the most highly respected of all literary forms and something which any educated person would be expected to be able to write; during certain periods it was even included as a section of the civil service examination. From its beginnings in the Chou dynasty it has been characterized by its heavy use of natural imagery, the importance of rhyme and other types of patterning, and a conciseness of expression. Certain themes have prevailed as well, in particular those concerning the poet's relationship to society, politics, and nature.

THE BOOK OF SONGS (SHIH CHING)

*This sixth-century anthology of 305 poems was traditionally believed
to have been selected by Confucius himself and was given canonical
status during the Han dynasty. The collection is a varied one, ranging from simple songs of courtship to ritual hymns and dynastic
legends.*

TRANSLATIONS

Karlgren, Bernhard, trans. *Shih Ching: The Book of Odes*. Stock-
 holm: Museum of Far Eastern Antiquities, 1950.

 Word-for-word scholarly translations of the *Shih ching*, in-
 cluding Chinese text, transliteration, and reconstruction of
 Chou period rhymes.
Legge, James, trans. *The Book of Poetry*. Reprint of 1931 ed.,
 New York: Paragon, 1967.

 Also includes examples of traditional commentaries, which
 interpreted the *Songs* as comments on or reflections of contemporary political and social conditions, influencing many
 later critical theories and methods.
Pound, Ezra, trans. *The Confucian Odes: The Classic Anthology
 Defined by Confucius*. Pbk ed., New York: New Directions,
 1954. Cambridge: Harvard University Press, 1954. Pbk ed.

 Translations of the *Shih ching*, "poetic" but often wide of
 the mark.
Waley, Arthur, trans. *The Book of Songs*. New York: Grove,
 1960. Pbk ed.

 Translations of almost all of the 305 poems, arranged by
 topic and rendered into accurate, graceful English.
Watson, Burton, trans. and ed. *The Columbia Book of Chinese*

Poetry, from Early Times to the Thirteenth Century. New York: Columbia University Press, 1984.

Includes superb translations from the *Book of Odes*.

SECONDARY READINGS

Holzman, Donald. "Confucius and Ancient Chinese Literary Criticism," in *Chinese Approaches to Literature from Confucius to Liang Ch'i-ch'ao*, pp. 29–38. Edited by Adele Rickett. Princeton University Press, 1978.

Liu, J. Y. *Chinese Theories of Literature.* University of Chicago Press, 1975.

McNaughton, William. *The Book of Songs.* Boston: Twayne, 1971.

Wang, C. H. *The Bell and the Drum: Shih Ching as Formulaic Poetry in an Oral Tradition.* Berkeley and Los Angeles: University of California Press, 1974.

Watson, Burton. *Early Chinese Literature.* New York: Columbia University Press, 1962; pbk ed., 1971.

The section on poetry includes a discussion of the *Book of Songs*.

Yu, Pauline. "Allegory, Allegoresis, and the *Classic of Poetry*," in *Harvard Journal of Asiatic Studies* 42 (December 1983)2:377–412.

—— *The Reading of Imagery in the Chinese Poetic Tradition.* Princeton University Press, 1987.

TOPICS FOR DISCUSSION

1. What are the main concerns of the poems and how are they expressed? What picture do they give us of the early Chou dynasty world?
2. What attitudes to nature are evident in the poems?

3. Discuss the major stylistic devices—imagery, repetition, refrains—and their effects. How are the various elements within an individual poem related to each other? How do the different forms relate to the varying subject matter?
4. What aspects of this text led to its appropriation by Confucian scholars for their canon? If you have read some of the traditional commentaries (in Legge), discuss their relationship to the poems.

THE SONGS OF THE SOUTH
(CH'U TZ'U)
BY CH'Ü YÜAN AND OTHER POETS

An anthology of seventeen works compiled in the second century C.E. on the basis of a tradition dating from the third century B.C. and associated with the great lyric poet Ch'ü Yüan.

TRANSLATIONS

Complete

Hawkes, David, trans. *The Songs of the South: An Anthology of Ancient Chinese Poems by Qu Yuan and Other Poets*. Harmondsworth: Penguin, 1985.

    Masterful translations with an extensive and authoritative introduction by an established authority.

Selections

Field, Stephen, trans. *Tian Wen: A Chinese Book of Origins*. New York: New Directions, 1984. Pbk ed.

Hawkes, David, trans. "Encountering Sorrow" (*Li Sao*) and selections from "The Nine Songs," "The Nine Declarations," "The Nine Arguments," "The Summons of the Soul," and "Summons for a Gentleman Who Became a Recluse," in Cyril Birch, ed., *Anthology of Chinese Literature*, 1:49–80. New York: Grove Press, 1965.

Waley, Arthur, trans. *The Nine Songs: A Study of Shamanism in Ancient China*. London: Allen and Unwin, 1955.

Watson, Burton, trans. "Encountering Sorrow" and selections from the "Nine Songs," in Burton Watson, trans. and ed., *The Columbia Book of Chinese Poetry*, pp. 45–66. New York: Columbia University Press, 1984.

SECONDARY READINGS

Ch'en Shih-hsiang. "The Genesis of Poetic Time: The Greatness of Ch'ü Yüan, Studied with a New Critical Approach," in *Tsinghua Journal of Chinese Studies* (n.s., June 1975):1–43.

Hawkes, David. "The Supernatural in Chinese Poetry," in *The Far East: China and Japan* (*University of Toronto Quarterly*, supplement no. 5, 1961), pp. 311–324.

—— "The Quest of the Goddess," in Cyril Birch, ed., *Studies in Chinese Literary Genres*, pp. 42–68. Berkeley and Los Angeles: University of California Press, 1974.

Hightower, James R. "Ch'ü Yüan Studies," in *Silver Jubilee Volume of the Zinbungaku-kenkyūsho*, Kyoto University, pp. 192–223. Kyoto, 1954.

Schneider, Laurence A. *A Madman of Ch'u: The Chinese Myth of Loyalty and Dissent.* Berkeley and Los Angeles: University of California Press, 1980.

Yu, Pauline. *The Reading of Imagery in the Chinese Poetic Tradition*, chapter 3. Princeton University Press, 1987.

TOPICS FOR DISCUSSION

1. How do the religious traditions of shamanism enter into the imaginative world of these poems?
2. What kind of journey is undertaken in "Encountering Sorrow," and with what result?
3. What may be learned from these poems about Chinese views of the political order and the issue of political responsibility? What is the concept of loyalty that Ch'ü Yüan represents?
4. What is the sense of death found in "Encountering Sorrow" and in "The Summons of the Soul"?
5. How does the poetic voice found in these poems differ from that found in the *Book of Odes* (*Shih ching*)?

CHINESE POETS AND POETRY

The period of the greatest poetic flowering, in a long tradition of high regard for poetry, was during the T'ang dynasty (618–907), which is emphasized here.

TRANSLATIONS

Anthologies

Ayling, Alan and Duncan R. Mackintosh. *A Collection of Chinese Lyrics*. London: Routledge and Kegan Paul, 1965; Nashville: Vanderbilt University Press, 1967.

    Pleasing translations of *tz'u* poetry done in rhyme and with accompanying Chinese texts.

Birrell, Anne. *New Songs from a Jade Terrace: An Anthology of Early Chinese Love Poetry*. London: Allen and Unwin, 1982.

    Translations of Six Dynasties love poetry.

Bynner, Witter. *The Jade Mountain: A Chinese Anthology, Being Three Hundred Poems of the T'ang Dynasty*. London: Allen and Unwin, 1929; New York: Knopf, 1929, 1967.

    Translation of a popular anthology.

Chang, H. C. *Chinese Literature: Nature Poetry*. Vol. 2. New York: Columbia University Press, 1977.

    Includes translations of important prose texts as well.

Chaves, Jonathan, ed. and trans. *The Columbia Book of Later*

Chinese Poetry: Yüan, Ming, and Ch'ing Dynasties, 1279–1911.
New York: Columbia University Press, 1986.

A representative selection of a hitherto neglected, yet very large, body of poetry.

Cheng, Francois, *Chinese Poetic Writing.* Translated from the French by Donald A. Riggs and Jerome P. Seaton, with an Anthology of T'ang poetry translated from the Chinese by Jerome P. Seaton. Bloomington: Indiana University Press, 1982. Pbk ed.

Three theoretical essays and an anthology of translations of T'ang dynasty poems.

Davis, A. R., ed. *The Penguin Book of Chinese Verse.* Translated by Robert Kotewall and Norman L. Smith. Harmondsworth and Baltimore: Penguin, 1962.

This anthology includes over 120 poets, most of them represented by one short lyric.

Frodsham, J. D. *An Anthology of Chinese Verse: Han, Wei, Chin, and the Northern and Southern Dynasties.* Oxford: Clarendon Press, 1967.

An ample selection of pre-T'ang poetry, faithfully rendered.

Fusek, Lois. *Among the Flowers: A Translation of the Tenth-Century Anthology of Tz'u Lyrics, the Hua-Chien Chi.* New York: Columbia University Press, 1982.

Graham, A. C. *Poems of the Late T'ang.* Baltimore: Penguin, 1965.

Selections from one of the most interesting periods of Chinese poetry; excellent translations of poets from 750 to 907, with a valuable introductory essay on translating Chinese poetry and on how the poetry works.

Liu, James J. Y. *Major Lyricists of the Northern Sung.* Princeton University Press, 1972.

A guide to six *tz'u* poets of the Northern Sung dynasty, with translation and critical analysis of their representative poems.

Liu Wu-chi and Irving Yucheng Lo, eds. *Sunflower Splendor: Three Thousand Years of Chinese Poetry*. Garden City, NY: Doubleday, Anchor Books, 1975. Pbk ed.

Comprehensive but uneven anthology.

Rexroth, Kenneth and Ling Chung, trans. and eds. *The Orchid Boat*. New York: McGraw-Hill, 1972; Seabury, 1972. Reissued as *Women Poets of China*. New York: New Directions, 1982.

Waley, Arthur. *Chinese Poems*. London: Allen and Unwin, 1946. Pbk ed., 1982.

Includes selections from *170 Chinese Poems, More Translations from the Chinese, The Temple*, and *The Book of Songs*. An ample representation of Waley's skill as a translator of Chinese verse, though, in Waley's own words, "not a balanced anthology of Chinese poetry." Half of the book is devoted to Po Chü-i.

Watson, Burton. *Chinese Lyricism: Shih Poetry from the Second to the Twelfth Century*. New York: Columbia University Press, 1971. Pbk ed.

An excellent introduction to *shih* poetry from the Han to the Sung dynasty. Able translation of some 200 representative poems accompanied by illuminating comments.

—— *Chinese Rhyme-Prose: Poems in the Fu Form from the Han and Six Dynasties Periods*. New York: Columbia University Press, 1971. Pbk ed.

Brilliant translations of thirteen works of the genre.

—— *The Columbia Book of Chinese Poetry, from Early Times to the Thirteenth Century*. New York: Columbia University Press, 1984.

Superb translations from the *Book of Odes*, the *Ch'u Tz'u*, early songs and *yüeh-fu* ballads, poems of the Han and Wei, T'ao Yüan-ming, Chin, Six Dynasties, and Sui poets, T'ang and Sung poets, and *tz'u* poets from the eighth to thirteenth centuries.

Yip, Wai-lim, ed. and trans. *Chinese Poetry: Major Modes and Genres*. Berkeley: University of California Press, 1976.
   Includes original texts.

Major Chinese Poets

Han Shan. *Cold Mountain: 100 Poems by the T'ang Poet Han-shan*. Translated by Burton Watson. New York: Columbia University Press, 1962.

Hsieh Ling-yün. *The Murmuring Stream: The Life and Works of the Chinese Nature Poet Hsieh Ling-yün (385–433)*. 2 vols. Translated by J. D. Frodsham. Kuala Lumpur: University of Malaya Press, 1967.

Hsin Ch'i-chi. *Hsin Ch'i-chi*. Translated by Irving Yucheng Lo. New York: Twayne, 1971.

Juan Chi. *Poetry and Politics: The Life and Works of Juan Chi, AD 210–263*, by Donald Holzman. Cambridge and New York: Cambridge University Press, 1976.

Li Ho. *Li Ho*. Translated by Kuo-ch'ing Tu. Boston: Twayne, 1979.
   The Poems of Li Ho (791–817). Translated by J. D. Frodsham. Oxford: Clarendon Press, 1970.

Li Po. *Li Po and Tu Fu*. Translated by Arthur Cooper. Harmondsworth: Penguin, 1973.
   The Poetry and Career of Li Po. Translated by Arthur Waley. London: Allen and Unwin, 1950.
   Somewhat disapproving and biased account of the eighth-century poet.

Li Shang-yin. *The Poetry of Li Shang-yin, Ninth-century Baroque Chinese Poet*, by James J. Y. Liu. University of Chicago Press, 1969.

Meng Chiao. *The Poetry of Meng Chiao and Han Yü*, by Stephen Owen. New Haven: Yale University Press, 1975.

Meng Hao-jan. *Meng Hao-jan*, by Paul Kroll. Boston: Twayne, 1981.

Po Chü-i. *The Life and Times of Po Chü-i,* by Arthur Waley. London: Allen and Unwin, 1949; New York: Macmillan, 1950.

Su T'ung-po. *Su Tung-p'o: Selections from a Sung Dynasty Poet.* Translated by Burton Watson. New York: Columbia University Press, 1965. Pbk ed.

T'ao Ch'ien. *The Poetry of T'ao Ch'ien.* Translated by J. R. Hightower. Oxford: Clarendon Press, 1970.

T'ao the Hermit: Sixty Poems by T'ao Ch'ien (365–427). Translated, with an Introduction and annotations, by W. R. B. Acker. London and New York: Thames and Hudson, 1952.

T'ao Yüan-ming. Study by A. R. Davis. 2 vols. Cambridge University Press, 1983.

Tu Fu. *Tu Fu, China's Greatest Poet,* by William Hung. 2 vols. Cambridge: Harvard University Press, 1952; London: Oxford University Press, 1952.

Selected Poems. Compiled by Feng Chih. Translated by Rewi Alley. Peking: Foreign Languages Press, 1962.

Li Po and Tu Fu. Translated by Arthur Cooper. Harmondsworth: Penguin, 1973.

A Little Primer of Tu Fu. Translated by David Hawkes. Oxford: Clarendon Press, 1967.

Wang Wei. *Poems of Wang Wei.* Translated by G. W. Robinson. Harmondsworth: Penguin, 1973.

Wang Wei, by Marsha Wagner. Boston: Twayne, 1981.

Hiding the Universe: Poems by Wang Wei, by Wai-lim Yip. New York: Grossman, 1972.

The Poetry of Wang Wei: New Translations and Commentary, by Pauline Yu. Bloomington: Indiana University Press, 1980. Pbk ed.

Includes original texts.

Yüan Chen. *Yüan Chen,* by Angela Palandri. Boston: Twayne, 1977.

SECONDARY READINGS

Birch, Cyril, ed. *Studies in Chinese Literary Genres*. Berkeley: University of California Press, 1975.

Essays on various literary genres; see especially David Hawkes' article on the songs of Ch'u, "Quest of the Goddess," pp. 42–68.

Bryant, Daniel. *Lyric Poets of the Southern T'ang: Feng Yen-ssu, 903–960, and Li Yü, 937–978*. Vancouver: University of British Columbia Press, 1982.

Chang, Kang-i Sun. *The Evolution of Chinese Tz'u Poetry: From Late T'ang to Northern Sung*. Princeton University Press, 1980.
—— *Six Dynasties Poetry*. Princeton University Press, 1986.

Chow Tsu-tsung, ed. *Wen-lin: Studies in the Chinese Humanities*. Madison: University of Wisconsin Press, 1968.

Seven of the twelve essays included are on poetry.

Frankel, Hans. *The Flowering Plum and the Palace Lady: Interpretations of Chinese Poetry*. New Haven: Yale University Press, 1976. Pbk ed.

Discussions and translations, arranged by topic, i.e., the major themes and methods of traditional poetry.

Hightower, J. R. *Topics in Chinese Literature,* chapters 4, 7–10, 14. Rev. ed., Cambridge: Harvard University Press, 1962.

Kao Yu-kung and Tsu-lin Mei. "Syntax, Diction, and Imagery in T'ang Poetry," in *Harvard Journal of Asiatic Studies* 31 (1971):51–136.

A major contribution to our understanding of recent style poetry (*lü-shih*).

—— "Meaning, Metaphor, and Allusion in T'ang Poetry," in *Harvard Journal of Asiatic Studies* 38.2 (December 1978):281–356.

Knechtges, David. *The Han Rhapsody: A Study of the Fu of Yang Hsiung, 53 B.C.-A.D. 18*. Cambridge and New York: Cambridge University Press, 1976.

Study of the Han *fu* ("rhyme prose," "prose poem").

——— *Wen Xuan; or, Selections of Refined Literature*. Vol. 1, *Rhapsodies on Metropolises and Capitals*. Princeton University Press, 1982.

Liu, James J. Y. *The Art of Chinese Poetry*. University of Chicago Press, 1962. Pbk ed.

An excellent guide to the forms, themes, and techniques of Chinese poetry. Ample references to Western poetry and criticism.

——— *Chinese Theories of Literature*. University of Chicago Press, 1979.

——— *The Interlingual Critic: Interpreting Chinese Poetry*. Bloomington: Indiana University Press, 1982.

MacLeish, Archibald. *Poetry and Experience*. Boston: Houghton Mifflin, 1961.

The author, a distinguished poet, defines the poetic experience with the help of a Chinese classic in poetics, Lu Chi's *Wen Fu*. Read the first four chapters. Chapter 3 discusses the imagery of several Chinese poems.

Owen, Stephen. *The Great Age of Chinese Poetry: The High Tang*. New Haven: Yale University Press, 1980.

——— *The Poetry of the Early T'ang*. New Haven: Yale University Press, 1977.

——— *Traditional Chinese Poetry and Poetics: Omen of the World*. Madison: University of Wisconsin Press, 1985.

Schafer, Edward. *The Divine Woman: Dragon Ladies and Rain Maidens in T'ang Literature*. Berkeley: North Point Press, 1980.

——— *The Golden Peaches of Samarkand: A Study of T'ang Exotics*. Berkeley: University of California Press, 1963. Pbk ed.

——— *Pacing the Void: T'ang Approaches to the Stars*. Berkeley: University of California Press, 1978.

——— *The Vermilion Bird*. Berkeley: University of California Press, 1963. Pbk ed., 1985.

Wagner, Marsha. *The Lotus Boat: The Origins of Chinese Tz'u*

Poetry in T'ang Popular Culture. New York: Columbia University Press, 1984.

On links between *tz'u* poetry and popular culture.

Waley, Arthur. *170 Chinese Poems.* New ed., London: Constable, 1962.

—— *The Temple and Other Poems.* London: Allen and Unwin, 1923; New York: Knopf, 1923. Reprint, New York: AMS, n.d.

The introductory section gives a historical survey of *fu* poetry.

Wang, C. H. *The Bell and the Drum: A Study of the Shih Ching as Formulaic Poetry.* Berkeley: University of California Press, 1975.

A study of the *Shih ching* as formulaic poetry in an oral tradition.

Watson, Burton. *Early Chinese Literature.* New York: Columbia University Press, 1962; pbk ed., 1971.

The section on poetry discusses the *Book of Songs,* the *Songs of the South,* and *fu* poetry of the Han period. Dazzling translations of several *fu* poems.

—— *Chinese Lyricism: Shih Poetry from the Second to Twelfth Century.* New York: Columbia University Press, 1970. Pbk ed.

The development of the *shih,* or short lyric poem, from the second to twelfth century.

—— *Chinese Rhyme-Prose: Poems in the Fu Form from the Han and Six Dynasties Periods.* New York: Columbia University Press, 1971. Pbk ed.

Yoshikawa Kōjirō. *An Introduction to Sung Poetry.* Translated by Burton Watson. Cambridge: Harvard University Press, 1967.

A survey of the subject by a great Japanese sinologist.

Yu, Pauline. *The Reading of Imagery in the Chinese Poetic Tradition.* Princeton University Press, 1987.

TOPICS FOR DISCUSSION

1. The Chinese language: its monosyllabic character, its concreteness, its elliptical economy. How do these qualities contribute to the pregnant density of Chinese verse?

2. The use of complementary or contrasting images in a given poem to enhance meaning. Is Western-style metaphor a regular feature of Chinese poetry? Among the poets you have read, is there a conscious use of symbolism?

3. The brevity of Chinese poems. Does the Chinese poet suffer in comparison with the Western poet because he is denied a wider choice of lyrical forms that offer larger scope? Do a close analysis of a Chinese poem, and then examine it again in the larger context of the poet's other works. Does the poem gain in meaning and consequence when seen as part of a larger whole?

4. The themes of Chinese poetry. Compare the love lyrics in *The Book of Songs* with later love poetry. Nature and friendship as themes. Does their habitual fondness for conventional themes and sentiments prevent Chinese poets from reaching the kinds of soul-searching honesty that distinguishes the best Western lyrical poetry?

5. The Chinese poet as philosopher. The momentary illumination of Confucian, Taoist, or Buddhist wisdom in the personal context of lyrical emotion.

6. The poet and his masks. Does the Chinese poet always speak in his own voice? How good is Chinese narrative poetry?

7. Chinese poetry and the musical tradition. The song quality of Chinese verse compared with the conversational style and colloquial rhythms of much English lyrical poetry.

IV. Classics of the Japanese Tradition

GENERAL WORKS

Kodansha Encyclopedia of Japan. 9 vols. Edited by Gen Itasaka. Tokyo and New York: Kodansha International, 1983.

Literature

Bownas, Geoffrey and Anthony Thwaite, eds. and trans. *The Penguin Book of Japanese Verse*. Baltimore: Penguin, 1964. Pbk ed.

> Selections from all periods in readable translations.

Brower, Robert H. and Earl Miner. *Japanese Court Poetry*. Stanford University Press, 1961.

> An excellent study of the development and aesthetics of Japanese poetry from the earliest times until the fourteenth century, illustrated with many translations.

de Bary, Wm. Theodore, ed. *Approaches to the Oriental Classics: Asian Literature and Thought in General Education*. New York: Columbia University Press, 1959; 2d rev. ed., 1989.

Hisamatsu Sen'ichi. *The Vocabulary of Japanese Literary Aesthetics*. Tokyo: Center for East Asian Cultural Studies, 1963.

Kato, Shuichi. *Form, Style, Tradition: Reflections on Japanese Art and Society*. Translated by John Bester. Berkeley: University of California Press, 1971.

—— *A History of Japanese Literature*. 3 vols. Vol. 1: *The First Thousand Years*. Translated by David Chibbett. Tokyo and New York: Kodansha International, 1979; pbk ed., 1982. Vol. 2, *The Years of Isolation,* and vol. 3, *The Modern Years*. Translated by Don Sanderson. Kodansha International, 1983.

Keene, Donald. *Dawn to the West: Japanese Literature in the Modern Era*. 2 vols. New York: Holt, Rhinehart and Winston, 1984.

> An extensive and readable study of major literary move-

ments and writers, in fiction, drama, poetry, and criticism, of the modern period.

—— *Japanese Literature: An Introduction for Western Readers*. London: John Murray, 1953. Pbk ed., New York: Grove, Evergreen, 1955.

A clear, brief introduction to the major genres and themes of Japanese literature.

—— *World Within Walls: Japanese Literature of the Pre-Modern Era, 1600–1867*. Holt, Rhinehart and Winston, 1976. Pbk ed., New York: Grove, Evergreen, 1978.

A complete and extremely readable history of the development of Japanese literature during the premodern period, with thorough discussions of major writers within the context of the period.

Keene, Donald, ed. *Anthology of Japanese Literature: from the Earliest Era to the Mid-Nineteenth Century*. New York: Grove, 1955. Pbk ed., Evergreen, 1960.

A very useful representative selection of major works of premodern Japanese literature by competent translators.

—— *Modern Japanese Literature: An Anthology*. New York: Grove, 1956. Pbk ed., Evergreen, 1960.

A representative selection of works by competent translators.

Konishi Jin'ichi. *A History of Japanese Literature*. Vols. 1–2. Edited by Earl Miner. Vol. 1, *The Archaic and Ancient Ages*. Translated by Aileen Gatten and Nicholas Teele. Vol. 2, *The Early Middle Ages*. Translated by Aileen Gatten. Princeton University Press, 1984–85. Pbk eds.

Translations of the first two volumes of a projected five-volume history of Japanese literature by a distinguished scholar.

LaFleur, William R. *The Karma of Words: Buddhism and the Literary Arts in Medieval Japan*. Berkeley: University of California Press, 1983.

Considers the influence of Buddhism on major works of Japanese literature from the ninth to the seventeenth century.

Marks, Alfred and Barry D. Bort. *Guide to Japanese Prose*. Boston: Hall, 1975; 2d ed., 1984.

Miller, Roy Andrew. *The Japanese Language*. University of Chicago Press, 1967.

Important not only for linguists but for students of literature who wish to learn how the Japanese language itself molded the literature.

Miner, Earl. *An Introduction to Japanese Court Poetry*. Stanford University Press, 1968; pbk ed., 1976.

A simplified version of Brower and Miner's *Japanese Court Poetry* (see above). It also includes a discussion of fifteenth-century poetry, not covered in the earlier book.

Miner, Earl, Hiroko Odagiri, and Robert E. Morrell. *The Princeton Companion to Classical Japanese Literature*. Princeton University Press, 1986.

Miner, Earl, ed. *Principles of Classical Japanese Literature*. Princeton University Press, 1985.

Essays on classical literature by a number of scholars.

Rimer, J. Thomas and Robert E. Morrell. *Guide to Japanese Poetry*. Boston: Hall, 1975; 2d ed., 1984.

Sato, Hiroaki and Burton Watson, eds. and trans. *From the Country of Eight Islands: An Anthology of Japanese Poetry*. Seattle: University of Washington Press, 1981. Pbk ed., New York: Columbia University Press, 1986.

Translations of selections drawn from the entire poetic tradition, by two very able translators.

Ueda, Makoto. *Literary and Art Theories in Japan*. Cleveland: Press of Case Western Reserve University, 1967.

An examination of different aspects of Japanese aesthetics as seen in the ideas and works of poets, dramatists, landscape gardeners, etc.

Japanese Thought and Religion

Kitagawa, Joseph. *Religion in Japanese History*. New York: Columbia University Press, 1966.

A series of lectures on the main themes of Japanese religious history, from the earliest times through the postwar period.

Matsunaga Daigan and Alicia Matsunaga. *Foundation of Japanese Buddhism.* 2 vols. Los Angeles: Buddhist Books International, 1974–76. Vol. 1, *The Aristocratic Age,* 1974. Pbk ed. Vol. 2, *The Mass Movement,* 1976. Pbk ed.

A history of Japanese Buddhist thought and institutions from the sixth to the sixteenth century.

Tsunoda Ryusaku, Wm. Theodore de Bary, and Donald Keene, eds. *Sources of Japanese Tradition.* New York: Columbia University Press, 1958. Pbk ed., 2 vols., 1964.

A source book covering the major developments in Japanese religion and thought from earliest times to the present, with extensive historical introductions to the translations.

Japanese History

Cambridge History of Japan. 6 vols. John W. Hall, Marius Jansen, Madoka Kanai, and David Twitchett, general eds. New York: Cambridge University Press, 1988– .

Fairbank, John K., Edwin O. Reischauer, and Albert M. Craig. *East Asia: The Great Tradition, New Impression.* Boston: Houghton Mifflin, 1973. See also Edwin O. Reischauer, John K. Fairbank, and Albert M. Craig. *East Asia: The Great Tradition.* Vol. 1 of *A History of East Asian Civilization.* Boston: Houghton Mifflin, 1960; London: Allen and Unwin, 1961.

The best available survey of institutional developments.

Hall, John Whitney. *Japan: From Prehistory to Modern Times.* New York: Delacorte Press, 1970. Pbk ed.

A general survey by a leading authority.

Hall, John Whitney and Toyoda Takeshi. *Japan in the Muromachi Age.* Berkeley: University of California Press, 1977. Pbk ed.

Morris, Ivan. *The Nobility of Failure: Tragic Heroes in the History of Japan.* New York: Holt, Rinehart and Winston, 1975. Pbk ed., New York: New American Library, Meridian, 1975.

Reischauer, Edwin O. *Japan, Past and Present.* 1st ed., London: Duckworth, 1947. 2d ed., New York: Knopf, 1953.

A brief, general survey by a leading authority.

Sansom, Sir George B. *A History of Japan to 1334*. Stanford University Press, 1958. Pbk ed.

—— *A History of Japan 1334–1615*. Stanford University Press, 1961. Pbk ed.

—— *A History of Japan 1615–1867*. Stanford University Press, 1963. Pbk ed.

These three volumes provide a much fuller account of the political, economic, and social development of Japan. The definitive work of its type.

—— *Japan, A Short Cultural History*. London: Cresset Press, 1931. 3d rev. ed., New York: Appleton-Century-Crofts, 1962. Pbk ed.

A standard work on Japanese cultural history from antiquity up to modern times. Excellent background reading for the works listed in this guide.

Schirokauer, Conrad. *A Brief History of Chinese and Japanese Civilizations*. New York: Harcourt, Brace, 1978, 2d rev. ed., 1988. Pbk ed.

Tiedemann, Arthur, ed. *An Introduction to Japanese Civilization*. New York: Columbia University Press, 1974. Pbk ed., New York: D. C. Heath, 1974.

Combines a survey of Japanese history with essays by specialists on various aspects of Japanese culture.

Varley, H. Paul. *Japanese Culture: A Short History*. 3d rev. ed. Honolulu: University of Hawaii Press, 1984. Pbk ed.

Traces the formation and evolution of Japanese culture from prehistory to the present.

—— *A Syllabus of Japanese Civilization*. Companion to Asian Studies. 2d ed. New York and London: Columbia University Press, 1972.

MAN'YŌSHŪ

The earliest extant anthology of Japanese poetry, containing over four thousand poems in twenty books, compiled about A.D. 770 by Ōtomo Yakamochi and others.

TRANSLATIONS

Inoue, S. and Kenneth Yasuda, trans and eds. *Land of the Reed Plains: Ancient Japanese Lyrics from the Manyoshu.* Rutland, VT: Tuttle, 1960; Tokyo: Tuttle, 1961.
Selections with illustrations.

Levy, Ian Hideo, trans. *The Ten Thousand Leaves: A Translation of the "Man'yōshū," Japan's Premier Anthology of Classical Poetry.* Vol. 1. Princeton University Press, 1981.
The first in a projected five-volume complete translation of the *Man'yōshū*, containing the first five books. The translations are accurate and lyrical, and convey some of the special qualities of the language.

Nippon Gakujutsu Shinkōkai, ed. and trans. *The Manyōshū.* Tokyo: Iwanami Shoten, 1940. Reprint, New York: Columbia University Press, 1965. Pbk ed., 1970.
A representative selection of one thousand poems, well translated into English verse with an extensive, if rather outdated, introduction.

SECONDARY READINGS

Brower, Robert H. and Earl Miner. *Japanese Court Poetry.* Stanford University Press, 1961.
Chapter 4, "The Early Literary Period," includes excellent translations of *Man'yōshū* poetry as well as a penetrating discussion of the anthology.

Doe, Paula. *A Warbler's Song in the Dusk: The Life and Works of Ōtomo Yakamochi (718–785)*. Berkeley and Los Angeles: University of California Press, 1982.

A thorough study of the life and works of a compiler and major poet of the *Man'yōshū*.

Levy, Ian Hideo. *Hitomaro and the Birth of Japanese Lyricism*. Princeton University Press, 1984.

A thorough examination of the poetic development of the most important *Man'yōshū* poet.

Konishi Jin'ichi. *A History of Japanese Literature*. Edited by Earl Miner. Chapter 7, "Waka Expression," and chapter 10, "Waka Composition," in Vol. 1, *The Archaic and Ancient Ages*. Translated by Aileen Gatten and Nicholas Teele. Princeton University Press, 1984. Pbk ed.

McCullough, Helen Craig. *Brocade by Night: "Kokin Wakashū" and the Court Style in Classical Japanese Poetry*. Stanford University Press, 1985.

Chapter 2, "Pre-Heian Song and Poetry," newly translates and analyzes a significant selection of *Man'yōshū* poems.

Philippi, Donald L., trans. *Kojiki*. University of Tokyo Press, 1969; Princeton University Press, 1969.

The *Kojiki,* the first Japanese "history," gives the traditional Shinto account of the Age of the Gods and of the foundation of the country. Although the literary interest is slight, the numerous poems provide an illuminating contrast with the *Man'yōshū* poetry.

—— *This Wine of Peace, This Wine of Laughter: A Complete Anthology of Japan's Earliest Songs*. New York: Grossman, 1968.

Translations of pre-*Man'yōshū* poetry.

TOPICS FOR DISCUSSION

1. The "Japaneseness" of the *Man'yōshū*. Choice of imagery and subject matter. Compare and contrast with Chinese poetry. Is there a distinctive Japanese aestheticism here?
2. The *Man'yōshū* as expressive of a polycentric, pluralistic, particularistic world view. Functions of poetry at the time; the court poets; poets away from the court. Patriotic attitudes.
3. Typical features of *Man'yōshū* poetic style, subject matter, and form. The *chōka* ("long poem") and its structure. The relation of the *hanka* (envoys) to the long poem.
4. Individual poets and their characteristic manners: Hitomaro, Akahito, Yakamochi, Okura. Emperors as poets. Women poets.

COURT POETRY: THE *KOKINSHŪ*
AND OTHER IMPERIAL ANTHOLOGIES

The organization, poetic form, vocabulary, tone, and themes in the
Kokinshū, *compiled in 905 by Ki no Tsurayuki (ca. 868–945) and*
others, set the standards of poetic expression for centuries.

TRANSLATIONS

Complete

McCullough, Helen Craig, trans. *Kokin Wakashū: The First Im-*
perial Anthology of Japanese Poetry. Stanford University Press,
1985.

Accurate translations of the complete anthology, including
Chinese and Japanese prefaces, *The Tosa Nikki,* and *Shinsen*
Waka, with excellent introductory material and notes. See
companion volume, below, on the period and its poetics.

Rodd, Laura Rasplica and Mary Catherine Henkenius, trans.
Kokinshū: A Collection of Poems Ancient and Modern. Princeton
University Press, 1984.

A complete translation with an emphasis on creating vi-
brant contemporary poetic texts; with helpful introductory
material for general readers and explanatory notes and essays.

Selections

Bownas, Geoffrey and Anthony Thwaite, eds. and trans. *The*
Penguin Book of Japanese Verse. Baltimore: Penguin, 1964. Pbk
ed.

Includes examples of *Kokinshū* poetry.

Keene, Donald, ed. *Anthology of Japanese Literature: From the*
Earliest Era to the Mid-Nineteenth Century. New York: Grove,
1955. Pbk ed., Evergreen, 1960.

Contains selections from the *Kokinshū* and several later Imperial anthologies.

LaFleur, William R., trans. *Mirror for the Moon: A Selection of Poems by Saigyō (1118–1190)*. New York: New Directions, 1978. Pbk ed.

A collection of poems by a great court poet of the late Heian period.

Rexroth, Kenneth, trans. *One Hundred Poems from the Japanese*. New York: New Directions, 1964. Pbk ed.

Rexroth, Kenneth and Itsuko Atsumi, eds. and trans. *Women Poets of Japan*. New York: New Directions, 1977. Pbk ed.

Both volumes contain work by *Kokinshū* poets and selections from other Imperial anthologies.

SECONDARY READINGS

Brower, Robert H. and Earl Miner. *Japanese Court Poetry*. Stanford University Press, 1961.

Chapter 5 of this standard work, "The Early Classical Period," is an analysis of the poetry of the *Kokinshū*, and includes translations of many poems.

—— "Formative Elements in the Japanese Poetic Tradition," in *Journal of Asian Studies* 16 (August 1957)4:503–27.

Konishi Jin'ichi. "Association and Progression: Principles of Integration in Anthologies and Sequences of Japanese Court Poetry, A.D. 900–1350." Translated and adapted by Robert H. Brower and Earl Miner, in *Harvard Journal of Asiatic Studies* 21 (December 1958):67–127.

A seminal work on the organization of Imperial anthologies and poetic sequences.

McCullough, Helen Craig. *Brocade by Night: "Kokin Wakashū" and the Court Style in Japanese Poetry*. Stanford University Press, 1985.

A treatment of the poetry, its heritage and legacy in depth

and at length. A companion to her translation of *Kokin Waka-shū* above.

Miner, Earl. *An Introduction to Japanese Court Poetry*, chapter 5. Stanford University Press, 1968. Pbk ed.

—— "The Techniques of Japanese Poetry," in *Hudson Review* 8 (Autumn 1955)3:350–66.

Ueda Makoto. *Literary and Art Theories in Japan*. Cleveland: Case Western Reserve University Press, 1967. Pbk ed.

Contains a chapter on Ki no Tsurayuki, the major compiler of the *Kokinshū,* and his theories of poetry.

Waley, Arthur. *Japanese Poetry: the "Uta."* Oxford: Clarendon Press, 1919. Reprint ed., Honolulu: University of Hawaii Press, 1976, and London: Allen and Unwin, 1976. Pbk ed.

TOPICS FOR DISCUSSION

1. The formation of a Japanese poetic in the *Kokinshū*. What were the occasions recognized as appropriate for composing poetry? How do they differ from occasions chosen by *Man'-yōshū* poets?

2. The *waka* (or *tanka*) as the classic Japanese verse form. What were some of the advantages and disadvantages of composing poetry in so brief a form? How did the choice of this form affect content?

3. The importance of the seasons in Japanese poetry; what does it imply about Japanese views of experience?

4. Differences between the *Man'yōshū* and the *Kokinshū* (and later court poetry) in form; in themes; in principles of organization; in language; in poetic usage.

5. The importance of poetic allusion; the close relation between the poet and the reader.

THE PILLOW BOOK
(MAKURA NO SŌSHI)
OF SEI SHŌNAGON

A collection of perceptive reflections and sharp and witty anecdotes, mainly concerned with court life in the late tenth century, by one of Japan's greatest literary stylists.

TRANSLATIONS

Complete

Morris, Ivan, trans. *The Pillow Book of Sei Shōnagon.* 2 vols. New York: Columbia University Press, 1967. Pbk ed., 1 vol., 1970.

    A complete translation of great literary distinction. The second volume is devoted to notes on the text and to many important items of background information.

Selections

Waley, Arthur, trans. Selections in *Anthology of Japanese Literature: From the Earliest Era to the Mid-Nineteenth Century,* pp. 137–44. Edited by Donald Keene. New York: Grove, 1955. Pbk ed., Evergreen, 1960.

—— *The Pillow-Book of Sei Shōnagon.* London: Allen and Unwin, 1928; Boston and New York: Houghton Mifflin, 1929. New York: Grove, 1953. Pbk ed., Evergreen, 1960.

    About a quarter of the original work, beautifully translated.

SECONDARY READINGS

Morris, Ivan. *The World of the Shining Prince: Court Life in Ancient Japan.* Cambridge: Oxford University Press, 1964;

New York: Knopf, 1964. Pbk ed., Harmondsworth: Penguin, Peregrine, 1969.

Sansom, Sir George B. *History of Japan to 1334*. Stanford University Press, 1958. Pbk ed.

  Chapter 9 is especially helpful.

Tsunoda Ryusaku, Wm. Theodore de Bary, and Donald Keene, eds. *Sources of Japanese Tradition*. New York: Columbia University Press, 1958. Pbk ed., 2 vols, 1964.

  Chapter 9 discusses Sei Shōnagon's characteristic vocabulary.

TOPICS FOR DISCUSSION

1. *The Pillow Book* as a genre.
2. The personality of Sei Shōnagon; why should a work so light in tone be considered one of the masterpieces of Japanese literature?
3. Sei Shōnagon's style and its importance in her work.
4. The Heian court as depicted in *The Pillow Book*; contrast with the world depicted in *The Tale of Genji*. Sei Shōnagon's judgment of her society.
5. The place of religion in Sei Shōnagon's life, and of aesthetics in religion. The dominant aesthetic attitude.
6. The wit of Sei Shōnagon. Would *The Pillow Book* bear out George Meredith's opinion (in *Essays on Comedy*) that wit can exist only in a society in which men and women associate as equals?
7. The function of the lists in *The Pillow Book*.

THE TALE OF GENJI
(GENJI MONOGATARI)
BY MURASAKI SHIKIBU

A long, psychologically insightful and moving novel written about 1010, dealing with Prince Genji and his descendants at the Japanese court of the tenth century. It is usually considered the supreme work of Japanese literature, influencing the visual and dramatic arts as well as later literary texts.

TRANSLATIONS

Complete

Seidensticker, Edward, trans. *The Tale of Genji*. 2 vols. New York: Knopf, 1976. Pbk ed., 1 vol., Borzoi Books, 1981.

An excellent complete translation, with lists of the principal characters, and a brief introduction.

Waley, Arthur, trans. *The Tale of Genji*. 2 vols. Boston: Houghton Mifflin, 1935; London: Allen and Unwin, 1935; 1 vol. eds., Houghton Mifflin, 1939; New York: Random House, Modern Library, 1960.

A superb rendering which captures beautifully the spirit of the original.

Selections

Seidensticker, Edward, trans. *The Tale of Genji*. Abridged. New York: Random House, Viking, 1985. Pbk ed.

Twelve chapters from among the first seventeen of the complete translation, selected to form a coherent narrative section.

Waley, Arthur, trans. "Yugao," in Donald Keene, ed., *Anthology of Japanese Literature: From the Earliest Era to the Mid-*

Nineteenth Century, pp. 106–36. New York: Grove, 1955. Pbk ed., Evergreen, 1960.

SECONDARY READINGS

Bowring, Richard. *Murasaki Shikibu: Her Diary and Poetic Memoirs.* Princeton University Press, 1982.

Complete translation and study of both Murasaki's Diary and the anthology of her autobiographical poems edited by Fujiwara Teika.

Gatten, Aileen. "Weird Ladies: Narrative Strategies in the *Genji monogatari,"* in *Journal of the Association of Teachers of Japanese* 20 (April 1986)1:29–48.

—— "A Wisp of Smoke: Scent and Character in *The Tale of Genji,"* in *Monumenta Nipponica* 32 (Spring 1977)l:35–48.

Kahan, Gail Capitol. "As a Driven Leaf: Love and Psychological Characterization in *The Tale of Genji,"* in Calvin L. French, ed., *Studies in Japanese Culture II,* pp. 157–73. Center for Japanese Studies, Occasional Papers No. 11. Ann Arbor: University of Michigan, 1969.

Keene, Donald. "The Tale of Genji," in Wm. Theodore de Bary, ed., *Approaches to the Oriental Classics,* pp. 186–95. New York: Columbia University Press, 1959.

McCullough, William H. "Japanese Marriage Institutions in the Heian Period," in *Harvard Journal of Asiatic Studies* 17 (1967):103–67.

A valuable study of the various forms of marriage described in *The Tale of Genji* and other works of the period.

McCullough, William H. and Helen Craig McCullough. *A Tale of Flowering Fortunes: Annals of Japanese Aristocratic Life in the Heian Period.* Stanford University Press, 1980.

A translation, with introduction and notes, of the *Eiga monogatari,* useful as an additional view of life contemporary to Murasaki and the world of *The Tale of Genji.*

McLeod, Dan. "Some Approaches to the Tale of Genji," in *Literature East and West* 18 (March 1974)2–4:301–313.

Discusses approaches for nonspecialists teaching *Genji* in a general education context.

Mathy, Francis, S. J. "Mono no aware," in Calvin L. French, ed., *Studies in Japanese Culture II,* pp. 141–53. Center for Japanese Studies, Occasional Papers No. 11. Ann Arbor: University of Michigan, 1969.

Morris, Ivan. *The World of the Shining Prince: Court Life in Ancient Japan.* Oxford University Press, 1964; New York: Knopf, 1964. Pbk ed., Harmondsworth: Penguin, Peregrine, 1969.

An informative and readable study of court life, values, and manners of the period.

Murase Miyeko. *The Iconography of the Tale of Genji.* Tokyo and Palo Alto, CA: Kodansha, 1983; New York: Weatherhill, 1985.

Pekarik, Andrew, ed. *Ukifune: Love in The Tale of Genji.* New York: Columbia University Press, 1982.

Essays by a number of scholars on various aspects of an important chapter in the last third of *Genji*.

Puette, William J. *A Guide to the Tale of Genji by Murasaki Shikibu.* Tokyo and Rutland, VT: Tuttle, 1983.

Rimer, J. Thomas. *Modern Japanese Fiction and Its Traditions: An Introduction,* chapters 5 and 11. Princeton University Press, 1978.

Sansom, Sir. George B. *A History of Japan to 1334.* Stanford University Press, 1958. Pbk ed.

Chapter 8 supplies the historical background of *The Tale of Genji*; Chapter 9, "The Rule of Taste," is an invaluable appreciation of it.

Shirane, Haruo. "The Aesthetics of Power: Politics in *The Tale of Genji,*" in *Harvard Journal of Asiatic Studies* 45 (1985)2:615–47.

—— *The Bridge of Dreams: A Poetics of the Tale of Genji*. Stanford, CA: Stanford University Press, 1987.

Stinchecum, Amanda Mayer. "Who Tells the Tale? 'Ukifune': A Study in Narrative Voice," in *Monumenta Nipponica* 35 (Winter 1980)4:375–403.

—— *Narrative Voice in the Tale of Genji*. Champaign: University of Illinois, 1985.

Tsunoda Ryusaku, Wm. Theodore de Bary, and Donald Keene, eds. *Sources of Japanese Tradition*. New York: Columbia University Press, 1958. Pbk ed., 2 vols, 1964.

Chapter 9 discusses the characteristic vocabulary of Murasaki Shikibu and her contemporaries. Chapter 22 gives Motoori Norinaga's memorable interpretation of *The Tale of Genji*.

Ueda, Makoto. Chapter 2, "Truth and Falsehood in Fiction: Lady Murasaki on the Art of the Novel," in *Literary and Art Theories in Japan,* pp. 25–36. Cleveland, OH: Press of Western Reserve University, 1967; Ann Arbor, MI: Books on Demand UMI, n.d.

Wakita, Haruko. "Marriage and Property in Premodern Japan from the Perspective of Women's History." Translated and Introduced by Suzanne Gay, in *Journal of Japanese Studies* 10 (Winter 1984)l:73–99.

TOPICS FOR DISCUSSION

1. *The Tale of Genji* as the first "novel" written anywhere in the world. How it differs from earlier adventure stories and romances. Its appeal to modern readers.

2. The world portrayed in the work: the court society; how its use of leisure differed from that of other court societies. The cult of beauty; the cult of love. Reasons for indifference to social conditions. The world of the novel compared to Sei Shōnagon's depiction of the Heian court in

The Pillow Book, or compared with *The Dream of the Red Chamber.*

3. The quality of love relationships; loyalty and infidelity.
4. The characters: what makes Prince Genji so appealing to some and so offensive to others? Sensitivity as the touchstone in relations. The individuality of other characters.
5. The purpose of the novel: Murasaki's own views; Motoori Norinaga's interpretation; other theories.
6. Structure of the novel. The shift in tone as it progresses. Differences in the world before and after Genji's death.
7. Religious themes and problems in the novel: the ideal of taking the tonsure; the question of the "religious life"; the tension between world renunciation and world involvement; the concept of death in the novel; the concept of fate.
8. The nature of marriage in the novel, and how it influences relationships and responses.
9. The authorial point of view; the quality of authorial comment.

POETIC DIARIES AND POEM TALES

The poetic diaries by the nobility, especially women of the Heian period, formed a new genre of fictionalized autobiography, influential in literary expression through the modern period.

TRANSLATIONS

Bowring, Richard, trans. *Murasaki Shikibu: Her Diary and Poetic Memoirs.* Princeton University Press, 1982.

A complete translation and study of both Murasaki's Diary and the anthology of her autobiographical poems edited by Fujiwara Teika.

Brazell, Karen, trans. *The Confessions of Lady Nijō.* Pbk eds., New York: Anchor Books, 1973; Stanford University Press, 1973.

A fine translation of a later (Kamakura period) poetic diary in the tradition of Heian court ladies.

Brewster, Jennifer, trans. *The Emperor Horikawa Diary: Sanuki no Suke Nikki by Fujiwara no Nagako.* Honolulu: University of Hawaii Press, 1977.

Cranston, Edwin A., trans. *The Izumi Shikibu Diary: A Romance of the Heian Court.* Cambridge: Harvard University Press, 1969.

A good translation with an extensive introduction and notes.

Harries, Phillip Tudor, trans. *The Poetic Memoirs of Lady Daibu.* Stanford University Press, 1980.

Translation and study of the autobiographical poetry collection composed by Kenreimon-in Ukyō no Daibu and covering a fifty-year period of her life during the opening years of the Kamakura period.

Harris, H. Jay, trans. *Tales of Ise.* Tokyo: Tuttle, 1972. Pbk ed.

Complete translation with illustrations from the first printed edition of 1608.

Keene, Donald, ed. *Anthology of Japanese Literature: From the Earliest Era to the Mid-Nineteenth Century*. New York: Grove, 1955. Pbk ed., Evergreen, 1960.

Contains selections from the *Tosa Diary,* Murasaki Shikibu's diary, and *The Sarashina Diary*.

McCullough, Helen Craig, trans. *Tales of Ise: Lyrical Episodes from 10th-Century Japan*. Stanford University Press, 1968.

A translation with an excellent introduction.

—— *Kokin Wakashū: The First Imperial Anthology of Japanese Poetry*. Stanford University Press, 1985.

Contains a well-annotated, complete translation of the *Tosa nikki*.

Miner, Earl, ed. and trans. *Japanese Poetic Diaries*. Berkeley and Los Angeles: University of California Press, 1969. Pbk ed., 1976.

Includes complete translations of the *Tosa Diary* and the *Izumi Shikibu Diary*, as well as later diaries in the tradition, plus an extensive introduction.

Morris, Ivan, trans. *As I Crossed the Bridge of Dreams*. New York: Dial Press, 1971.

A beautiful translation, with introduction, of *Sarashina nikki*.

Seidensticker, Edward, trans. *The Gossamer Years*. Tokyo and Rutland, VT: Tuttle, 1964. Pbk ed., 1974.

A translation of *Kagerō nikki*.

Tahara, Mildred, trans. *Tales of Yamato*. Honolulu: University of Hawaii Press, 1980.

Whitehouse, Wilfred and Eizo Yanagisawa, trans. *Lady Nijō's Own Story: The Candid Diary of a 13th-Century Japanese Imperial Concubine*. Tokyo and Rutland, VT: Tuttle, 1974. Pbk ed.

Has good supportive materials.

SECONDARY READINGS

Most of the above translations contain good, informative introductory material.

Keene, Donald. "Feminine Sensibility in the Heian Era," in *Landscapes and Portraits: Appreciations of Japanese Culture*, pp. 26–39. Tokyo and Palo Alto, CA: Kodansha International, 1971. Reprinted as *Some Japanese Portraits*. Tokyo and New York: Kodansha International, 1978. Pbk ed.

McCullough, William. "Japanese Marriage Institutions in the Heian Period," in *Harvard Journal of Asiatic Studies* 27 (1967):103–167.

Morris, Ivan. *The World of the Shining Prince: Court Life in Ancient Japan.* Oxford University Press, 1964; New York: Knopf, 1964. Pbk ed., Harmondsworth: Penguin, Peregrine, 1969.

Vos, Frits. *A Study of the Ise-monogatari.* 2 vols. The Hague: Mouton, 1957.

Wakita, Haruko. "Marriage and Property in Premodern Japan from the Perspective of Women's History." Translated and Introduced by Suzanne Gay. *Journal of Japanese Studies* 10 (Winter 1984)l:73–99.

TOPICS FOR DISCUSSION

1. The "poem tale" as a literary genre. Is the emphasis greater on the poetry or on the prose in *Tales of Ise*? How do the two relate?
2. The "poetic diary" as an important literary genre. What is the function of the poetry in these memoirs?
3. The line between fiction and fact in the diaries; the use of fiction to arrive at truth in expression.
4. The transition from the diary to the novel. Differences be-

tween a private diary and a public diary. The nature of autobiographical expression.
5. The social context of the diaries; the position of women in the Heian court. Differences in diaries by men and by women.
6. The religious underpinnings of the diaries.

TEXTS OF JAPANESE BUDDHISM

The Japanese first received advanced continental civilization through Korean Buddhist monks who knew written Chinese. Since Japanese knowledge of Buddhism was conveyed through Chinese sources, China became for Japan the "Land of the Buddha." All of the principal sects of Chinese Buddhism were transplanted in Japan; the scriptures were read in Chinese and most commentaries were composed in that language. Eventually, certain Japanese monks did choose to write important works in their native language. While Kūkai, in the Heian period, wrote in literary Chinese, the Buddhist masters of the Kamakura and later periods wrote in both Chinese and Japanese.

WRITINGS OF KŪKAI
(KŌBŌ DAISHI, 774–835)

Kūkai, greatest of the Heian period Buddhist teachers, studied esoteric Buddhism and Sanskrit in the T'ang capital Ch'ang-an and brought back to Japan a type of Buddhism that was to have an enormous impact on Heian culture.

TRANSLATIONS

de Bary, Wm. Theodore et al. *The Buddhist Tradition in India, China, and Japan.* New York: Modern Library, 1969; pbk ed., New York: Random House, Vintage, 1972.

Contains a section on Kūkai.

Hakeda, Yoshito S. *Kūkai: Major Works, translated with an Account of His Life and a Study of His Thought.* Records of Civilization, Sources, Studies, and Translations of the Oriental Classics. New York: Columbia University Press, 1972. Pbk ed.

Includes a biography of Kūkai, a study of his thought, and translations of his most important works.

SECONDARY READINGS

Kitagawa, Joseph. "Kūkai as Master and Savior," in Frank Reynolds and Donald Capps, eds., *The Biographical Process: Studies in the History and Psychology of Religion*, pp. 319–341. Religions and Reason: Method and Theory in the Study and Interpretation of Religion, no. 11. Paris: Mouton, 1976.

Traces the transformation of Kūkai the historical figure into a semidivine savior.

Kiyota Minoru. *Shingon Buddhism: Theory and Practice.* Los Angeles: Buddhist Books International, 1978.

Chapter 1 provides useful background information on the Indian foundations of Kūkai's esoteric Buddhism.

Matsunaga Daigan and Alicia Matsunaga. *The Mass Movement.* Vol. 2 of *Foundation of Japanese Buddhism.* Los Angeles: Buddhist Books International, 1976.

See chapter 48, "Shingonshū, Esoteric Buddhism," for a brief discussion of Kūkai's life and teachings.

Tajima Ryōjun. *Les Deux Grand Maṇḍalas et la Doctrine de l'Esoterisme Shingon.* Bulletin de la Maison Franco-Japonaise nouvelle série, no. 6. Tokyo: Maison Franco-Japonaise, 1959; Paris: Presses Universitaires de France, 1959.

—— *Étude sur le Mahāvairocana-sūtra (Dainichikyō), avec la traduction commentée du premier chapitre.* Paris: Maisonneuve, 1936.

Wayman, Alex. *The Buddhist Tantras.* New York: Weiser, 1973.

Read the first section, "Introductions."

See also *Supplementary Readings on Indian Buddhism.*

TOPICS FOR DISCUSSION

1. The aesthetic element in Kūkai's teachings: what role does it have in teaching? in worship?
2. Kūkai's attitude toward Confucianism, Taoism, and the exoteric Buddhist teachings.
3. How did Kūkai view the historical Buddha?
4. Usually, the ten stages to enlightenment were thought to take three *kalpas* (eons). In what way is Kūkai's esoteric Buddhism a "sudden" approach?
5. The literary form of the *Indications of the Goals of the Three Teachings;* how is it related to the content?

WRITINGS OF BUDDHIST MASTERS OF THE KAMAKURA PERIOD

In the twelfth and thirteenth centuries, five Buddhist leaders founded sects that served to spread the religion throughout Japanese society. These figures were Hōnen of the Pure Land sect, Shinran of the True Pure Land, Nichiren of the sect that bears his name, and the Zen masters Eisai and Dōgen.

TRANSLATIONS

Andres, Allen A. *The Teachings Essential for Rebirth: A Study of Genshin's Ōjōyōshū.* A Monumenta Nipponica monograph. Tokyo: Sophia University Press, 1973.

Bandō Shōjun and Harold Stewart. "Tannishō: Passages Deploring Deviations of Faith," in *The Eastern Buddhist* n.s., 13 (Spring 1980) 1:57–78.

The essential teachings of Shinran as remembered by a devoted disciple.

Cook, Francis. *How to Raise an Ox: Zen Practice as Taught in Zen Master Dōgen's Shōbōgenzō.* Los Angeles: Center Publications, 1979.

Gives special attention to the relationship between philosophy and practice in Dōgen's thought.

de Bary, Wm. Theodore et al. *The Buddhist Tradition in India, China, and Japan.* New York: Modern Library, 1969; pbk ed., New York: Random House, Vintage, 1972.

Selections, with Introductory remarks, from the writings of the central Kamakura Buddhist figures.

Gosho Translation Committee. *The Major Writings of Nichiren Daishōnin.* 3 vols. Tokyo: Nichiren Shōshū International Center, 1979–85.

Matsunaga Reihō. *A Primer of Sōtō Zen*. Honolulu: East-West Center Press, 1971.

A readable translation of Dōgen's *Shobōgenzō zuimonki*.

Yokoi Yūhō. *Zen Master Dōgen: An Introduction with Selected Writings*. New York and Tokyo: Weatherhill, 1976.

A good introduction to Dōgen's Zen.

SECONDARY READINGS

Anesaki Masaharu. *Nichiren, the Buddhist Prophet*. Cambridge: Harvard University Press, 1916. Reprint ed., Gloucester, MA: Peter Smith, 1966.

An intellectual biography of one of the most fascinating personalities in Japanese history.

Bloom, Alfred. *Shinran's Gospel of Pure Grace*. Tucson: University of Arizona Press, 1965.

Provides a brief discussion of the background of Pure Land Buddhism in addition to an analysis of Shinran's thought.

Dumoulin, Heinrich. *Zen Enlightenment: Origins and Meanings*. New York and Tokyo: Weatherhill, 1979.

Chapters 9 and 10 treat Dōgen's life and the distinctive features of his teachings.

Matsunaga Daigan and Alicia Matsunaga. *Foundation of Japanese Buddhism*. Vol. 2. Los Angeles: Buddhist Books International, 1976.

Contains lengthy sections on each of the Kamakura sects.

Weinstein, Stanley. "The Concept of Reformation in Japanese Buddhism," in *Studies in Japanese Culture II*. Edited by Saburō Ōta. Tokyo: P.E.N. Club, 1973.

TOPICS FOR DISCUSSION

1. The concept of the Latter-Day Dharma (*mappō*).
2. The concepts of "self-power" (*jiriki*) and "other-power" (*ta-*

riki) in Pure Land Buddhism; the Pure Land argument in favor of salvation by grace; and the differences between Hō-nen's and Shinran's teachings.

3. Nichiren's search for "true" Buddhism, his special reverence for the *Lotus Sutra,* and his sense of mission.
4. Esoteric Buddhist elements in Nichiren Buddhism and in Eisai's Zen.
5. Dōgen's stress upon the importance of constant effort; the identity of practice and enlightenment in his thought.
6. The common ground of Kamakura Buddhism; the distinctive tendencies of the various sects.

WRITINGS OF THE ZEN MASTER HAKUIN (1686–1769)

Hakuin, greatest of the Tokugawa period Zen Masters, restored Rinzai Zen to the purity of its T'ang and Sung traditions.

TRANSLATIONS

de Bary, Wm. Theodore et al. *The Buddhist Tradition in India, China, and Japan.* New York: Modern Library, 1969. Pbk ed., New York: Random House, Vintage, 1972.

Contains excerpts from Hakuin's *Orategama.*

Wadell, Norman, trans. "Wild Ivy (*Itsumadegusa*): The Spiritual Autobiography of Hakuin Ekaku," in *The Eastern Buddhist,* n.s. Part 1, 15 (Autumn 1982)2:71–109; part 2, 16 (Spring 1983)1:107–39.

Yampolsky, Philip B., trans. *The Zen Master Hakuin: Selected Writings.* Records of Civilizations, Studies and Sources, no. 86. New York: Columbia University Press, 1971. Pbk ed.

Contains a translation of the *Orategama* in its entirety along with two of Hakuin's other writings. The introduction provides a succinct historical survey of the various Zen transmissions to Japan.

SECONDARY READINGS

Dumoulin, Heinrich. *A History of Zen Buddhism.* New York: McGraw-Hill, 1965. Pbk ed., Boston: Beacon Press, 1969.

Contains a useful chapter on Hakuin.

Miura Isshū and Ruth Fuller Sasaki. *Zen Dust.* New York: Harcourt, Brace and World, 1968.

This is an expanded version of *The Zen Kōan* and contains

a wealth of information on Zen and Chinese Buddhism in general.

—— *The Zen Kōan.* New York: Harcourt, Brace and World, 1965.

Deals with the history of the *kōan* in Rinzai Zen and *kōan* study as it is now carried on in Japan.

Shibata Masumi. *Les Maitres du Zen au Japan.* Paris: Maisonneuve and Larose, 1969.

In addition to Hakuin, deals with Yōsai, Dōgen, Musō, Ikkyū, Takuan, Suzuki Shōsan, and Bankei.

TOPICS FOR DISCUSSION

1. Meditation in the midst of activity and meditation in quietude.
2. The two levels of truth (the absolute truth and the worldly truth) in Hakuin's sermons.
3. Alchemy and Taoism in Hakuin's letters.
4. *Kōan* study versus "dead sitting."
5. Similarities between meditation on "*mu*" (emptiness) and the Mindfulness meditation of the *Mahāsatipaṭṭhana sutta* (see Indian section); Hakuin's praise of Hīnayāna adepts.

SUPPLEMENTARY READINGS ON
JAPANESE BUDDHISM

Readers may wish to consult other texts, surveys, and histories of Japanese Buddhism. Among these the following should prove useful.

Anesaki, Masaharu. *History of Japanese Religion*. London: Kegan Paul, Trench, Trubner, 1930. Reprint, Rutland, VT and Tokyo: Charles E. Tuttle, 1963.

   A standard although somewhat dated work by an outstanding Japanese scholar of religion.

Collcutt, Martin. *Five Mountains: The Rinzai Zen Monastic Institution in Medieval Japan*. Cambridge: Harvard University Press, 1981.

   Describes the institutional development and organization of Rinzai Zen in the twelfth through fifteenth centuries.

de Bary, Wm. Theodore et al. *The Buddhist Tradition in India, China, and Japan*. New York: Modern Library, 1969. Pbk ed., New York: Random House, Vintage, 1972.

   Contains a number of important selections from Japanese Buddhist literature.

Earhart, H. Byron. *Japanese Religion: Unity and Diversity*. Belmont, CA: Dickenson, 1969; 3d rev. ed., 1982. Pbk ed.

   Aims at highlighting themes within Japanese religious history that cut across Shinto, Buddhist, Confucian, and folk traditions.

Eliot, Sir Charles. *Japanese Buddhism*. London: E. Arnold, 1935. Reprint, London: Routledge and Kegan Paul, 1959; New York: Barnes and Noble, 1959.

   A somewhat outdated study, covering India and China as well as Japan.

Fujiwara Ryōsetsu. *The Tanni Shō*. Kyoto: Ryukoku Translation Center (Ryukoku University), 1962.

The *Tanni Shō* is one of the most beautiful expressions of Amidist devotional literature. Other works of Shinran (including his *Kyō Gyō Shin Shō, Jōdo Wasan,* and *Shōshin Ge*) have been published in this series.

Groner, Paul. *Saichō: The Establishment of the Japanese Tendai School.* Berkeley Buddhist Studies Series. Berkeley: Institute of Buddhist Studies, 1984.

A fine study of the life and thought of the founder of Japanese Tendai Buddhism.

Haskel, Peter, trans. *Bankei Zen: Translations from the Record of Bankei.* New York: Grove, 1984. Pbk ed.

Introductory material on Bankei's life and times and good translations.

Hori, Ichiro. *Folk Religion in Japan: Continuity and Change.* Edited and translated by Joseph M. Kitagawa and Alan L. Miller. University of Chicago Press, 1968.

Insightful essays by a distinguished authority.

Hurvitz, Leon, trans. *Scripture of the Lotus Blossom of the Fine Dharma: Translated from the Chinese of Kumārajīva.* New York: Columbia University Press, 1976. Pbk ed.

A text whose popularity has transcended sectarian boundaries.

Kamstra, J. H. *Encounter or Sycretism.* Leiden: Brill, 1967.

A detailed study of the initial period of Buddhism in Japan. Though Kamstra's arguments are not universally accepted, they are interesting and useful.

Matsunaga Daigan and Alicia Matsunaga. *Foundation of Japanese Buddhism.* 2 vols. Vol. 1, *The Aristocratic Age,* 1974; vol. 2, *The Mass Movement,* 1976. Los Angeles: Buddhist Books International, 1974. Pbk eds.

—— *The Buddhist Concept of Hell.* New York: Philosophical Library, 1972.

McMullin, Neil. *Buddhism and the State in Sixteenth Century Japan.* Princeton University Press, 1984.

Morris, Ivan. "Religion," in *The World of the Shining Prince,* pp.

103–155. Oxford University Press, 1964; Harmondsworth: Penguin, Peregrine, 1969.

Reischauer, Edwin O. *Ennin's Travels in T'ang China*. New York: Ronald Press, 1955.

A fascinating mosaic of ninth-century China drawn from the diary of an itinerant Japanese monk. Provides insight into Japanese attitudes toward China as the homeland of Buddhism. Companion volume to Reischauer's translation of Ennin's Diary.

Saunders, E. Dale. *Buddhism in Japan, with an Outline of Its Origins in India*. Philadelphia: University of Pennsylvania Press, 1964; reprint, 1977.

Takakusu Junjiro. *The Essentials of Buddhist Philosophy*. Honolulu: University of Hawaii Press, 1947; 3d ed., 1956.

Tanabe, Willa J. *Paintings of the Lotus Sutra*. Tokyo and New York: Weatherhill, 1987.

Waddell, Norman, trans. *The Unborn: The Life and Teaching of Zen Master Bankei, 1622–1693*. San Francisco: North Point Press, 1984. Pbk ed.

AN ACCOUNT OF MY HUT (HŌJŌKI)
BY KAMO NO CHŌMEI (1153–1236)

A short account of the choice of a reclusive life, with meditations on the vicissitudes of worldly life, the beauties of nature, and the satisfactions of simplicity, by an important literary figure; the opening paragraph is particularly well known and loved.

TRANSLATIONS

Keene, Donald, ed. *Anthology of Japanese Literature: From the Earliest Era to the Mid-Nineteenth Century,* pp. 197–212. New York: Grove, 1955. Pbk ed., Evergreen, 1960.

Includes a complete translation of *An Account of My Hut (Hōjōki),* as well as selections from other medieval prose works.

Sadler, A. L., trans. *The Ten Foot Square Hut and Tales of the Heike.* Westport, CT: Greenwood, 1970. Pbk ed., Tokyo and Rutland, VT: C. E. Tuttle, 1971.

SECONDARY READINGS

Kato, Hilda. "The Mumyōshō of Kamo no Chōmei and Its Significance in Japanese Literature," in *Monumenta Nipponica* 23 (1968)3–4:321–430.

Translation of an important collection of short essays on the art of Japanese poetry by the author of the *Hōjōki.*

Sansom, Sir George B. *A History of Japan to 1334.* Stanford University Press, 1958. Pbk ed.

Chapter 14, "The Gempei War," describes the military and political events that formed the background for much of the literature of the medieval period.

Tsunoda Ryusaku, Wm. Theodore de Bary, and Donald Keene,

eds. *Sources of Japanese Tradition*. New York: Columbia University Press, 1958. Pbk ed., 2 vols., 1964.

Chapter 10, "Amida and the Pure Land," deals with the variety of Buddhism most characteristic of this period.

Ury, Marian. "Recluses and Eccentric Monks: Tales of the *Hosshinshū* by Kamo no Chōmei," in *Monumenta Nipponica* 27 (1972)2:149–73.

Chōmei's venture into the genre of *setsuwa* literature, religious accounts designed to enlighten and convert the reader.

Wilson, William R. *Hōgen monogatari: Tale of the Disorder in Hōgen*. Monumenta Nipponica Monograph. Tokyo: Sophia University Press, 1971.

TOPICS FOR DISCUSSION

1. *An Account of My Hut* as confessional or apologetic literature; as romantic idyll or contemplative reflection.
2. The tension between Buddhist world renunciation, world acceptance, and Japanese love of nature.
3. Discuss the change in tone between the Heian masterpieces and those of the Kamakura period.
4. Kamo no Chōmei's view of life in the capital and life in the midst of nature. His omission of the political upheavals of his time from the enumeration of disasters in *An Account of My Hut*, and its significance for his world view.
5. The influence of Esoteric Buddhism, Amida Buddhism, and Shintō in *An Account of My Hut*. What does it tell us about the Japanese experience of Buddhism?
6. Compare the form of *An Account of My Hut* with autobiographical diaries; what are the similarities? the differences?

ESSAYS IN IDLENESS
(TSUREZUREGUSA)
BY YOSHIDA KENKŌ (1283–1350)

Observations in journal form on life, nature, and art, with especially important articulations of Japanese aesthetic values, written about 1330 by a worldly priest and classic literary stylist.

TRANSLATIONS

Keene, Donald, trans. *Essays in Idleness: The Tsurezuregusa of Kenkō*. New York: Columbia University Press, 1967. Pbk ed.
   An excellent complete translation, with an introduction and notes.
Sansom, Sir George B., trans. "Essays in Idleness," in Donald Keene, ed., *Anthology of Japanese Literature: From the Earliest Era to the Mid-Nineteenth Century*, pp. 231–41. New York: Grove, 1955. Pbk ed., Evergreen, 1960.

SECONDARY READINGS

Sansom, Sir George B. *Japan: A Short Cultural History*. Stanford University Press, 1952. Pbk ed.
   Chapter 18 treats Kenkō's time.
Tsunoda Ryusaku, Wm. Theodore de Bary, and Donald Keene, eds. *Sources of Japanese Tradition*. New York: Columbia University Press, 1958. Pbk ed., 2 vols, 1964.
   Chapter 14 discusses some of the aesthetic concepts of the *Essays in Idleness*.

TOPICS FOR DISCUSSION

1. Kenkō as an arbiter of Japanese taste: his views on houses, interior decoration, gardens, tradition in art.

2. Kenkō as an arbiter of Japanese manners: the behavior of the gentleman and of the boor.
3. Aesthetic theories: beginnings and ends; the importance of the perishability of beauty. How are these aesthetic ideals related to religious roots?
4. The conflict between Kenkō's insistence on strict standards of taste—aesthetic and social—and Buddhist views on impermanence and indeterminism.
5. Kenkō's personality and concerns: his friends; the nature of his daily life; are his attitudes this-worldly or other-worldly? What evidence is there of his religious commitment?
6. What resemblances and points of difference are there between *The Pillow Book* and *Essays in Idleness?*
7. Compare the concerns of the *Essays in Idleness* with those of *An Account of My Hut*; how are they similar or different in theme? in style?
8. Why should this book have become one of the most popular of all Japanese literary works?

THE TALE OF THE HEIKE
(HEIKE MONOGATARI)

Great medieval military tales grew from both written and oral traditions, with The Tale of the Heike *the most representative and influential. Its stories and interpretations of historical characters significantly influence later literature and drama.*

TRANSLATIONS

Complete

Kitagawa Hiroshi and Paul Tsuchida, trans. *The Tale of the Heike: "Heike Monogatari."* University of Tokyo Press, 1975. Pbk ed., 2 vols, 1977.

McCullough, Helen Craig, trans. *The Tale of the Heike.* Stanford University Press, 1988.

Selections

Keene, Donald, ed. *Anthology of Japanese Literature: From the Earliest Era to the Mid-Nineteenth Century.* New York: Grove, 1955. Pbk ed., Evergreen, 1960.

Includes selected episodes from *The Tale of the Heike* and other medieval prose works.

Sadler, A. L. *The Ten Foot Square Hut and Tales of the Heike.* Westport, CT: Greenwood, 1970. Pbk ed., Tokyo and Rutland, VT: Tuttle, 1971.

SECONDARY READINGS

Butler, Kenneth Dean. "The *Heike monogatari* and the Japanese Warrior Ethic," in *Harvard Journal of Asiatic Studies* 29 (1969):93–108.

—— "The Textual Evolution of the Heike Monogatari," in *Harvard Journal of Asiatic Studies* 26 (1966):5–51.

Ruch, Barbara. "Medieval Jongleurs and the Making of a National Literature," in John W. Hall and Toyoda Takeshi, *Japan in the Muromachi Age*, pp. 279–309. Berkeley and Los Angeles: University of California Press, 1977.

A pioneering study of the oral transmission of *Heike monogatari* and other works of medieval literature.

—— "The Other Side of History: In Search of the Common Culture of Medieval Japan," in *Cambridge History of Japan*, vol. 3, John W. Hall, Marius Jansen, Madoka Kanai, and David Twitchett, general eds. New York: Cambridge University Press, forthcoming, 1989.

A thought-provoking study of medieval culture, of the place of women in it, and of the author of the *Heike*.

Sansom, Sir George B. *A History of Japan to 1334*. Stanford University Press, 1958. Pbk ed.

Chapter 14, "The Gempei War," describes the military and political events that formed the background for much of the literature of the period.

Tsunoda Ryusaku, Wm. Theodore de Bary, and Donald Keene, eds. *Sources of Japanese Tradition*. New York: Columbia University Press, 1958. Pbk ed., 2 vols., 1964.

Chapter 10, "Amida and the Pure Land," deals with the variety of Buddhism most characteristic of this period.

TOPICS FOR DISCUSSION

1. The attitude toward warfare displayed in the *Heike monogatari* and other military tales. Are these works celebrations of victories or commemorations of defeats, or neither? Is the tone epic?

2. Structure of the *Heike monogatari*: can it be considered a novel? The claims of history versus the claims of literature.

Why should the *Heike monogatari* have provided the materials for innumerable works of the theater?

3. Historical fiction and fictionalized history: how does the *Heike* influence views of the past?

4. How is the form of the *Heike monogatari* influenced by its tradition of oral performance? What is the role of the writer of the *Heike* in its final form?

5. What is the role of women in the *Heike*? Why does it end with a woman's memories?

6. The religious underpinnings of the tale: what Buddhist themes are most prominent? How do religious attitudes differ from those in *The Tale of Genji*?

THE NŌ PLAYS

The classic drama of Japan, mixing poetry and prose, music, choreography, and masks, written chiefly in the fourteenth and fifteenth centuries and now much admired in the West as well.

TRANSLATIONS

Keene, Donald, ed. *Twenty Plays of the Nō Theatre.* New York: Columbia University Press, 1970. Pbk ed.

Reliable, literate translations of major plays, most of which were previously untranslated, with introductions, stage directions, and figures in the text, and notes to help clarify the presentation.

Nippon Gakujutsu Shinkōkai, ed. *Japanese Noh Drama.* Vols. 1 and 2. Tokyo: Nippon Gakujutsu Shinkōkai, 1955, 1959. Vol. 3, *The Noh Drama.* Tokyo and Rutland, VT: Tuttle, 1960.

Translations of thirty plays with valuable introductions and figures in the text illustrating the movements of the actors. The language of the translations is somewhat old-fashioned.

Peri, Noël, trans. *Le Nō.* Tokyo: Maison Franco-Japonaise, 1944.

Ten Nō plays and eleven *kyōgen* with valuable introductory material.

Ueda Makoto, trans. *The Old Pine Tree and Other Noh Plays.* Lincoln: University of Nebraska Press, 1962.

A program of five plays well translated with a good introduction.

Waley, Arthur, trans. *The Nō Plays of Japan.* London: Allen and Unwin, 1921; New York: Knopf, 1922. Pbk ed., New York: Grove, Evergreen, 1957.

Graceful renderings of nineteen plays with summaries of others.

SECONDARY READINGS

Hare, Thomas Blennan. *Zeami's Style: The Noh Plays of Zeami Motokiyo*. Stanford University Press, 1986.

A full-length study of Zeami as playwright and stylist with complete translations and analysis of three of Zeami's most celebrated plays, *Takasago, Izutsu,* and *Tadamori*.

Keene, Donald. *Japanese Literature: An Introduction for Western Readers*. London: John Murray, 1953. Pbk ed., New York: Grove, Evergreen, 1955.

—— *Nō: The Classical Theatre of Japan*. Tokyo and Palo Alto, CA: Kodansha, 1966; rev. pbk ed., 1973.

A discussion of the background of Nō theater, the history and the presentation, illustrated with many photographs.

Komparu, Kunio. *The Noh Theater: Principles and Perspectives*. Tokyo: Weatherhill/Tankosha, 1983.

O'Neill, Patrick G. *Early Nō Drama: Its Background, Character and Development, 1300–1450*. London: Lund Humphries, 1959.

A scholarly examination of the background, character, and development of the Nō.

Raz, Jacob. *Audiences and Actors: A Study of Their Interaction in the Japanese Traditional Theatre*. Leiden: Brill, 1983.

Rimer, J. Thomas and Yamazaki Masakazu, trans. *On the Art of the Nō Drama: Major Treatises of Zeami*. Princeton University Press, 1984. Pbk ed.

Translations of nine of Zeami's major treatises on the art of Nō theater.

Shidehara Michitarō and Wilfred Whitehouse, trans. "Seami's Sixteen Treatises," in *Monumenta Nipponica* 4 (1941)2:204–39; 5 (1942)2:180–214.

Sieffert, René. *La tradition secrète du Nō*. Paris: Gallimard, 1960.

An excellent translation of works of criticism by Zeami

(Seami), together with the translation of a typical Nō program of plays.

Tsunoda Ryusaku, Wm. Theodore de Bary, and Donald Keene, eds. *Sources of Japanese Tradition*. New York: Columbia University Press, 1958. Pbk ed., 2 vols, 1964.

Chapter 14 includes translations of representative works of criticism by Zeami.

Ueda Makoto. *Zeami, Bashō, Yeats, Pound: A Study in Japanese and English Poetics*. The Hague: Mouton, 1965.

The chapter on Zeami has the subtitle: "Imitation, *Yūgen*, and the Sublime."

—— *Literary and Art Theories in Japan*. Cleveland, OH: Press of Western Reserve University, 1967; Ann Arbor, MI: Books on Demand UMI, n.d.

The chapter on Zeami is a revised version of the above.

Zeami. *Kadensho*. Translated by Sakurai Chūichi, and others. Kyoto: Foundation of Sumiya-Shinobe Scholarship, 1968.

TOPICS FOR DISCUSSION

1. The structure and the language of the plays: what is the function of a conventional framework? What is the point of the many poetic allusions?
2. What creates tension in the plays? How is the tension, or conflict, resolved?
3. How can plays that give little or no attention to character development, conflict, or even plot, manage nevertheless to move audiences? What of the plays is lost when we read the text instead of seeing them?
4. How do stage conventions of Nō restrict the expression of dramatic ideas? How do they make possible types of expression not generally found in other theaters? If you can hear or see a tape of the play, discuss the relation between movement and text; between music and text.
5. Is the form of the Nō as characteristically Japanese as other

art and literary forms (e.g., *The Pillow Book*, *Essays in Idleness*, haiku, etc.)? Compare with other dramatic forms in India, China, and the West.

6. The functions of ghosts in the Nō plays; the connection between spirits and the absence of character development.

THE FICTION OF IHARA SAIKAKU
(1642–1693)

Fiction, chiefly about love and money in the new culture of townspeople in seventeenth-century Japan, by the greatest prose writer of the late premodern period.

TRANSLATIONS

de Bary, Wm. Theodore, trans. *Five Women Who Loved Love.* Tokyo and Rutland, VT: Tuttle, 1956. Pbk ed.
  A complete translation into readable English of Saikaku's masterpiece, *Kōshoku gonin onna.*
Keene, Donald, ed. *Anthology of Japanese Literature: From the Earliest Era to the Mid-Nineteenth Century,* pp. 335–62. New York: Grove, 1955. Pbk ed., Evergreen, 1960.
Leutner, Robert, trans. "Saikaku's Parting Gift: Translations from *Saikaku Okimiyage,*" in *Monumenta Nipponica* 30 (Winter 1975) 4:357–91.
Morris, Ivan, trans. *The Life of an Amorous Woman and Other Writings.* New York: New Directions, 1963. Pbk ed., 1969.
  Selections from Saikaku's principal works, translated fluidly into an idiom reminiscent of Saikaku's contemporary, Defoe.
Nosco, Peter, trans. *Some Final Words of Advice.* Tokyo and Rutland, VT: Tuttle, 1980.
  A translation of a posthumously published work of Saikaku's later period, somewhat darker in tone than earlier works.
Sargent, G. W., trans. *The Japanese Family Storehouse (Nihon Eitagura); or, The Millionaires' Gospel Modernised.* London: Cambridge University Press, 1959.

A complete translation of a collection of tales about merchants who made and lost fortunes.

Takatsuka Masanori and David C. Stubbs, trans. *This Scheming World*. Tokyo and Rutland, VT: Tuttle, 1965.

A good translation of one of Saikaku's last works, a series of short tales about the desperate stratagems men employ in order to pay their annual debts at New Year.

SECONDARY READINGS

Most of the above volumes of translations are equipped with excellent introductions and other explanatory material that afford the best guide to Saikaku and his age.

Hibbett, Howard. *The Floating World in Japanese Fiction*. London: Oxford University Press, 1959. Pbk ed., Tokyo and Rutland, VT: Tuttle, 1975.

Has a lengthy description and analysis of the *ukiyo-zōshi* genre, and includes selections from the work of Ejima Kiseki and Saikaku's *Kōshoku ichidai onna* (The life of an amorous woman).

Keene, Donald. *World Within Walls: Japanese Literature of the Pre-Modern Era, 1600–1867*. New York: Holt, Rhinehart and Winston, 1976. Pbk ed., New York: Grove, Evergreen, 1978.

Chapters 7, "Kana-zōshi," and 8 "Saikaku," discuss the social and literary context of the period and the works of Saikaku in detail.

Lane, Richard. "The Beginnings of the Modern Japanese Novel: *Kana-zōshi*, 1600–1682," in *Harvard Journal of Asiatic Studies* 20 (December 1957)3 and 4:644–701.

TOPICS FOR DISCUSSION

1. The emergence of a major popular commercial literature in Japan; compare and contrast with the works read previously as to continuity of themes and canons of taste.
2. Saikaku as a master stylist: his lightness of touch, wit, brevity, and poetic expression.
3. Saikaku's attitude toward his characters—a mixture of detachment and affection.
4. Saikaku's attitude toward love. Contrast with *The Tale of Genji*.
5. Saikaku's attitudes toward money and commercialism.
6. Saikaku's humor; its relation to his characterizations.
7. Saikaku's morality, or lack of it; how does it relate to prevailing moral standards of his age?

THE POETRY AND PROSE OF MATSUO BASHŌ (1644–1694)

New genres of poetry and prose by the master of the haiku, and one of the greatest of all Japanese poets.

TRANSLATIONS

Corman, Cid and Kamaike Susume, trans. *Back Roads to Far Towns: Bashō's Oku-no-Hosomichi.* New York: Grossman, 1968; pbk ed., Fredonia, NY: White Pine Press, 1986.

A translation into a jagged, modern English that attempts to suggest the elliptical qualities of the original text.

Henderson, Harold G. *An Introduction to Haiku: An Anthology of Poems and Poets from Bashō to Shiki.* New York: Doubleday, Anchor, 1958. Pbk ed.

Includes graceful translations of haiku by Bashō and his school.

Keene, Donald, ed. *Anthology of Japanese Literature: From the Earliest Era to the Mid-Nineteenth Century.* New York: Grove, 1955. Pbk ed., Evergreen, 1960.

Contains excerpts from *The Narrow Road of Oku* and other writings by Bashō and his disciples.

Miner, Earl, ed. and trans. *Japanese Poetic Diaries.* Berkeley and Los Angeles: University of California Press, 1969. Pbk ed., 1976.

Includes a complete translation of *Narrow Road Through the Provinces (Oku no hosomichi).*

Yuasa Nobuyuki, trans. *The Narrow Road to the Deep North and Other Travel Sketches.* Baltimore: Penguin, 1966. Pbk ed.

Complete translations of Bashō's five travel accounts, with an introduction and maps.

SECONDARY READINGS

Blyth, R. H. *Haiku*. 4 vols. Tokyo: Kamakura Bunko, 1949–52.

Includes many haiku by Bashō with lengthy explanations.

Keene, Donald. "Bashō's Journey to Sarashina," in *Landscapes and Portraits: Appreciations of Japanese Culture*, pp. 94–108. Tokyo and New York: Kodansha International, 1971.

A translation of one of Bashō's travel accounts, with a description of its importance.

—— "Bashō's Journey of 1684," in *Landscapes and Portraits* (see above), pp. 109–30.

Translation of Bashō's first travel account.

—— *World Within Walls: Japanese Literature of the Pre-Modern Era, 1600–1867*. New York: Holt, Rinehart and Winston, 1976. Pbk ed., New York: Grove, Evergreen, 1978.

Chapters 1 through 3 trace the development of early *haikai* poetry, but see especially chapters 4, "The Transition to Bashō," and 5, "Matsuo Bashō (1644–1694)."

McKinnon, Richard N. "Tanka and Haiku: Some Aspects of Classical Japanese Poetry," in H. Frenz and G. L. Anderson, eds., *Indiana University Conference on Oriental-Western Literary Relations*, pp. 67–84. Chapel Hill: University of North Carolina Press, 1955.

Nippon Gakujutsu Shinkōkai, ed and trans. *Haikai and Haiku*. Tokyo: Nippon Gakujutsu Shinkōkai, 1958.

Tsunoda Ryusaku, Wm. Theodore de Bary, and Donald Keene, eds. *Sources of Japanese Tradition*. New York: Columbia University Press, 1958. Pbk ed., 2 vols, 1964.

Chapter 20, "The Haiku and the Democracy of Poetry in Japan," includes translations of works by Bashō and a discussion of the haiku as a social phenomenon in Japan.

Ueda, Makoto. *Literary and Art Theories in Japan*. Cleveland, OH: Press of Western Reserve University, 1967. Ann Arbor, MI: Books on Demand UMI, n.d.

—— *Matsuo Bashō*. Boston: Twayne, 1970. Pbk ed., Tokyo and Palo Alto, CA: Kodansha International, 1982.

—— *Zeami, Bashō, Yeats, Pound: A Study in Japanese and English Poetics*, pp. 35–64. The Hague: Mouton, 1965.

TOPICS FOR DISCUSSION

1. What makes a good haiku? What are the strengths of the form? its limitations?
2. The eternal and the ever-changing in haiku: Bashō's insistence that the haiku must include both.
3. Buddhist impermanence and the idea of enduring art; immutability of language in the haiku.
4. Bashō's appreciation of Chinese literature.
5. Bashō and the Japanese cultural tradition: to what degree does his poetry reflect his own society? How did Bashō see his relation with earlier poets and other artists?
6. The subjects Bashō treated; is it proper to speak of him as a "poet of nature?"

THE PLAYS OF CHIKAMATSU
MONZAEMON (1653–1725)

Plays written by Japan's leading dramatist for the popular puppet theater, performed as well in the Kabuki theater, which are mainly concerned with conflict between love and duty in the lives of city-dwelling commoners and low-ranking samurai.

TRANSLATIONS

Keene, Donald, ed. *Anthology of Japanese Literature: From the Earliest Era to the Mid-Nineteenth Century,* pp. 386–409. New York: Grove, 1955. Pbk ed., Evergreen, 1960.
     One play plus "Chikamatsu on the Art of the Puppet Stage."
Keene, Donald, trans. *Major Plays of Chikamatsu.* New York: Columbia University Press, 1961.
     Fine translations of eleven plays with an extensive and informative introduction.
—— *Four Major Plays of Chikamatsu.* Pbk ed., New York: Columbia University Press, 1964.
     Four of the eleven plays in the preceding volume, including the introductory materials.
Mueller, Jacqueline. "A Chronicle of Great Peace Played Out on a Chessboard: *Goban Taiheiki,*" in *Harvard Journal of Asian Studies* 46 (June 1986)1:221–67.
Shively, Donald H., trans. *The Love Suicide at Amijima.* Cambridge: Harvard University Press, 1953.
     A translation with extensive notes of one of Chikamatsu's most important plays.

SECONDARY READINGS

Adachi, Barbara. *The Voices and Hands of Bunraku*. Tokyo and New York: Kodansha International, 1978.

A study of the artists of the puppet theater today, richly illustrated with color photographs.

Bowers, Faubion. *Japanese Theatre*. New York: Hermitage House, 1952.

Includes a discussion of Chikamatsu's plays.

Dunn, C. J. *The Early Japanese Puppet Drama*. London: Luzac, 1966.

A scholarly examination of the history of the puppet theater from its origins up to the time of Chikamatsu, including translations of some early plays.

Gerstle, C. Andrew. *Circles of Fantasy: Convention in the Plays of Chikamatsu*. Cambridge, MA and London: Council on East Asian Studies, Harvard University, 1986.

Analyzes musical and dramatic conventions of the time as well as literary form.

Jones, Stanleigh H., ed. and trans. *Sugawara and the Secrets of Calligraphy*. New York: Columbia University Press, 1985. Pbk ed.

Contains a short essay on the internal workings of the puppets, as well as an Introduction and translation.

Keene, Donald. *The Battles of Coxinga: Chikamatsu's Puppet Play, Its Background and Importance*. London: Taylor's Foreign Press, 1951.

Includes a history of the puppet theater.

—— *Bunraku: The Art of the Japanese Puppet Theatre*. Tokyo and Palo Alto, CA: Kodansha, 1965.

A study of all aspects of the puppet theater, illustrated with many excellent photographs.

—— *World Within Walls: Japanese Literature of the Pre-Modern Era*. New York: Holt, Rhinehart and Winston, 1976. Pbk ed., Grove, Evergreen, 1978.

Chapters 10, "The Beginnings of Kabuki and Jōruri," and 11, "Chikamatsu (1653–1725)," deal with the cultural context, literary heritage, and works of Chikamatsu.

Tsunoda Ryusaku, Wm. Theodore de Bary, and Donald Keene, eds. *Sources of Japanese Tradition.* New York: Columbia University Press, 1958. Pbk ed., 2 vols, 1964.

See especially chapter 19, "The Vocabulary of Japanese Aesthetics, III."

TOPICS FOR DISCUSSION

1. The characteristics of the Japanese popular theater: how Chikamatsu's dramas differ from Nō in intent and audience; how Chikamatsu's dramas differ from Shakespeare's in characters and subjects.
2. Is it proper to speak of Chikamatsu's dramas as tragedies? What might Aristotle have said about them? What gives the characters their stature? To what degree do they determine their own fates?
3. The function of the narrator in creating dramatic situation and character; compare with the function of the chorus in Nō drama.
4. The conflict between duty and love (*giri* and *ninjō*) found in the plays.
5. Differing attitudes of Chikamatsu and Saikaku toward their characters; toward the social conditions and attitudes of their time.
6. Chikamatsu's special concessions to the requirements of the puppet stage.
7. The relation of style, form, and content in Chikamatsu. How integral are they to one another? How distinctively Japanese, and how unique with Chikamatsu?

THE TREASURY OF LOYAL RETAINERS (CHŪSHINGURA, ca. 1748), BY TAKEDA IZUMO, MIYOSHI SHŌRAKU, AND NAMIKI SENRYŪ

The most popular of all Japanese plays, this was originally written for the puppet stage, but is now best known in Kabuki productions, as well as film and television versions.

TRANSLATIONS

Keene, Donald, trans. *Chūshingura: The Treasury of Loyal Retainers*. New York: Columbia University Press, 1971. Pbk ed.
    An excellent translation with introductory material on the play, its authorship, and the times.

SECONDARY READINGS

Brandon, James, ed. *Chūshingura: Studies in Kabuki and the Puppet Theater*. Honolulu: University of Hawaii Press, 1982.
    Essays by a number of scholars, with a Kabuki version of the play.
Brandon, James, trans. *Kabuki: Five Classic Plays*. Cambridge: Harvard University Press, 1975.
Dunn, Charles and Bunzō Torigoe, trans. and eds. *The Actors' Analects (Yakusha rongo)*. New York: Columbia University Press, 1969.
Ernst, Earle. *The Kabuki Theatre*. New York: Grove, 1956. Honolulu: University of Hawaii Press, 1974. Pbk ed.
Gunji, Masakatsu. *Kabuki*. Translated by John Bester. Tokyo and New York: Kodansha International, 1969; 1985.
    Contains photographs of Kabuki performances of *Chūshingura*.

Kawatake Mokuami. *The Loves of Izayoi and Seishin*. Translated by Frank T. Motofuji. Tokyo and Rutland, VT: Tuttle, 1966.

Keene, Donald. *Bunraku: The Art of the Japanese Puppet Theatre*. Tokyo and Palo Alto, CA: Kodansha, 1965.

Contains ten pages of photographs of *Chūshingura* as performed in the puppet theater.

—— *World Within Walls: Japanese Literature of the Pre-Modern Era, 1600–1867*. New York: Holt, Rinehart and Winston, 1976. Pbk ed., New York: Grove, Evergreen, 1978.

Chapter 12, "Drama: Jōruri After Chikamatsu," contains a detailed discussion of *Chūshingura* as well as its literary historical context.

Leiter, Samuel L. *The Art of Kabuki: Famous Plays in Performance*. Berkeley and Los Angeles: University of California Press, 1979.

Leiter, Samuel L. and Jiro Yamamoto, eds. *Kabuki Encyclopedia: An English Language Adaptation of Kabuki jiten*. Westport, CT: Greenwood, 1979.

Raz, Jacob. *Audiences and Actors: A Study of Their Interaction in the Japanese Traditional Theatre*. Leiden: Brill, 1983.

Richie, Donald, and Miyoko Watanabe. *Six Kabuki Plays*. Tokyo: Hokuseido, 1963.

Includes a translation of four scenes of *Chūshingura*.

TOPICS FOR DISCUSSION

1. Reasons for the immense popularity of this play with all classes of Japanese.
2. The "feudal" morality of the play. How feudal, how Confucian, how Japanese? Why were its ideals so absorbing to audiences in eighteenth-century Japan? Why should they still be absorbing today, when the "feudal" morality has seemingly been rejected?
3. Characters in the play: are they believable as individuals, or

do they tend to be types? Comparison with characters in Chikamatsu's plays. The variety of persons in the play.
4. Violence and delicacy: characteristic aspects of Japanese life found in this play. How are they resolved?
5. Dramatic structure of *Chūshingura*.

KOKORO, BY NATSUME SŌSEKI (1867–1914)

The Meiji period (1868–1912), which represents the transition from the pre-modern to the modern era, produced several major novelists, one of the most important and widely read being Natsume Sōseki.

TRANSLATIONS

Kokoro

McClellan, Edwin, trans. *Kokoro*. Chicago: Henry Regnery, 1967. Pbk ed.

Other Works by Sōseki

Keene, Donald, ed. *Modern Japanese Literature*. New York: Grove Press, 1955. Pbk ed., Evergreen, 1960.
    Contains the first chapter of *Botchan,* translated by Burton Watson.

Natsume Sōseki. *And Then: Natsume Sōseki's Novel Sorekara.* Translated with an Afterword and Selected Bibliography by Norma Moore Field. New York: Putnam, Perigee, 1978. Pbk ed.

—— *Botchan*. Translated by Alan Turney. Tokyo and New York: Kodansha International, 1972.

—— *Botchan*. Translated by Umeji Sasaki. Tokyo and Rutland, VT: Tuttle, 1968. Pbk ed.

—— *Grass on the Wayside*. Translated by Edwin McClellan. University of Chicago Press, 1969. Pbk ed.

—— *I Am a Cat*. Translated by Katsue Shibata and Motonari Kai. Tokyo: Kenkyusha, 1961.

—— *Light and Darkness: An Unfinished Novel by Natsume Sōseki.*

Translated with a critical essay by V. H. Viglielmo. London: Peter Owen, 1971.

—— *Mon* (The Gate). Translated by Francis Mathy. London: Peter Owen, 1972.

—— *Sanshiro*. Translated with a critical essay by Jay Ruben. Seattle and London: University of Washington Press, 1977. Pbk ed.

—— *The Three-Cornered World*. Translated by Alan Turney. London: Peter Owen, 1965. Chicago: Henry Regnery, 1967. Pbk ed.

—— *Ten Nights of Dream, Hearing Things, the Heredity of Taste*. Translated by Aiko Itō and Graeme Wilson. Tokyo and Rutland, VT: Tuttle, 1974.

—— *The Wayfarer*. Translated by Beongcheon Yu. Detroit: Wayne State University Press, 1967.

SECONDARY READINGS

Biddle, Ward William. "The Authenticity of Natsume Sōseki," in *Monumenta Nipponica* 28 (Winter 1973)4:391–426.

Doi, Takeo. *The Psychological World of Natsume Sōseki (Sōseki no shinteki sekai)*. Translated by William Jefferson Tyler. Cambridge, MA: East Asia Research Center, Harvard University, 1976.

Etō Jun. "Natsume Sōseki: A Japanese Meiji Intellectual," in *American Scholar* 39 (1965)4:603–619.

Hibbett, Howard S. "Sōseki and the Psychological Novel," in Donald H. Shively, ed., *Tradition and Modernization in Japanese Culture,* pp. 305–46. Princeton University Press, 1971. Pbk ed.

Keene, Donald. *Dawn to the West: Japanese Literature in the Modern Era*. Vol. 1: *Fiction*. New York: Holt, Rinehart and Winston, 1984.

Chapters 1 through 11 provide the literary history of the

Meiji period preceding Sōseki; see especially chapter 12, "Natsume Sōseki."

—— *Modern Japanese Novels and the West*. Charlottesville: University of Virginia Press, 1961.

McClellan, Edwin. *Two Japanese Novelists: Sōseki and Tōson*. University of Chicago Press, 1969.

Matsui, Sakuko. *Natsume Sōseki as a Critic of English Literature*. Tokyo: Centre for East Asian Cultural Studies, 1975.

Miyoshi, Masao. *Accomplices of Silence: The Modern Japanese Novel*. Berkeley and Los Angeles: University of California Press, 1974. Pbk ed.

Okazaki Yoshie. *Japanese Literature in the Meiji Era*. Translated and adapted by V. H. Viglielmo. Tokyo: Obunsha, 1955.

An extremely detailed work, useful for reference rather than as an introduction to the literature of the period.

Rubin, Jay. "Sōseki on Individualism," in *Monumenta Nipponica* 34 (Spring 1979)1:21–48.

—— "The Evil and the Ordinary in Sōseki's Fiction," in *Harvard Journal of Asiatic Studies* 46 (December 1986)2:333–52.

Ueda, Makoto. *Modern Japanese Writers and the Nature of Literature*. Stanford University Press, 1976.

Chapter 1 discusses Sōseki's work and literary theories.

Walker, Janet. *The Japanese Novel of the Meiji Period and the Idea of Individualism*. Princeton University Press, 1979.

Yamanouchi, Hisaaki. *The Search for Authenticity in Modern Japanese Literature*. Cambridge University Press, 1978. Pbk ed., 1980.

See chapter 3, "The Agonies of Individualism: Natsume Sōseki."

Yu, Beongcheon. *Natsume Sōseki*. Boston: Twayne, 1969.

TOPICS FOR DISCUSSION

1. In what ways does *Kokoro* most immediately reveal Western influence? What is the significance of Sensei's foreign friend?

315

What historical and social information is contained in the novel? How does it influence the characters?

2. What patterns are repeated in the major relationships in *Kokoro?* Discuss the relationship of the student with Sensei, with his family; the relationship of Sensei with his family, with his friend K, with his wife.

3. What are the major themes of the novel? What is the dominant atmosphere?

4. Consider the style and structure of the novel in relation to its themes. Does the work have a plot? a resolution? What is the point of the three-part division? of the first-person narrations? What do you think are the author's attitudes to his characters?

5. What is the significance in the novel of the Emperor Meiji's death? How does the suicide of General Nogi compare with the other suicides in the novel?

COMPANIONS TO ASIAN STUDIES

Approaches to the Oriental Classics, ed. Wm. Theodore
de Bary   1959
Early Chinese Literature, by Burton Watson. Also in
paperback ed.   1962
Approaches to Asian Civilization, ed. Wm. Theodore
de Bary and Ainslie T. Embree   1964
The Classic Chinese Novel: A Critical Introduction, by
C. T. Hsia. Also in paperback ed.   1968
*Chinese Lyricism: Shih Poetry from the Second to the Twelfth
Century*, tr. Burton Watson. Also in paperback ed.   1971
A Syllabus of Indian Civilization, by Leonard A. Gordon
and Barbara Stoler Miller   1971
Twentieth-Century Chinese Stories, ed. C. T. Hsia and
Joseph S. M. Lau. Also in paperback ed.   1971
A Syllabus of Chinese Civilization, by J. Mason Gentzler,
2d ed.   1972
A Syllabus of Japanese Civilization, by H. Paul Varley,
2d ed.   1972
An Introduction to Chinese Civilization, ed. John Meskill,
with the assistance of J. Mason Gentzler   1973
An Introduction to Japanese Civilization, ed. Arthur E.
Tiedemann   1974
Ukifune: Love in the Tale of Genji, ed. Andrew Pekarik   1982
The Pleasures of Japanese Literature, by Donald Keene   1988
A Guide to Oriental Classics, ed. Wm. Theodore de Bary
and Ainslie T. Embree; third edition ed. Amy
Vladeck Heinrich   1989

NEO-CONFUCIAN STUDIES

Instructions for Practical Living and Other Neo-Confucian Writings by Wang Yang-ming, tr. Wing-tsit Chan   1963

Reflections on Things at Hand: The Neo-Confucian Anthology, comp. Chu Hsi and Lü Tsu-ch'ien, tr. Wing-tsit Chan   1967

Self and Society in Ming Thought, by Wm. Theodore de Bary and the Conference on Ming Thought. Also in paperback ed.   1970

The Unfolding of Neo-Confucianism, by Wm. Theodore de Bary and the Conference on Seventeenth-Century Chinese Thought. Also in paperback ed.   1975

Principle and Practicality: Essays in Neo-Confucianism and Practical Learning, ed. Wm. Theodore de Bary and Irene Bloom. Also in paperback ed.   1979

The Syncretic Religion of Lin Chao-en, by Judith A. Berling   1980

The Renewal of Buddhism in China: Chu-hung and the Late Ming Synthesis, by Chun-fang Yu   1981

Neo-Confucian Orthodoxy and the Learning of the Mind-and-Heart, by Wm. Theodore de Bary   1981

Yüan Thought: Chinese Thought and Religion Under the Mongols, ed. Hok-lam Chan and Wm. Theodore de Bary   1982

The Liberal Tradition in China, by Wm. Theodore de Bary   1983

The Development and Decline of Chinese Cosmology, by John B. Henderson   1984

The Rise of Neo-Confucianism in Korea, by Wm. Theodore de Bary and JaHyun Kim Haboush   1985

Chiao Hung and the Restructuring of Neo-Confucianism in the Late Ming, by Edward T. Ch'ien   1985

Neo-Confucian Terms Explained: Pei-hsi tzu-i, by Ch'en Ch'un, ed. and trans. Wing-tsit Chan   1986

Knowledge Painfully Acquired: K'un-chih chi, by Lo Ch'in-shun, ed. and trans. Irene Bloom   1987

To Become a Sage: The Ten Diagrams on Sage Learning, by Yi T'oegye, ed. and trans. Michael C. Kalton   1988

The *Message of the Mind in Neo-Confucianism*, by Wm.
Theodore de Bary   1989

INTRODUCTION TO ORIENTAL CIVILIZATIONS
Wm. Theodore de Bary, EDITOR

Sources of Japanese Tradition 1958; paperback ed.,
   2 vols., 1964
Sources of Indian Tradition 1958; paperback ed., 2 vols.,
   1964; second edition, 1988
Sources of Chinese Tradition 1960; paperback ed., 2 vols., 1964

TRANSLATIONS FROM THE ORIENTAL CLASSICS

Major Plays of Chikamatsu, tr. Donald Keene. Also in
   paperback ed.   1961
Four Major Plays of Chikamatsu, tr. Donald Keene. Paper-
   back text edition   1961
*Records of the Grand Historian of China, translated from the
   Shih chi of Ssu-ma Ch'ien*, tr. Burton Watson, 2 vols.   1961
*Instructions for Practical Living and Other Neo-Confucian
   Writings by Wang Yang-ming*, tr. Wing-tsit Chan   1963
Chuang Tzu: Basic Writings, tr. Burton Watson, paper-
   back ed. only   1964
The Mahābhārata, tr. Chakravarthi V. Narasimhan.
   Also in paperback ed.   1965
The Manyōshū, Nippon Gakujutsu Shinkōkai edition   1965
Su Tung-p'o: Selections from a Sung Dynasty Poet, tr.
   Burton Watson. Also in paperback ed.   1965
Bhartrihari: Poems, tr. Barbara Stoler Miller. Also in
   paperback ed.   1967
Basic Writings of Mo Tzu, Hsün Tzu, and Han Fei Tzu,
   tr. Burton Watson. Also in separate paperback eds.   1967
The Awakening of Faith, Attributed to Aśvaghosha,
   tr. Yoshito S. Hakeda. Also in paperback ed.   1967

Reflections on Things at Hand: The Neo-Confucian Anthology,
comp. Chu Hsi and Lü Tsu-Ch'ien, tr. Wing-tsit Chan 1967

The Platform Sutra of the Sixth Patriarch, tr. Philip B.
Yampolsky. Also in paperback ed. 1967

Essays in Idleness: The Tsurezuregusa of Kenkō, tr. Donald
Keene. Also in paperback ed. 1967

The Pillow Book of Sei Shōnagon, tr. Ivan Morris, 2 vols. 1967

*Two Plays of Ancient India: The Little Clay Cart and the
Minister's Seal*, tr. J. A. B. van Buitenen 1968

The Complete Works of Chang Tzu, tr. Burton Watson 1968

The Romance of the Western Chamber (Hsi Hsiang chi), tr.
S. I. Hsiung. Also in paperback ed. 1968

The Manyōshū, Nippon Gakujutsu Shinkōkai edition.
Paperback text edition 1969

*Records of the Historian: Chapters from the Shih chi of Ssu-
ma Ch'ien*. Paperback text edition, tr. Burton Watson 1969

Cold Mountain: 100 Poems by the T'ang Poet Han-shan,
tr. Burton Watson. Also in paperback ed. 1970

Twenty Plays of the Nō Theatre, ed. Donald Keene. Also
in paperback ed. 1970

Chūshingura: The Treasury of Loyal Retainers, tr. Donald
Keene. Also in paperback ed. 1971

The Zen Master Hakuin: Selected Writings, tr. Philip B.
Yampolsky 1971

*Chinese Rhyme-Prose: Poems in the Fu Form from the Han
and Six Dynasties Periods*, tr. Burton Watson. Also in
paperback ed. 1971

Kūkai: Major Works, tr. Yoshito S. Hakeda. Also in
paperback ed. 1972

*The Old Man Who Does as He Pleases: Selections from the
Poetry and Prose of Lu Yu*, tr. Burton Watson 1973

The Lion's Roar of Queen Śrīmālā, tr. Alex and Hideko
Wayman 1974

*Courtier and Commoner in Ancient China: Selections from the
History of the Former Han by Pan Ku*, tr. Burton Watson.

Also in paperback ed. 1974

Japanese Literature in Chinese, vol. 1: *Poetry and Prose in Chinese by Japanese Writers of the Early Period,* tr. Burton Watson 1975

Japanese Literature in Chinese, vol. 2: *Poetry and Prose in Chinese by Japanese Writers of the Later Period,* tr. Burton Watson 1976

Scripture of the Lotus Blossom of the Fine Dharma, tr. Leon Hurvitz. Also in paperback ed. 1976

Love Song of the Dark Lord: Jayaveda's Gītagovinda, tr. Barbara Stoler Miller. Also in paperback ed. Cloth ed. includes critical text of the Sanskrit. 1977

Ryōkan: Zen Monk-Poet of Japan, tr. Burton Watson 1977

Calming the Mind and Discerning the Real: From the Lam rim chen mo of Tsoṅ-kha-pa, tr. Alex Wayman 1978

The Hermit and the Love-Thief: Sanskrit Poems of Bhartrihari and Bilhaṇa, tr. Barbara Stoler Miller 1978

The Lute: Kao Ming's P'i-p'a chi, tr. Jean Mulligan. Also in paperback ed. 1980

A Chronicle of Gods and Sovereigns: Jinnō Shōtōki of Kitakabe Chikafusa, tr. H. Paul Varley 1980

Among the Flowers: The Hua-chien chi, tr. Lois Fusek 1982

Grass Hill: Poems and Prose by the Japanese Monk Gensei, tr. Burton Watson 1983

Doctors, Diviners, and Magicians of Ancient China: Biographies of Fang-shih, tr. Kenneth J. DeWoskin. Also in paperback ed. 1983

Theater of Memory: The Plays of Kālidāsa, ed. Barbara Stoler Miller. Also in paperback ed. 1984

The Columbia Book of Chinese Poetry: From Early Times to the Thirteenth Century, ed. and tr. Burton Watson. Also in paperback ed. 1984

Poems of Love and War: From the Eight Anthologies and the Ten Songs of Classical Tamil, tr. A. K. Ramanujan. Also in paperback ed. 1985

The Columbia Book of Later Chinese Poetry, ed. and tr.
Jonathan Chaves. Also in paperback ed.   1986

MODERN ASIAN LITERATURE SERIES

Modern Japanese Drama: An Anthology, ed. and tr. Ted
Takaya. Also in paperback ed.   1979
*Mask and Sword: Two Plays for the Contemporary Japanese
Theater,* by Yamazaki Masakazu, tr. J. Thomas Rimer   1980
Yokomitsu Rüchi, Modernist, by Dennis Keene   1980
*Nepali Visions, Nepali Dreams: The Poetry of Laxmiprasad
Devkota,* tr. David Rubin   1980
Literature of the Hundred Flowers, vol. 1: *Criticism and
Polemics,* ed. Hauling Nieh   1981
Literature of the Hundred Flowers, vol. 2: *Poetry and Fiction,*
ed. Hualing Nieh   1981
Modern Chinese Stories and Novellas, 1919–1949, ed.
Joseph S. M. Lau, C. T. Hsia, and Leo Ou-fan Lee.
Also in paperback ed.   1984
A View by the Sea, by Yasuka Shōtarō, tr. Kären Wigen
Lewis   1984
*Other Worlds: Arishima Takeo and the Bounds of Modern
Japanese Fiction,* by Paul Anderer   1984
Selected Poems of Sŏ Chŏngju, tr. with intro. by David R.
McCann   1989

STUDIES IN ORIENTAL CULTURE

1. *The Ōnin War: History of Its Origins and Background,
with a Selective Translation of the Chronicle of Onin,*
by H. Paul Varley   1967
2. *Chinese Government to Ming Times: Seven Studies,* ed.
Charles O. Hucker   1969
3. *The Actors' Analects (Yakusha Rongo),* ed. and tr. by
Charles J. Dunn and Bungō Torigoe   1969

4. *Self and Society in Ming Thought,* by Wm. Theodore de Bary and the Conference on Ming Thought. Also in paperback ed. 1970

5. *A History of Islamic Philosophy,* by Majid Fakhry, 2d ed. 1983

6. *Phantasies of a Love Thief: The Caurapañcāśikā Attributed to Bilhaṇa,* by Barbara Stoler Miller 1971

7. *Iqbal: Poet-Philosopher of Pakistan,* ed. Hafeez Malik 1971

8. *The Golden Tradition: An Anthology of Urdu Poetry,* by Ahmed Ali. Also in paperback ed. 1973

9. *Conquerors and Confucians: Aspects of Political Change in the Late Yuan China,* by John W. Dardess 1973

10. *The Unfolding of Neo-Confucianism,* by Wm. Theodore de Bary and the Conference on Seventeenth-Century Chinese Thought. Also in paperback ed. 1975

11. *To Acquire Wisdom: The Way of Wang Yang-ming,* by Julia Ching 1976

12. *Gods, Priests, and Warriors: The Bhṛgus of the Mahābhārata,* by Robert P. Goldman 1977

13. *Mei Yao-ch'en and the Development of Early Sung Poetry,* by Jonathan Chaves 1976

14. *The Legend of Semimaru, Blind Musician of Japan,* by Susan Matisoff 1977

15. *Sir Sayyid Ahmad Khan and Muslim Modernization in India and Pakistan,* by Hafeez Malik 1980

16. *The Khilafat Movement: Religious Symbolism and Political Mobilization in India,* by Gail Minault 1980

17. *The World of K'ung Shang-jen: A Man of Letters in Early Ch'ing China,* by Richard Strassberg 1983

18. *The Lotus Boat: The Origins of Chinese Tz'u Poetry in T'ang Popular Culture,* by Marsha L. Wagner 1984

19. *Expressions of Self in Chinese Culture,* ed. Robert E. Hegel and Richard C. Hessney 1985

20. *Songs for the Bride: Women's Voices and Wedding Rites of Rural India,* by W. G. Archer, ed. Barbara Stoler

Miller and Mildred Archer   1986

21. *A Heritage of Kings: One Man's Monarchy in the
    Confucian World,* by JaHyun Kim Haboush   1988